Did Adam and Eve act rationally in eating the fruit of the forbidden tree? That can seem to depend solely on whether they had found the best means to their ends, in the spirit of the 'economic' theories of rationality. Martin Hollis respects the elegance and power of these theories but judges their paradoxes endemic. He argues that social action cannot be understood by viewing human beings as abstract individuals with preferences in search of satisfaction, nor by divorcing practical reason from questions of the rationality of norms, principles, practices and ends. These essays, focused on the themes of 'rational choice', 'roles and reasons' and 'other cultures, other minds', make the point and explore alternative approaches. Culled in revised form from twenty-five years' work, they range across periods and disciplines with a philosophical imagination and vivid prose, which will engage philosophers and social scientists alike.

REASON IN ACTION

Essays in the philosophy of social science

MARTIN HOLLIS

*Professor of Philosophy in the School of Economic and Social Studies,
University of East Anglia, Norwich*

CAMBRIDGE
UNIVERSITY PRESS

Published by the Press Syndicate of the University of Cambridge
The Pitt Building, Trumpington Street, Cambridge CB2 1RP
40 West 20th Street, New York, NY 10011-4211, USA
10 Stamford Road, Oakleigh, Melbourne 3166, Australia

© Cambridge University Press 1996

First Published 1996

Printed in Great Britain at the University Press, Cambridge

A catalogue record for this book is available from the British Library

Library of Congress cataloguing in publication data
Hollis, Martin
Rationality in action: essays in the philosophy of social science / Martin Hollis
p. cm.
Includes bibliographical references and index.
ISBN 0 521 44263 X (hardback).   ISBN 0 521 44779 8 (paperback)
1. Social sciences – Philosophy.   I. Title.
H61.H666   1996
300′.1–dc20   95–8138   CIP

ISBN 0 521 44263 X hardback
ISBN 0 521 44779 8 paperback

Contents

Acknowledgements

These essays, except the first, are revised versions of articles whose original sources are given in the first note at the beginning of each. Here I would like to thank the following journals and publishers for their kind permission to reprint copyright material: the Cambridge University Press (2, 4, 7, 11, 15), *Philosophical Forum* (3), *Analysis* (5), *Journal of Philosophy* (6), The British Academy (8), *The British Journal of Political Studies* (9), *Ethics* (10), *The European Journal of Sociology* (12), *Philosophy* (13), Basil Blackwell (14) and The Aristotelian Society (16 and 17).

Since the original publications span twenty-five years of work on aspects of rationality in philosophy and the social sciences, I owe large debts to more colleagues and critics than I can mention here; but particular thanks are offered in notes to particular essays.

CHAPTER 1

Prologue: reason in action

Linking these essays is a simple conviction that people act, for the most part, rationally and that the social sciences depend on it. Neither proposition stays simple for long. People's reasons for action are so various that one soon wonders whether there can be any single account of practical reason for all species of rational action or single definition of rationality for all purposes of social science. Philosophical disputes about practical reason and *Methodenstreit* among social scientists encourage the doubt. Enlightenment thinkers held that, as Hobbes put it in chapter V of *Leviathan*, 'reason is the pace, increase of science the way, and the benefit of mankind the end'. This remains my motto too. But it is a cryptic one, as this prefatory essay will demonstrate. In what follows, I shall sketch the analysis of rational action best established in the social sciences, air objections to it, introduce possible alternatives and identify three themes which run through the subsequent essays.

Did Eve make a rational choice, when she was beguiled by the serpent and ate of the forbidden tree? The theory of rational choice answers obliquely by saying what an ideally rational agent would do. She would compare the expected utility of the actions open to her and choose the best alternative. Each action involves consequences, which she would rank in order of preference. If these consequences were certain, she would simply choose the most preferred. In so far as they were not certain, she would assign probabilities to them and discount their utility

I am warmly grateful to Rüdiger Bittner and Timothy O'Hagan for their helpful comments on an earlier draft of this prologue.

accordingly, in the spirit of a gambler balancing winnings against risks at roulette. That would yield her expected utility for each action. An ideally rational agent never chooses *a* when *b* offers greater expected utility.

Here rationality is concerned solely with the choice of means to ends. The ends are taken as given. They enter the story as desired outcomes and then, since the future is uncertain and the causes of action must already be present, they are translated into given preferences. This givenness has important, if diverse, implications. It blocks questions of the rationality of ends and whether preferences are virtuous, rightful or tend to the common good. It ensures that whether an action is rational does not depend on how agents come by their preferences. It sees to it that preferences can be cited to explain actions without then turning out to be the product of what they explain. Also, since preferences are the motivating element and are always addressed to the consequences of actions, it gives the theory of choice a forward-looking, consequentialist slant.

Older versions of the approach aimed for a universal science of human nature, which included a psychological story about desires as appetites in search of psychic satisfaction. For instance, Hobbes and Hume specified a list of universal passions and set reason the task of serving them, or, at any rate, serving those most useful to us. Bentham opened *An Introduction the Principles of Morals and Legislation* by remarking that 'Nature has placed mankind under the governance of' two sovereign masters, *pleasure* and *pain*. It is for them alone to point out what we ought to do, as well as to determine what we shall do.' He then declared that 'the principle of utility' recognises this sovereignty and hence sees to it every action is assessed by 'its tendency to augment or diminish the happiness of the party whose interest is in question'. That allowed a single scale for assessing satisfactions: 'By utility is meant that property in any object, whereby it tends to produce benefit, advantage, pleasure, good or happiness, (all this in the present case comes to the same thing)...' With this guarantee that forms of utility are commensurable (since they all come to the same thing), a complete felicific calculus was in prospect.

Recently, however, rational choice theorists have become wary of setting up as psychologists. They have tended to bleach all psychology out and to replace it by a logic alone. This logic defines rationality austerely as consistency among preferences, together with correctness in the calculations which link preferences to actions. Preference itself is more like an avowal of a ranking than a desire for a feeling of satisfaction. In the most austere versions, introspection also drops out as a form of special access to inner states, and preferences are simply imputed to an agent by reading them off behaviour as revealed in the actual choices made. That makes it hard to see how action can be *explained* by citing preferences. But, leaving for later questions of whether a sheer logic of practical reason can explain action, we can readily see why austerity can be attractive.

The attraction is that the account of action offered by game theory is all the more elegant, if uncluttered with psychology. The key idea, luminously simple and immensely fertile, is that of strategic choice. Rational choice theory starts with parametric choice: a single individual, Adam, choosing in an independent environment. This environment sets parameters for his calculations of expected utility. It need not be static, but its changes are not due (solely) to him. Now introduce Eve. While, initially, she is an independently moving figure in the environment, she is merely a complication. But, as soon as what it is rational for Adam to choose comes to depend on what it is rational for Eve to choose and vice versa, the situation is transformed. They are playing a game, as game theory puts it, in which the pay-off to each player's choice depends on what the other player chooses. Such choices are strategic.

Everyday examples need not be complex. Whether Adam does well to keep to the left of the path depends on whether Eve keeps left, which she is wise to do only if she expects him to keep left. Equally, each does well to keep right, if the other keeps right. They face a coordination problem with more than one solution. If they do not care which solution emerges, the one which does emerge is plausibly thought of as a convention or, more grandly, since no one has a reason to deviate from it, as a self-perpetuating consensual norm. Deeper thoughts start to

stir, including one about the basis of language. We could go on
to suggest that, since it does not matter whether we call a spade a
spade, provided that we all give it the same name, different
languages embody different solutions to a problem of coordination
among a group of people seeking to communicate. More
ambitiously still, we could fancy that society too, and at least
some of its norms and institutions, can be traced to conventions
which allow coordination to mutual advantage. Even if we
hesitate to build so much on a game-theoretic analysis of
conventions, we can readily grant that strategic choices which
coordinate to mutual advantage are commonplace and instructive.

So also, however, are strategic choices which fail to achieve
mutual benefits. If we picture Adam and Eve as inhabitants of
the state of nature which Hobbes postulates in *Leviathan*, they
will both do better to live at peace than at war. Peace would give
them the prospect of 'commodious living', which they would
much prefer to a life which is 'solitary, poor, nasty, brutish and
short'. Yet, if each most prefers to steal a march on the other, or
cannot trust the other not to behave in this way, they will
continue in 'that condition which is called war; and such a war
as is of every man against every man'. The mutual advantages of
peace cannot give rise to self-sustaining conventions among
players with conflicting interests; and, even if they were proposed
and agreed to, they would not be stable. Hence, Hobbes argues
in chapter XIII, the only escape is to create 'a common power to
keep them all in awe'. This is the Leviathan of the book's title, a
sovereign authority or 'artificial man', created by convention
but constitutionally armed with a sword and composed of
individuals who benefit from giving up their own swords in
return for a guarantee that others have done the same. With
Leviathan in place, otherwise fragile covenants and contracts
can be relied on, since lapses will be punished by law.

This suggests a different analysis of convention, at least for
some cases, and sets an enduring puzzle, if one holds that social
life depends on trust and not solely on fear of reprisal. The crux is
that individually rational choices need not sum to an outcome
which anyone intends or wants. The game which best illustrates
it is the Prisoner's Dilemma. Adam and Eve both do better if

both choose *b* than if both choose *a*, but, for each of them, *a* scores higher than *b*, if the other chooses *a*, and higher also, if the other chooses *b*. Hence each finds it rational to choose *a*, *whatever the other chooses*; and the benefits of both choosing *b* elude them. Here too deeper thoughts soon stir. Restated with several players, the game sets the sort of 'free rider' problem, which illuminates much in social life. For instance whaling nations presumably have a mutual interest in making and keeping an agreement to limit catches, thus preserving a stock for the future. But, although this suits all better than anarchy, each may still find it rational to catch more whales, whatever the others do. The sum of such choices is the anarchy no one wants. More generally, public goods will not be provided and collective action will not be undertaken, whenever they depend on voluntary contributions which each player rationally avoids making, whatever other players do. Hobbes smiles dourly.

Yet objections also start to stir. In practice, people do often act contrary to this logic. They often act in concert, contribute voluntarily, keep their word and trust one another in such situations. Why? Some answers to this leading question enhance the approach, others subvert it; and it is not always plain which do which. Thus the logic which says 'Defect!' may lose determinacy when the game is played in particular settings or embedded in a series. For example, litterbugs are less likely to leave litter on their own village green; and economists who conduct experiments involving trust and occasions for cheating find that players cheat less when paired with the same player several times. (Enjoyably, they also find that economics students cheat more than others.) Whether such findings are consistent with the model or limit its scope or invite an amendment or challenge its assumptions radically is a deep question.

More generally, people do not always act rationally, by the test of what one would predict from the axioms of rational choice theory and game theory. Departures are too common, even in simple situations, and too systematic to be shrugged off. Here too discrepancies can be interpreted in ways which range from squaring the data with the axioms to abandoning the whole approach. One line of defence is to grant that not all actions are rational by the test proposed, but to add that rational choice theory is normative as well as descriptive: in so far as people do not make rational choices, they would fare better if they did. This defence offers much to think about, not least when reflecting on the basis of trust in social life. In so far as the model is normative, does it endorse or scotch the idea that fully rational agents will take so enlightened a view of their mutual self-interest that they will choose a cooperative strategy even on some occasions when logic seems to say 'Defect!'? If it endorses the idea, are we thereby offered the makings of a rational choice theory of ethics? If it scotches it, what does that show about the workings of trust and other moral engagements in social life?

Whatever the answers, the widely remarked mismatch between what people ordinarily think it reasonable to do and what theory deems it rational to do invites fresh thinking about the descriptive and explanatory potential of the whole approach. There are three ways to go. One is to restore some explicit psychology to flesh out the schematic character of preferences. The second is to replace instrumental rationality as the primary or only definition of rationality worth relying on. The third is to challenge the individualism which pervades the game-theoretic treatment of social interaction as a sum of strategic choices by rational individuals. I shall next offer a brief word about each, thus putting down markers for later essays.

The first way looks promising, if the result of relying solely on logic is to make rational agents into what Amartya Sen has termed 'rational fools', condemned to self-defeating choices and self-destructive social relations.[1] One might start by distinguishing between psychological and philosophical egoism. The former deems us selfish, self-seeking and self-regarding, and has inspired the familiar but disputable view that 'the first principle of economics is that every agent is actuated solely by self-interest'[2]. The latter holds merely that the only desires which can move us are our own. In that case philosophical egoism has room for a

---

[1]　A. K. Sen, 'Rational Fools', *Philosophy and Public Affairs*, 6, 1977, pp. 317–44, reprinted in his *Choice, Welfare and Measurement*, Oxford: Basil Blackwell, 1982, and in F. Hahn and M. Hollis, eds., *Philosophy and Economic Theory*, Oxford: Oxford University Press, 1979.

[2]　F.Y. Edgeworth, *Mathematical Psychics*, London: Routledge and Kegan Paul, 1881, p. 16.

more generous psychology, which can credit us with less selfish passions, like sympathy for others, love of our fellows or altruistic concern. Hume, for instance, while insisting that reason alone cannot be a motive to any action of the will, allows a variety of passions to move us:

It is universally acknowledged that there is a great uniformity among the actions of men, in all nations and ages, and that human nature remains still the same, in its principles and operations. The same motives produce the same actions: the same events follow from the same causes. Ambition, avarice, self-love, vanity, friendship, generosity, public spirit: these passions, mixed in various degrees, and distributed through society, have been, from the beginning of the world, and still are, the source of all actions and enterprises, which have ever been observed among mankind. (*An Enquiry Concerning Human Understanding*, VIII.I.65)

One can query the list and its claim to universal validity, or wonder at Hume's omniscience, without disputing his underlying philosophy of mind. Indeed the thesis that action is the product of desire plus belief, with desire supplying the motor, is commonplace among philosophers who do not accept that 'human nature remains still the same' or can serve as the foundation of a social science. Whereas a switch from 'passions' to 'preferences' creates an illusion that no psychology at all is needed, a switch from psychological to philosophical egoism makes room for useful debate about human psychology.

Hume's philosophical egoism can certainly be disputed, however, as can his claim that 'reason alone cannot be a motive to any action of the will'. Do we not sometimes act contrary to our desires? Moral choices are often experienced as a conflict between inclination and duty. In Kant's account of practical reason, action which is instrumentally rational in furthering a desire is contrasted with action on principle. Principled action is guided by judgements made from the moral point of view, which is impersonal, impartial and universal: when judging what I should do, I must ask what it would be right for anyone in the same position to do, thus giving myself a universal maxim to act on. Such maxims are reasons for action. They become reasons which can motivate us not because we have a desire to be moral but because, in recognising that a particular maxim provides a relevant reason, we make that reason our own.

Can we not have a desire to be moral? Hume includes some high-minded passions on his list and sometimes suggests, like Adam Smith, that we have an impartial spectator in our breasts to give us pause. Yet, when discussing trust, respect for property and our sense of justice, he does not leave all the work to an extended set of passions. Having identified 'partiality' towards ourselves and those closest to us as an obstacle to social arrangements designed to remove the 'inconveniences' which spring from human nature and our 'natural uncultivated ideas of morality', he opines that it can be overcome by the emergence of conventions of justice and property.

The remedy, then, is not derived from nature, but from *artifice*, or, more properly speaking, nature provides a remedy, in the judgement and understanding, for what is irregular and incommodious in the affections. (*A Treatise of Human Nature*, Book III, Part II, Section 2)

The suggestion that we need artifice is intriguing. It reflects a general reluctance, shared by his descendants, to broaden the passions to include a desire to be moral or rational, for fear, I fancy, that his moral psychology would thereby lose all distinctiveness. But it puts reason in charge sometimes and thus, as in Kant, enables rational agents to override their preferences.

The second way to make us less like rational fools is to challenge the primacy of instrumental reason. Here one might start from Kant's idea that, at least in moral matters, it is rational to act on a relevant and universal maxim, like 'everyone should keep their promises'. Reason, emancipated from slavery to the passions, is concerned for the rationality of ends. Ends, and hence maxims, provide reasons for action not because of the good consequences of pursuing them but because of the connection which Kant claims to discern between duty and autonomy. I act autonomously when I freely accept the moral law and therefore do what any moral agent in my situation should do. As an autonomous agent, acting from duty and regarding my own interests with an impartial eye, I am bound to respect the autonomy of others. I cannot treat them as means to my ends, since I recognise that I and they are equally members of 'the kingdom of ends'. Although this is not the moment to try unpacking Kant's moral philosophy, it has directly relevant attractions. One is that morally autonomous agents can trust one another not to take advantage, whenever it would seemingly pay to defect, since they act on maxims which ensure their compliance with bargains struck and promises made. The moral psychology involved is at least interesting.

On the other hand, to model rational choice on a Kantian notion of moral judgement seems unduly high-minded. Even in ethics it is not plainly right or rational to follow a universal maxim when one knows that other people will not. Kantian morality forbids the telling of lies; but might I not have better reason to lie to the secret police in a banana republic? More to the point, many problems of rational choice seem to be a matter of prudence rather than morality, as, for instance, when I am choosing whether to park my new car in a run-down area. The difference is that prudence pays heed to consequences and to what other people will do. So, even if there are imperatives of prudence, they are not to be assessed simply from a moral point of view. Yet I would not wish to deny that prudence may involve virtues as well as calculations, and hence that a picture of rational agents as pure calculators of the consequences which best satisfy their given preferences lacks a vital spark for this reason.

Meanwhile, Kantian autonomy goes with an idea of free agency to set against the idea that freedom consists in the absence of constraints. A standard *homo economicus* is merely a computerised throughput between the determinants of given preferences and the resulting actions. Autonomous agents can override their preferences or intervene between input and output, thus, we might hope, rejoicing in a kind of freedom which seems oddly missing from the instrumentalist notion of rational choice. But this is a tendentious comment, since, on further reflection, it is not plain that a Humean slave of the passions has not become a Kantian slave to maxims. That gives more to think about than I shall attempt for the moment.

The third way to go is to replace the atomic individuals of the standard model with agents who are essentially social. *Homo sociologicus* takes the stage. Having just objected to *homo economicus* as a mechanical throughput, I shall not try substituting an equally mechanical *homo sociologicus*, who is a creature of determining social positions and roles, and hence another throughput. A fertile alternative might start from Wittgenstein's portrait of us as players of the 'games' of social life, whose actions are moves in the game of the moment and whose reasons for action are internal to the games we play. Whereas game theory conceives games as sums of strategic choices by individuals, Wittgensteinian games have so different a character that it can seem idle to make comparisons. Yet, with all due caution, it is instructive to contrast their very different ideas of norms and reasons for action.

The most obvious fact about games, in the everyday sense of the word, is that they have rules. The rules of chess, for example, define the purpose of the game, the powers of the pieces and their permissible moves. Moves are events in a constructed, rule-governed space of sixty-four related locations. In defining what is permissible, the rules establish the construct and make chess possible. They constitute the game. They are not a solution to a prior problem of coordination in a world of hitherto frustrated chess players who have been vainly shifting pawns around to no effect. Then, secondarily, there are also regulative rules of varying authority and importance, which guide the players in making wise choices ('castle early', 'keep control of the central squares') or specify the etiquette of the game ('a piece, if touched, must be moved', 'don't fidget'). Such rules are secondary, in that they presuppose the constitution of the game. Chess thus illustrates an instructive distinction between constitutive rules, which are prior to a particular class of actions and make them possible, and regulative rules, which guide choice among possible actions. It also hints at a much pricklier thought: without rules of chess there could be no chess players; without games and practices, no players of any kind.

The distinction between two kinds of rule is suggestive on other fronts too. Words, to take a deeper but more elusive case, are mere noise without linguistic rules to constitute their meaning. We could mean nothing by our words, unless some of them had meaning already. Given these constitutive rules, there are many ways to achieve a single speech-act; but none could succeed in their absence. Speakers' individual intentions thus depend on social conventions. There can have been no moment in the dawn of history when Eve said to Adam 'Let's invent language!' and he replied 'What a good idea!'

Could she have had ideas nevertheless, although lacking the language to express them? The priority between language and thought is not to be settled by hasty analogies with chess. Even if language were prior to thought, we need not grant that its rules are all-encompassing. They may constitute what we can say and regulate how to say it; but it would be a bold leap to conclude that they exhaust our reasons for saying what we say or thinking what we think. Yet there is a case to be made for this bold conclusion, or at least for a general view of social games and practices, which might favour it.

There are contexts where all the rules, taken together, seem to tell each player exactly how to go on. Codes of honour, to pick an enticing example, are pervasive in some forms of life. For instance, musketeers may be so thoroughly honour-bound that an insult not only warrants a challenge to a duel but also demands one. Duels are fought in a 'grammatical' space whose rules tell musketeers exactly how to go on. Here, perhaps, normative expectations are strong enough to create a definite obligation. In that case, to understand the code might be to understand not only what D'Artagnan was doing in throwing down a gauntlet but also why he did it. That would make him *homo sociologicus* to his very core – so deeply a man of honour that he always does what is expected of him *because* it is expected. Thence one might argue that the case illustrates the general proposition that action in a normative context derives its motive, as well as its meaning and intention, from the rules of the game. *Homo sociologicus* even lurks in the preference order of *homo economicus*. Indeed the latter is finally a further example of the former: in the last analysis marketeers and musketeers are equally the embodiments of institutions, practices and, in short, forms of life.

These are wild leaps, however. The obvious objection is that not even musketeers are so mindless. Even if their actions are, or indeed must be, in some sense 'grammatical', neither in practice nor philosophically are they slaves to the rules of the game. In practice no code could specify what is required for every situation, and there is always room for judgement in deciding which of its rules are relevant and how they are to be applied. Rules are never complete in advance and any image of a handbook able to cover all situations would be profoundly misleading. They acquire a definite interpretation only in the course of applying them in situations which are never straight-forwardly identical to previous ones. Actors are always active, always helping to shape the rules which bind and guide them, never wholly passive when deciding how to go on.

Here the prickly character of the thought that there are no chess players prior to the constitutive rules of chess becomes critical. We now have a different *homo sociologicus*, more attractive than a puppet on social strings, but not necessarily more reassuring. The games we play become open-textured and our motives or real reasons for making our moves can be distinguished from the intentions expressed in the act of making them. But that leaves an ambiguity, if we, the actors, hoped to emerge as persons whose identity is not defined by any or all of the games of social life. Talk of motives or real reasons may signal only a deeper level of intentions, as when a chess master who seems to be merely defending against a threat is really setting a trap. Or, where motives are external to the game of the moment, they may still belong to another game. A musketeer might fight a duel for his honour because he needed respect as part of his plot to become king of France. But the throne would be a prize in another game, not an aspiration outside all social space and grammar. That someone speaking in English may be thinking in Japanese is no evidence that we can think in a linguistic vacuum.

So far, then, none of the three ways to stop the standard model from making rational fools of us is compelling. The shortcomings of *homo economicus* are fully remedied neither by revamping the psychology nor by claiming primacy for an analysis of reasons for action inspired by a moral point of view nor by regarding social action as the work of an intelligent *homo sociologicus*. Since all these lines have their merits, we might try combining them. But they are incompatible, in my view, and that leaves me pulled in two directions. One is towards a universal standpoint from which to judge whether an agent has acted, prudently or morally, on rational preferences or as anyone so placed would rationally act. The other is towards recognising that reasons for action are relative to roles and contexts, thus suggesting that rationality can be a matter of following a local rule in an appropriate way.

This tension between the universal and the relative is palpable, when we invoke the hermeneutic imperative that the social world can be understood only from within and raise the problem of Other Minds. At first sight, there is no knowing *a priori* what other people and other cultures believe, especially granted that they may hold beliefs which are incoherent or empirically false. There seems to be no alternative to a patient empiricism. Furthermore, if there is also no knowing *a priori* what criteria of coherence and truth particular people and cultures employ, there also seems to be no alternative to an accompanying relativism. Yet the pull to the universal proves resistant. Even though diversity is a plain fact of social life, one can still maintain that there are limits to it.

The case for universally held beliefs and universal criteria for the coherence and truth of beliefs can be made on either empirical or *a priori* grounds. Here, for instance, is Hume. 'It is universally acknowledged', he observed in the passage quoted earlier, 'that there is a great uniformity among the actions of men, in all nations and ages, and that human nature remains still the same, in its principles and operations.' He continues:

Mankind are so much the same, in all times and places, that history informs us of nothing new or strange in this particular. Its chief use is only to discover the constant and universal principles of human nature.

That yields a ready-made test for deciding whether an interpretation is plausible, as his next paragraph illustrates:

Should a traveller, returning from a far country, bring us an account of men, wholly different from any with whom we were ever acquainted; men, who were entirely divested of avarice, ambition or revenge; who knew no pleasure but friendship, generosity, and public spirit; we should immediately, from these circumstances, detect the falsehood and prove him a liar, with the same certainty as if he had stuffed his narration with stories of centaurs and dragons, miracles and prodigies.

Yet are such constant and universal principles, as Hume supposed, principles of human nature, known to us by observation? If so, eighteenth-century Edinburgh offered an astonishing gazebo. Or is the case for uniformity finally one for *a priori* principles of interpretation? Since that is my own view, my verdict is for rationality over relativism.

The essays which follow have three principal themes and I have grouped the texts by which is uppermost. The first theme, 'rational choice', explores the instrumental notion of practical reason central to microeconomics and critical for 'economic' theories of social action at large. Although I do not claim to have blocked all ways of nuancing the notion through clever technical manoeuvres or by enriching its psychology.[3] I do not believe that such moves can be effective, given a basic moral psychology where reason is the slave of the passions.

The second theme, 'roles and reasons', addresses what Kant called 'man's asocial sociality' by contrasting two of the remedies for what is incommodious in the affections. Shall we liberate the judgement and understanding from them? Or shall we make social actors essentially social persons, for whom rationality consists in conforming to a contextually appropriate rule? Both lines have much to offer, but they are not easily reconciled. In upshot, our asocial sociality means that, although we need social relations, there is mysteriously more to persons than even a creative account of social relations can provide.

The third theme, 'other cultures, other minds', turns to anthropology and epistemology. Hume bids us reject astonishing narratives, when it is likelier that they are false than that other minds and other cultures are as they claim. I endorse this advice, after recasting it as an *a priori* principle of interpretation: all understanding presupposes a 'bridgehead' of true and rational

---

[3] For more on both lines, see M. Hollis and R. Sugden, 'Rationality in Action', *Mind*, 102.405, 1993, pp. 1–35.

beliefs. The criteria of truth and rationality being universal and objective, relativism yields. Finally the three themes come together in the last essay on 'reasons of honour'.

So did Eve make a rational choice, when she ate of the forbidden tree? It may seem no. She saw that the tree was good for food and pleasant to the eyes and she knew that eating of its fruit would make her wise. But she also knew that the Lord God had forbidden it on pain of death. Prudence apparently said 'Don't!'. Yet there is more to rational action than the correct calculation of consequences. That is not because the penalty turned out to be expulsion from the garden of Eden, rather than death. A deeper reason to hesitate can be found in the serpent's insinuation that 'Ye shall not surely die . . . but shall be as gods, knowing good and evil.' Such wisdom may or may not have been worth acquiring, but she was no person to be the judge of that, until she had acquired it.

I

Rational choice

CHAPTER 2

Three men in a drought

Water was short in the torrid summer of 1976 and there were soon calls for restraint. Where I live, the Anglian Water Authority quickly threatened to ban garden hoses if the calls went unheeded. The sun blazed down in emphasis and the Authority made an ostentatious purchase of standpipes for the streets in case households had to be cut off. Philosophising amid my limp lettuces, I wondered how much notice it was rational for me to take. It was plainly in the general interest that water be saved and this premise will not be challenged. But was it rational for me to save water? This is the common or garden problem to be pondered here.

The question is one about collective goods, meaning goods which can be provided only by collective or central action. They benefit all yet it seems that, if contributions are voluntary and if everyone acts rationally, they will never be provided. Examples are parks, schools, trade unions, national defence and democracy, but I pick my own to save getting embrangled in a cluttered landscape. I shall rehearse two standard ways with collective goods, usually dubbed the economic and the sociological, and shall complain about both. This is the middleground of the essay. There is also a background in the nature of rational action and its bearing on method in the social sciences, and we shall

This essay first appeared under the title 'Rational Man and Social Science' in R. Harrison, ed., *Rational Action: Studies in the Philosophy of Social Science*, Cambridge: Cambridge University Press, 1979, with warm thanks to Amartya Sen, to Quentin Skinner and to those at the meeting of the Thyssen Philosphy Group, where it was first presented, for their criticisms of an earlier draft. But that version made *homo economicus* too selfish and *homo sociologicus* too much a puppet. So I have here made both more flexible (and changed the title), thus creating tensions which later essays will explore further.

have to touch some hard puzzles in epistemology and ethics. But let us start in the foreground with a lazy gardener growing his own lettuces during a drought. He is asked to save water. Is he to respond?

The Water Authority opened on a gentlemanly note of logic and ethics, with only an offhand gesture to my self-interest. All (good) citizens should save water, I was told; you are a (good) citizen; so you should save water. I granted the minor premise with smug alacrity. Undoubtedly I was a (good) citizen. But I disputed the major. Why should all (good) citizens save water? The aim was for enough water to be saved in sum now to see us through later. That was the collective good whose value to all citizens, including me, will not be challenged. But it did not depend on whether all citizens save water. Enough is enough; why should I help? Well, came the soft answer, very little is being asked of you. It would not hurt you to put half a brick in your cistern, for instance, and, if a million households do the same, the region will be a million gallons a day to the good. Nor would you really miss the odd bath and, if you showered with a friend, you might even enjoy it. At worst any marginal unpleasantness will be outweighed by your marginal self-satisfaction. Every little helps postpone the crisis and so benefits you too. Virtue brings its own reward, you see.

As a philosopher with lettuces at risk, I was unmoved. The question being initially not what was right but what was rational, it was too soon to appeal to virtue. My beautiful friendships might survive the odd bath skipped but my lettuces would die. Bluntly, my costs would outweigh my benefits and so, by an 'economic' definition of rationality, it was irrational to incur them. The reason was not that a dead lettuce now would outweigh my present joy in contemplating an uncertain future gallon of water. It was that the Authority's case involved a flaw akin to a fallacy of distribution. I stood to gain, only if a million others saved water too. Unless they did, my efforts would be vain. But, if they did, my efforts would be unnecessary. Hence my efforts would be either vain or unnecessary. Since they cost me something, however little, it was not rational for me to make them. It was fallacious for the Authority to argue that what all would rationally want to have provided each would rationally help to provide.

Meanwhile a lady wrote in sorrow to the local paper to lament 'the odd person who thinks that washing his car or watering his garden cannot make all that difference'. Yes, but was he so odd? Taking the question numerically, the Authority found that he was not; and so doubled its exhortations and put a formal ban on hoses. The letter columns of the paper began to glow with the Dunkirk spirit, as citizens pooled tips on bathing in a bucket and boiling eggs in the tea pot. One man reported that his dahlias were blooming on dishwater as never before and was printed under the heading 'Virtue Rewarded'. But the figures told another story. Surveys showed that, while 10 per cent were saving like mad, 40 per cent were making only token economies and 50 per cent none at all. Let us invent a random citizen from each group, called, respectively, Lock, Stock and Barrel. Lock is one of the 10 per cent all but keeping their taps locked. Stock is one of the 40 per cent making a few stock gestures but no more. Barrel is one of the 50 per cent using water by the barrel. Let us suppose that all grow flowers and lettuces but none earns his living from his garden or has any other special claim to water. Also none is a magistrate, councillor or local bigwig, with a special need to set an example (or not to be caught out). Lock loses both flowers and lettuces, Stock loses his flowers but waters his lettuces by hand. Barrel hoses both impartially. Which is the rational man?

In so far as three men have resolved the same problem in different ways, logic suggests that at most one is rational. Nonetheless it can be argued that all are, since each had objectively good reasons for his response. Lock and his 10 per cent had the reasons considerately supplied by the Water Authority. Stock and his 40 per cent had the legal ban on hoses as a reason for abandoning the flowers and economic reasons for saving the lettuces. Barrel and his 50 per cent kept rather quiet (except for a man who announced that he had paid his water rates for unlimited water and meant to have what he had paid for) but there were reasons to hand. For instance the City Council was still visibly watering lawns, flowerbeds and even hard tennis courts. Besides, domestic water consumption is trivial compared with what industry uses. Also the argument about the fallacy of distribution could itself be cited by Barrel as a reason.

But, I reply, even though all had their reasons, it does not follow that all were rational. We need to ask who had the best reasons. It can turn out that all had equally inconclusive reasons but not that all had sufficient reasons, when a sufficient reason for doing x is also sufficient for not doing y. Admittedly Buridan's ass, placed midway between two bushels of hay, has a sufficient reason for eating either. But it does not have one for preferring a named bushel; and, in any case, Lock, Stock and Barrel are not in the same fix. If they all face the same problem set by the drought and solve it differently, we need a way of arbitrating between them.

The reply depends on the problem's being the same for each and this can be doubted. Each had his own projects, desires and beliefs. Each did what appeared best to him and could report, like the legendary fellow who leapt naked into a bed of nettles, that it seemed a good idea at the time. Each had apparently scored 100 per cent in a private examination which he alone sat. Economists often give this answer and it taps one common interpretation of utility theory. Here each agent faces a situation defined by the subjective utilities of various combinations of services or goods and is blessed with a complete, reflexive and transitive scheme of preferences. In trading off the utility of plants saved against that of freedom from sanctions, Lock, Stock and Barrel all act differently and each consistently. Or so it may be said.

In simple form, this approach sounds vapid but I am not trying to poke fun. Even if the universal fact of ordered preferences in each agent is the merest of tautologies, it cannot be known *a priori* how much of what a particular agent would prefer to what at what prices, and empirical work is still needed. Also, like drones in a beehive, tautologies are nowadays seen to be useful on their own account as categorial axioms or statements introducing paradigmatic concepts and it need not be trite or vapid to say that explanation should be concerned with individuals' preferences and their satisfaction. Nonetheless the circularity should not pass unnoticed. Indifference maps are drawn by taking actions as signs of pairwise comparisons and then projecting the comparisons on the assumption that the agent has a consistent scheme of transitive preferences and maximises expected utility accordingly. Any apparent discrepancy between the assumption and actual choices is removed by drawing distinctions among apparently similar occasions of choice. The distinctions are regulated by a principle of producing the simplest map consistent with the assumption. Yet, even if the process recalls a traditional culture preserving its belief in witchcraft, oracles and magic, that need not be to condemn it.

Nevertheless any purported explanation of action becomes a redescription, premised on making all agents not just equally rational but necessarily so. With more space I would argue that such redescriptions are not explanatory. As it is, I must be content to note that they cannot answer the original question. How much notice was it rational for me to take of the drought? I refuse to accept the answer that, however much or little notice I take, I shall always have acted rationally. Fortunately there is another way to read utility theory, which supports this refusal. Many economists, still subscribing to Edgeworth's dictum that 'the first principle of economics is that every agent is actuated only by self-interest',[1] would urge that Lock, Stock and Barrel could not all have succeeded in maximising their self-interest. They put a hard-headed gloss on 'self-interest' and the question is who gained the highest benefit at lowest cost. The hard-headed reply is clear. Since each individual saving of water is either vain or unnecessary and since it involves some cost, however small, Barrel is the outright winner, until hoses are banned. Thereafter the judges must decide whether there has been a change in the price of water. If penalties and risks of detection are low, then the price is still effectively zero and Barrel retains his title. If they are high, Stock moves into first place. A change of price does not affect the principle, however, which is that it is more rational to gain a fixed benefit at lower cost.

---

[1] *Mathematical Psychics*, London: Routledge and Kegan Paul, 1881, p. 16.

The moral for government is equally clear. The water campaign used the terse slogan 'Save It', borrowed from the campaign to save energy when oil prices doubled. In both cases each consumer could reason rightly that his saving would be either vain or unnecessary as a contribution to the total. In both cases the total benefit is shared among all, whether they have contributed or not. Yet the energy campaign had far more success. Why? Unlike water, energy is usually metered and we each pay for what we use. So there is a selective incentive, even if not one of quite the sort which confines a subscription concert to those who have paid the subscription. It could only weaken the energy campaign to extend the 'Save It' slogan to water or, for that matter, chastity. There has to be an effective spur, like a real risk of a huge fine or an outbreak of VD among teenagers. Without one, it is merely irrational to work for charity, pay bills, vote in elections, take litter home from picnics or volunteer in a national emergency. In all such matters Reason stands like a proverbial sergeant-major, inviting those who can play the violin to step forward and marching them off to scrub the latrines.

In fact, of course, people do vote in safe seats on wet nights without Australian-style fines. They do demonstrate amid hostile crowds, collect money for spastics, speak out against tyrants and bathe in five inches of water. But they are being stupid, given the hard-headed economic argument. While they are stupid, the moral does not apply and there is no need for selective incentives. Yet the moral is still there, only waiting for the spread of education and enlightened self-interest. Theories of the social contract sometimes fancy that human beings need law because they are irrational. On the contrary, by the economic account they need law because they are too often rational.

Before exploring the social implications, however, we need to be clear about the assumptions of this economic account. Three are especially significant. First, rationality is taken as *Zweck-rationalität*, a matter strictly of the means to a given end. The rationality of ends does not arise, except in so far as ends can be means to further ends. The criterion for what is a better means needs not be in crude cash. For instance, the value of a lovingly tended lettuce may be more than the few pence the greengrocer would charge for an apparent substitute. Anyone whose ends are better served by saving his lettuces is irrational to do as the Water Authority wants.

Secondly, an egoism has been assumed. There is no fallacy in arguing, 'The public will need water later; there will be none later, unless the public saves it now; so it is rational for the public to save water now.' The same holds, although with diminishing force, as we substitute smaller units, like industries, still large enough to affect their own future supply. The flaw emerges, when we argue, 'Each person will need water later; so it is rational for each to save it now.' Egoism exposes the flaw by pointing out that it is irrational to contribute to a desired result, unless the result depends on one's contribution. This is not to say that I have no interest in the interests of others, since I often have goals which I can attain only by cooperation. Also the fact that I love my mother, for instance, may both condition my goals and act as a selective incentive. But the crux is that other people's concerns affect *me* only in so far as they bear on *my* concerns. This makes the central puzzle one of identifying conditions under which the interests of each will coincide with the interests of all. To seek its solution by means of selective incentives, is to assume that we are self-regarding in a philosophical sense, whether or not we are selfish in an everyday sense.

There is also, thirdly, a social atomism. Lock, Stock and Barrel have featured throughout as abstract atoms or individuals. They could be picked at random from their groups, because it made no difference who they were. Each was simply a member of the set comprising all like him, and the sets differed merely in the skill with which they tackled the same problem. This is not the only way to conceive human beings. For instance, had Lock been made a social atom but not an egoist or an egoist but not a social atom, other solutions might have emerged. We get the 'economic' solution only if he is both an atom and an egoist and therefore stupid. But with these three assumptions it truly follows, I submit. It is irrational to contribute to a collective good at positive cost, even though the good benefits each and will not be provided for anyone if all act rationally. The secret of harnessing the General Will is then to find the selective incentives which force men to be free.

Those who dislike the solution must challenge the assumptions. Let us start with the third by making more of the thought that Lock, Stock and Barrel are citizens. Could it be that Lock is not a stupid atom but a rational citizen? Certainly the fact that he is a citizen helps explain why he saves water. There are norms of citizenship, exploited in the original appeal to all (good) citizens to economise and evidenced by the indignant tone of letters to the paper. So far a citizen has been merely a member of the set of individuals attached to the national water supply; but, if the idea of norms is introduced into the argument, a fresh inference emerges:

1 Citizens are required to do their 'duty'.
2 Their 'duty' at present is to save water.
3 So each citizen 'should' save water.

Previously there was no valid step from: 'It is in the interest of all that water be saved' to 'It is in the interest of each to save it'. Now it looks as if we might pass validly from 'It is the duty of all' to 'It is the duty of each'.

There is, admittedly, a doubt about the meaning and truth of the premises. 'Duty' in the first two and 'should' in the conclusion bear a special sense deriving from the concept of a norm. Whether this is a proper sense is too long a story to unravel here. To set the sociologist off, I shall simply assume that there is a social position of citizen with normative expectations attached, which every citizen has a 'duty' (in quotes) to discharge. I shall also assert that citizens did truly have a 'duty' to save water. Someone may protest that this is preposterous, when half the population was taking no notice and another 40 per cent very little. But in that case why should the Locks be so smug and the Barrels so silent? At any rate, assuming that talk of 'duties' (in quotes) is licit, we can see the difference between economist and sociologist by citing the fate of Lord Finchley as immortalised by Hilaire Belloc:

> Lord Finchley tried to mend the electric light
> Himself. It struck him dead and serve him right.
> It is the business of the wealthy man
> To give employment to the artisan.

To the economist, Lord Finchley's fault was that of a wealthy man who forgets in a situation of choice under uncertainty that the hire of an electrician would be worth the opportunity cost. To the sociologist, his lordship erred in transgressing the bounds of his station and found that *noblesse oblige* was reinforced by lethal electric sanctions.

At first sight there is nothing here to embarrass economists. They can grant that each citizen has a 'duty' to save water and simply ask why that makes it rational to do so. The prize still goes to Barrel, who has calculated that the costs of doing his 'duty' outweigh the benefits and has therefore rationally shirked the 'duty'. But sociologists have a fresh answer. It is that each citizen has the goal of doing his 'duty' and saving water is the only means to this end. Rationality being taken as *Zweckrationalität*, of course it is rational for a citizen to save water. Similarly, citizens may or may not have a duty to vote; but, if they do, then it is rational for them to trundle to the poll, whatever the weather.

Economists are now awkwardly placed. In so far as they have disclaimed all interest in the source and rationality of goals, it seems that they must concur. To do so does not put them out of a job, since it not always so plain what 'duty' demands of citizens. The Chancellor of the Exchequer, for instance, has a duty to combine a high level of GNP with high employment and will need the best economists in the Treasury to divine how. Equally, with a looser test for what counts as an economic problem, most social policy offers scope for cost-benefit analysis in implementing it. But, on the other hand, economists have now forfeited their claim to judge between Lock, Stock and Barrel. Instead of ruling clearly in favour of Barrel, they must suspend judgement until told what goal is being sought and what sociological constraints there are on the rational economic choice of means. For the particular case of a typical householder in a drought, there is then nothing further to do, since it does not take a degree in economics to decide what to do about a few buckets of water.

This raises a hard question about rationality assumptions in neo-classical economics. They are usually claimed to specify what makes an allocation of resources rational, without reference to whether the goal thus pursued is worth pursuing. But it is not plain that questions of rationality reduce to those of efficiency. For instance the theory assumes that producers aim to maximise profit and consumers to maximise consumer surplus, and it then shows how to assess alternative actions by the test of whether they achieve these aims. When experience suggests, as it does, that few agents are successful maximisers, theory has various options. It might admit to being descriptively false but insist that it is still normatively valid: would-be maximisers should pay more attention to its prescriptions. Or it might maintain that it is indeed descriptively accurate, when account is taken of particular circumstances as perceived by the agents themselves. Or it might settle for the suggestion that economic agents are usually 'satisficers', rather than maximisers, and are content with 'good enough' solutions to problems of choice. This last alternative subdivides into satisficing because it is not worth the time, effort or expense of acquiring better information, and satisficing because the agent has plural goals or roles and would not care to pursue one, for example profit, at the exclusion of others, for example social esteem.

These options are indeed various. The first makes us ponder the relevance and merit of maximising advice given to agents who seem not to have the maximising urge. The second creates a suspicion that the theory is vacuous or, at any rate, so well equipped to redescribe all contrary evidence that it is unfalsifiable. The third allows a trade-off between imperfect information and plural goals which leaves it unclear whether satisficing and maximising are rival or complementary ideas. That in turn makes us ask whether 'utility' can possibly serve as a universal goal or universal currency for comparing goals or, indeed, what work exactly it is doing at all. With all these balls in the air, it ceases to be plain both when an allocation is efficient and whether an efficient allocation is always a rational one.

Conversely, if the economist is to give the clear initial ruling in favour of Barrel as the individual who has responded most rationally to the drought, it can only be by making specific assumptions which reduce the options in ways open to challenge. These assumptions did not obtrude earlier because they were dressed as universal propositions about human nature. Rational economic man is *homo sapiens* at large, an egoistic social atom who answers an appeal to save water only if it is in his own self-interest. But, in that case, the judges cannot award the prize to Barrel without knowing the real interests of egoistic social atoms. Lock, saving every spoonful, is utterly efficient in pursuing the goal set by the Water Authority and either he is mistaken about where his self-interest lies or the judges are mistaken. Either way, awkward questions spring up. But we shall be better placed to pursue them, when we have said more about a sociological perspective.

Whereas *homo economicus* is an abstract, individual, yet universal, homunculus, *homo sociologicus* is a social being, essentially located in a scheme of positions and roles. It is important to see how very strong the accompanying postulates must be, if sociology is to bid successfully for the explanatory trumps. At first sight positions are merely abodes and roles merely trappings: if someone dislikes being a nun she can change her job or not pray so hard, rather as others can move house or wear new clothes. But so detached a role-player will also find herself wondering whether it is rational for her to do what is expected of a nun. Yet a fully and finally sociological solution depends on an inference from 'It is her "duty" to do what her order expects' to 'It is rational for her to obey.' The inference is invalid if the goal internal to her way of life is a means to an external goal which could be better served in some other way. Hence pre-social atoms are replaced *essentially* by role-bearers, *constituted* by the social positions to which the roles belong. Otherwise the economist springs back with utility calculations about when it is rational to do one's 'duty'. Ultimately, failure to perform must be failure to be oneself.

I stress the word 'ultimately'. The point is not that a nun cannot rationally resign but that she cannot escape all positions and roles and remain human. A rational nun need not be a totally obsessive nun. Being perhaps also a doctor, daughter, historian and second trombone, she may rationally consider how best to combine these roles. A sociological scheme has room for doubt within it and, witness the Chancellor of the Exchequer, scope for economists to resolve the doubt. But, ultimately, there can be no extra-social goals to judge the return on role-playing against. For the solution to work uncompromisingly, *homo sociologicus* must lay a very strong claim to encapsulate our identity as persons.

Nor can *homo sociologicus* be an egoist. The economic solution assumed *Zweckrationalität*, egoism and atomism. The sociologist cannot be content to reject the atomism, in so far as egoism implies a substantive thesis about real interests and the rationality of self-regarding action. In disputing that real interests are independent of social institutions, the sociologist rejects both egoism as an external measure of interests and the claim that action is rational in so far as it is instrumental in pursuing them. The problem which arose in the drought, because the self-interest of each does not sum to a collective self-interest, is supposed to be solved by working back from the collective, socially defined interest to what each person therefore has a duty to contribute. Admittedly this is no magic resolution. We may well distrust the idea of a collectivity set above individuals' own independent aspirations; and, on a practical note, centralised states which govern by fiat are notoriously incompetent at devising rules which, when obeyed by all, realise the collective aim. This version of *homo sociologicus* may turn out to be no improvement on the previous *homo economicus*.

Nevertheless, we now have two schematic answers to the hose-pipe problem. One makes it rational for Barrel to use as much water as he can get away with. The other makes it rational for Lock to use as little as an obedient citizen is permitted. I myself like Lock no better than Barrel and, even as he receives his embossed scroll from the Lord Mayor, I shall try to strike him down. It is tempting to challenge this version of *homo sociologicus* directly, by denying flatly that all questions of rationality arise within a role and are settled by working out the demands of the role. But that would be to counter dogma with dogma; and there is more virtue in a fresh look at the idea of rationality itself.

Both answers started by assuming that rationality is an instrumental notion, relating means to ends but neutral among ends. Yet both make assumptions about human nature, which, in stating what we essentially are, imply a thesis about where our real interests lie. Having postulated a substantive view of our proper ends, both turn out to imply that action directed to the wrong end is irrational, if the alternative was action which would serve the correct end. This suggests that there is more to *Zweckrationalität* than the instrumentality that meets the eye. I shall suggest that *Zweckrationalität*, as standardly defined is neither the sole nor even the primary notion of rationality.

What, then, are the conditions for an action to be *zweckrational*? They are often said to be that the agent must believe, after deliberation among alternatives, that he is doing what is likeliest to achieve whatever he happens to want. Let us start by spelling these conditions out too weakly and then tighten them, until we reach a defensible answer. Too weakly, then, *S* acts rationally in doing *a*, if and only if:

1 *S* wants to achieve *g*.
2 *S* has a choice among alternative ways of achieving *g*.
3 *S* believes that *a* is the best way to achieve *g*.

Such an account says too much and too little. It includes too much by specifying a conscious choice among alternatives. The minor objection is that there need not be alternatives. Whether drinking water is the rational way to stay alive in the desert does not depend on whether there is an inferior way to stay alive, nor on whether there is anything else to drink. The major objection is that to insist on conscious deliberation is to miss the place of habit in rational action. The rational way to drive a car is precisely not to deliberate each change of gear but to master the skill so well that no deliberation is needed. There are rational habits and, were there not, we could not talk, plan, associate, build, reason or perform many other tasks which make social life possible. Rational action is a skill requiring habit and, if the point is missed, large areas of social action are wrongly classed as non-rational, with great harm to the social sciences.

The conditions include too little by resting content with the agent's wants and beliefs. The lesser objection is that mere belief that *a* is the best way is not enough to make the doing of *a* rational. Since knowledge would be too strong a condition, what is required to distinguish subjectively from objectively rational action is rational belief. Much hangs on the definition. During the 1970s a Labour government passed a law requiring local authorities to introduce comprehensive education in their schools, to replace the existing selective scheme of grammar, technical and secondary modern schools. The Labour council in the borough of Tameside duly set about it but lost control to the Conservatives just before the new scheme was to start. The new council began unscrambling the scheme, whereupon the Minister tried to stop them on the grounds that they were interfering unreasonably with children's education. The matter went to court, where the Minister's case was not that selective schooling is unreasonable (although he thought it was) but that it was too late to organise it before the school year started. He won, but the Law Lords overruled him on appeal, not because the new council did have a viable scheme and time enough but because, they said, the law recognises that a man may be reasonable, although wrong. The only limit to reasonable error, in the eyes of the law, is that a man cannot be 'so wrong that no reasonable person could sensibly take that view'. Blatant circularity aside, the judgement is surely mistaken. It holds people to act reasonably, provided that they have some warrant for their view, even though they have ignored or not bothered to check for better warrant against. The Tameside council indisputably had the weight of expert evidence against them and so resembled someone who shuts one ear and protests that he is doing his best with the other. Objectively rational belief is belief justified by the balance not of evidence actually taken into account but of evidence which should be taken into account. Otherwise irrational actions are wrongly classed as rational, with harm to, for example, the study of mental illness.

The larger objection is to treating what the agent wants as

given *desideranda*. It is tempting to do so, since it seems to explain why what is sauce for the goose is not automatically sauce for the gander – why, for instance, one person will rationally holiday in Spain while another climbs Mount Everest. Indeed, if rationality were a purely instrumental notion, it should be possible to infer straight from '*S* wants to achieve *g*' and '*a* is the most effective means' to '*S* would act rationally in doing *a*.' The temptation may also make us doubt whether Lock, Stock and Barrel are in competition. Nonetheless the inference is to be resisted. The most effective way for me to get rapturously high, let us suppose, is taking heroin. Does that make it rational to do so? Well, I must first realise that addiction is likely and an early death. But, provided I want this result, or at least accept it as the price of the kicks, am I not rational to go ahead?

An instrumental notion of rationality does not imply an unqualified Yes. I act irrationally in seeking to satisfy a desire which I shall foreseeably regret having acted upon. For example, addiction will frustrate the satisfaction of other desires, which will matter more later than they do now. Economists can distinguish between immediately urgent preferences and preferences ordered consistently over time, and thus between what is merely desired and what is rationally desired. But 'rationally desired' here turns solely on what is achievable and any set of consistently satisfiable desires will do. Utility maps have an engagingly named 'bliss point' in the top right corner, where satisfaction is maximised and, one imagines, the bloated consumer puts paws in the air with a stupefied sigh. Desires which can achieve this equilibrium can be deemed more rational than others.

Admittedly bliss points are purely notional, especially in a social system which depends on our always wanting more than we get. As Hobbes observes;

Continual success in obtaining those things which a man from time to time desireth, that is to say, continual prospering, is that men call FELICITY; I mean the felicity of this life. For there is no such thing as perpetual tranquillity of mind, while we live here; because life itself is but motion, and can never be without desire, nor without fear, no more than without sense. (*Leviathan*, ch. VII)

This restless kind of felicity, whether due to human nature or to capitalism, is unsettling for the notion that a rational desire is a satisfiable desire. Indeed it invites the sociological comment that economically rational egoists are doomed to alienation from their fellows and themselves. But, in principle, frustration is the measure of irrationality. The most attainable set of goals is the rational set; and the most efficient way to close the gap between what is desired and what is achieved is the rational way. The implication is squarely that rational individuals adjust their goals to what the system delivers, if that is easier than changing the system.

I wish to contend that, on the contrary, it is not always rational to lower one's ceiling, rather than raising one's floor. This possibility is not allowed in the previous answers. The economists who gave Barrel the prize must maintain that action which brings about a lasting match between desire and reward is *eo ipso* rational. They are squarely committed to a thesis about real human interests, one which, because no question of the essential identity of social atoms arises, cannot object to turning a discontented man into a pig satisfied. What is rational for me cannot depend in principle on who I am, while my identity is in principle a variable open to social or psychic engineering. Sociologists, however, seem at first more resistant, since they take identity as something closer to a constant. If I am defined in terms of positions and roles, then to dislocate me is to destroy me. (Admittedly identity is not quite a constant since the nun could rationally change position; yet neither is it quite a variable, since the nun survives only if her new position is somehow concordant with the old.) But, although sociologists thus have a fresh view of human nature and, with it, of human interests, it is still more rational to be a happy slave than a frustrated citizen. The transition is still advantageous, even if it can only be made gradually. No sense yet attaches to the idea that rational persons need an identity in which they can be fully themselves.

The contentious issue is thus whether there can be desires which a person could act on without regretting the result and yet be irrational to act on. There is a science fiction story where human civilisation comes finally to rest with what seem to be bunches of shimmering grapes. On closer inspection, the time traveller sees that each grape is a cosy, iridescent envelope and inside it there lies a happy, slug-like human forever stroked by a mechanical arm. These creatures would never regret their terminal state, if only because they had programmed themselves not to regret it. Yet it is not obvious that a human being would act rationally in choosing this irreversible happiness. That depends on where our real interests lie; and real interests, I submit, are bound up not with what we want but with what we are.

This line is appealing but ambiguous. Does it claim that each of us has our own identity and destroys it at our own peril? Or does it claim more grandly that everyone, in virtue of being human, has the same real interests? Fortunately we need not establish the latter in order to show that *Zweckrationalität* is not the primary kind of rationality. We need only show that it might be in our interests to change our desires, our projects, our character, or whatever it is that tempts us to say there is no single criterion for Lock, Stock and Barrel. Nonetheless the weaker claim is too weak, since it makes us into monads, all essentially different and each entitled to rejoice in our uniqueness. When Barrel is found with his hand on the tap, we have already refused to let him settle the argument by saying 'I would not be me if I did not turn it on.' Yet we cannot just give Lock's reason that orders are orders, since an analogous argument would make it rational for a member of the Gestapo to torture obediently and with enthusiasm, provided that he is happy in his work, has a proper career structure and enjoys the esteem of his peers. Rationality has to consist in identifying with some set of principles neither merely because one wants to nor merely because they are the going norms of one's station but because, whatever it may mean to say so, they are in one's real interest.

We are not far from the idea that action is rational when it is expressive. Is it rational to climb Mount Everest? Instrumentally it is, for someone who wants to get to the top and has no more efficient way up. But that answer sees action as a way of achieving. An expressive view sees it as a way of being and becoming, of expressing and developing the self. Cost-effectiveness is no longer crucial and people can act rationally from, for instance, honour, respect or gratitude without having to be found a goal rationally thus achieved.

The idea is attractive enough to have invaded political sociology, where exponents of an 'economic' theory of democracy sometimes invoke it to deal with the puzzle of the determined voter. This is the stubborn citizen, who turns out to vote regardless of discomfort or prospect of affecting the result. Since such persons make up most of the electorate, they are an embarrassment to a theory premised on the postulate that individuals are instrumentally rational. But that, it is often said, is solely because voting is often not an instrumental act; hence all is resolved when we see that determined voters are acting rationally by acting expressively.

Yet mere labelling explains nothing, and we may still ask what is rational about the voters' gesture. If the answer is either that they merely feel moved by a desire to record their true preference or are mere creatures of the electoral norms, we are still just where we were. There has to be a reason to explain why it is rational to act on the desire or to accept the norm. I do not mean that it is never rational to do what one desires because one wants to or to follow a rule because it is the rule. But, in acting expressively, we affirm the value both of the desire which constitutes us what we are and of the rule which constitutes the action what it is. To deem the gesture rational, we need good reason for the affirmation. Otherwise it is the idlest sleight of hand to classify determined voters as *wertrational* economic agents. So far Barrel is merely consistently selfish and Lock merely oversocialised. Neither is made more intelligible by dubbing his actions expressive.

Hence I prefer to keep to the notion of real interests, with the suggestion that it may be in one's real interest to affirm an identity. The case is the minimal one, that 'a is the best means to g' does not entail 'a is a rational action', since the inference requires that g be in one's real interest, which in turn is a matter of who one is. Since I shall not be more specific here, a formal statement must suffice. Catching up the earlier points, I propose that S acts rationally in doing a if and only if:

1 *a* is likeliest to realise *g*.
2 It is in *S*'s overall real interest to realise *g*.
3 Conditions (1) and (2) are *S*'s reasons for doing *a*.

Those willing to support me can now pass judgement on the lettuce problem. The economist's strategy is sound enough, since it seeks the candidate who best advances his real interests, whereas the sociologist affects not to judge the norms in terms of the interests of the citizens. But the economist ascribes rationality to a notional sort of atom who cannot have real interests, whereas the sociologist has at least the makings of a connection between the rationality of ends and the identity of the agent. Yet, for a *homo sociologicus* of the sort considered so far, the connection is that it is always rational to conform to the norms of one's culture, just because they are the norms. Those disliking both Lock and Barrel can therefore award the prize to Stock, on the grounds that he alone is a rational citizen. He is detached enough from the norms to make place for economic calculation but not so detached that he ceases to be essentially a citizen. Unlike Barrel, he heeds the public good. Unlike Lock, he leaves a distance between himself and the role the Water Authority has scripted for him. He alone emerges as a rational person with an essential social identity and his prizewinning solution is to take as little notice of the Water Authority as a rational citizen should.

There is one further ambiguity to resolve, however, before Stock can claim his prize. Although the trio were picked at random from actual groups of people, they are not yet flesh and blood. In the abstract I prefer persons conceived as citizens distanced from the norms. But it does not follow that Stock will always abandon his flowers and save his lettuces. Sometimes he will act like Barrel, on the un-Barrelish grounds that the government needs to be provoked into enforcing a norm properly in the interests of all. Thus fervent humanitarians will sometimes refuse to give money to charity, because charities do just enough good to let the state shirk its responsibility to do more. Conversely Stock will act like Lock, when he finds the norms excellent or deems the national crisis urgent enough to forgo his distance. Indeed the doctrine of collective responsibility depends on getting mutinous Stocks to act like Locks for the larger good. In the abstract, we conclude that the rationality of the ends justifies the means; that ends are rational in so far as they serve the real interests of the agent; that real interests are to be gauged by making a true model of human nature; and that social science must take note in explaining no less than social ethics in justifying. But the model is one question and the rational way for Stock to act in a drought another.

Nonetheless I submit also that Stock was right to abandon his flowers and save his lettuces. Unlike Barrel, he is essentially a citizen and so party in principle to the enterprise of providing collective goods. Whereas Barrel thinks of himself as a shopper in a supermarket, free to spurn the amazing offers on the shelves and the appeal of the Spastics' box at the door, Stock sees a duty not to let the side down. Consequently Barrel cannot urge directly that it is rational for Stock to pay less for everything. Instead he must argue either that it would be rational for Stock to think of himself like Barrel or that even a citizen, who is essentially a citizen, is a fool to save water. Stock can then reply that he is essentially a citizen and so can find it rational to act expressively at small inconvenience. Against Lock, however, he contends that blind obedience is no virtue. It is indeed foolish to let used bath water drain into the sea, when it could be siphoned into the garden, thus reducing the need for foreign imports. As an unsentimental contributor to the pluralist state, he offers up his thirsty flowers and keeps his lettuces. And so I picture the three of them riding into the sunset at the end of the debate, Barrel in the middle of the road in his well-washed Mercedes, Stock with a dusty saloon and a tankful of unleaded petrol, Lock about to be knocked off his bicycle into the ditch as a reward for saving energy too. But notice that it is not Stock on the bicycle. In the old dispute between herbivores and carnivores, Stock is temperately carnivorous.

Meanwhile the seasons advanced, the rains came, the reservoirs filled and England enjoyed the wettest autumn for years. The Water Authority could still be heard shouting through the cascade that the drought was as serious as ever. But the Dunkirk spirit had gone from the papers, washed out by sight of the collective good being provided from on high. Lock felt cheated of his virtue, Stock mourned his lost chrysanthemums and Barrel reached for the salad cream. The saving of water had turned out both vain and unnecessary. But that was merely a quirk of fate, whereas our task is to deliver the judgement of Reason.

CHAPTER 3

Rational preferences

In *The Golden Treasury of Microeconomic Legends* the ancient tale of the Judgement of Paris goes perhaps like this:

The previous story told how Paris, son of King Priam of Troy, was secretly handed over to shepherds as a baby and brought up as a shepherd. One day while out with his sheep, he was maximising his utility by substituting leisure for work, when three goddesses invaded the domain of his preferences. They handed him a golden apple and bade him award it to whichever of them he judged the most beautiful. That gave him three feasible options and he set about ranking them by pairwise comparisons of the consequences of each in the light of his current tastes. Since all effort is a cost, he might not have got far with the task, had not each goddess in turn whispered an improper suggestion in his startled ear. Athena promised him wisdom and, for good measure, victory in all his battles, if he would award her the apple. Hera undertook to make him lord of all Asia in return for the prize. Aphrodite offered him the hand of the loveliest mortal woman in the world.

Paris settled down to calculate. 'I rate Athena's offer at an initial 100 utils', he mused, 'and Hera's at 100 utils too. But Athena is too devious to be trusted and Hera would be the more dangerous to offend. So Athena's 100 reduces to 80, given a 20 per cent chance of non-delivery, and then to 50 with the hidden cost of displeasing Hera; whereas Hera's 100, discounted, is still 91.33 utils (to two decimal places). Aphrodite's offer, however, weighs in at 200 utils and, even after discounting, is the one which does most for my consumer surplus. She, therefore, will win the golden apple for beauty.'

This caricature of Rational Economic Man is not meant with malice. It exaggerates some crucial features of the stock notion

This essay first appeared in *The Philosophical Forum*, 14, 1983.

of rational choice in economics but only so as to make them readily visible. Before picking them out, however, let me sketch a line of thought to guide the essay and indicate what is intended to emerge from it.

Microeconomic theory is pivotal for the economics standardly taught in Western universities and of huge interest to other social sciences. It commands attention especially for its powerful species of individualism and for the elegance and force of its mathematical techniques. The former grounds an analysis of market transactions between individuals of all sorts (including, for instance, firms). The latter achieve a precision unmatched elsewhere in the social sciences. Together they seem not only to explain a vital part of the social system but also to do so in a way which can be generalised. They are linked by an elegant notion of rational choice, which can appear to make microeconomics a seamless whole. But, on reflection, it is not seamless. The individualism can be challenged and the notion of rational choice can be adapted to an essentially social kind of actor, while retaining the glory of the techniques. The essay explores this thought by reflecting on the idea of rational preferences, its aim being a fresh portrait of the rational agent.

If Paris is to do duty as a typical microeconomic agent, some preliminary comment is needed. The textbook usually stipulates perfect information in the ideal case and he certainly lacked that. Aphrodite quite forgot to mention that the loveliest woman in the world was married already and that abducting her would lead to the Trojan War and the death of Paris himself. But I shall simply shirk the thorny question of information by assuming that he did his honest best on incomplete evidence and under conditions of uncertainty. The canon of deliberative rationality does not guarantee correct answers and he had followed it properly. I shall argue that he calculated on the wrong base but not that he miscalculated on the base which he used.

The utility numbers also need a preliminary word. I put them in partly as a tease and, to that extent, ordinal utilities would do at least as well. Plainly one could query both the number of utils offered by each option and any figure for the likelihood of getting it. But the numbers also hint at a serious point by gesturing to some old hopes of the felicific calculus. Utils started life as units of inner satisfaction or, so to speak, microwatts of inner glow. I doubt if anyone ever took them literally. The idea was, rather, that a science of mind must in principle make all alternative actions comparable and, ideally, quantitatively so, thus providing a basis for exact predictions. The mind worked in accordance with precise mental laws governing the satisfactions to be had, given various initial conditions. The psychological detail of the old account has since dropped away, leaving only the broad mathematical requirement that a rational agent be some sort of maximiser. But, it seems to me, a mathematical psychics still needs its ontology. It still matters what is maximised and I shall resist the idea that terms like 'preference' and 'self-interest' can function merely as dummies.

The legend also credits Paris with complete and consistent preferences. This is certainly true to the stock economic model but invites the complaint that the model is not true to life. Real people do not have such ordered preferences and, if we really made $\frac{n(n-1)}{2}$ pairwise comparisons for every n feasible options (even without allowing for the several consequences of varying likelihood involved in each), we would get nothing done at all. Most of us muddle through with inconsistent or incomplete preferences and partial orderings. That is undeniable and economists know it too. But it does not debar the textbook model as a useful ideal type. Were we not at least broadly systematic about relevant ranges of alternatives, social life would collapse. The model idealises this fact by abstracting and then projecting to an instructive limiting case. It also idealises in the sense of prescribing what a fully rational agent would do and hence, in so far as it fails to capture our actual habits, shows us how to do better. So economists can agree that life is messier and less competent than in their model, but can then turn criticism by adjusting the balance of descriptive and prescriptive. Perhaps that threatens to leave the model too immune to falsification; but, although I would take this very seriously on another occasion, I shall acquiesce here. It is no vice to idealise, provided that lifelines are not entirely cut, and I shall not pursue charges of oversimplification.

My caricature is thus meant to isolate the core of the model – the relation between preferences, actions and outcomes. A rational agent, microeconomically speaking, is one whose actions are well calculated, in the light of their likely consequences (and costs) best to satisfy his existing preferences. To quote Frank Hahn, 'given the set of available actions, an agent chooses rationally, if there is no other action available to him the consequence of which he prefers to that of the chosen action'.[1] This is so much the core that it is worth pausing to dissect it. Apart from their general completeness and consistency, Paris' preferences have four particular characteristics, which mark out the idea of rational choice involved. His preferences are *given, current, homogeneous* and *determining*. I shall work through this list and then use it to raise doubts about the stock notion of economic rationality.

Paris' preferences are *given*. The goddesses' offers act basically like the arrival of a mail-order catalogue, by changing the options open to someone with prepared tastes. Like a catalogue, they may change the price lines on the agent's utility map but (subject to what will be said presently) they do not change the indifference curves and other schedules. This is not to pretend that his preferences have no explanation at all. It means only that explaining them is not the job of economists. Microeconomics relies on various givens, which include the external social context and internal psychic dispositions. It is left to other sciences to account for these extraneous factors and economics need not wait for the results. Admittedly there has to be some scope for preferences to vary with events in the market and I shall return to that. But the scope cannot be large enough to subvert the underlying relation between preferences, actions and outcomes, which marks the textbook agent; nor can the findings of other sciences subvert the notion of rational choice involved.

[1] This sentence comes from the introduction to F. Hahn and M. Hollis, eds., *Philosophy and Economic Theory*, Oxford: Oxford University Press, 1979, p. 4, where some rather more technical points (for which I claim no credit) are made about economic rationality.

Secondly, the preferences which motivate Paris are *current*. He
is not directly moved by past or by future or by hypothetical
preferences. That seems obvious at first blink but so odd at the
next that it needs spelling out. Paris seems clearly to be moved
by a past taste for shepherdesses and by a future taste for the
delights promised by Aphrodite. But he is not directly so moved.
The past taste matters partly because he still has it and partly
because its previous results inform the assignment of utilities.
The future taste operates by strengthening his present confidence
and perhaps his present desire. Similarly, other people's desires
move him only in so far as he has a present taste for satisfying
them. Equally, hypothetical desires, which he would have if this
or that were to occur, affect him only by way of beliefs which
feed present motivations. How odd – or how natural – this
sounds depends on how it is worded but the reasons for insisting
on it go very deep. They derive from a Humean philosophy of
mind, which treats action as the product of present desire plus
present belief, with desire as the motor and reason firmly the
slave of the passions. Just as beliefs, although often no doubt
about past or future or other people's beliefs, cannot affect
calculation, unless they are the agent's own present beliefs, so
too desires must be current. To doubt it (as I shall later) is to
subvert the motivational component of the model.

Thirdly, preferences are *homogeneous*, in the sense that they
have to be ordered in a common coin, despite the whiff of
incommensurability. Paris can compare pushpin with poetry,
bingo with Beethoven, guns with butter and sex with wisdom.
(He may be indifferent, but never baffled.) My version of the
legend puts the point carelessly by suggesting that he was
untroubled by ethics. He needed to know that Helen was
married, it seemed, only because that would raise his costs and
reduce his chances. But the model itself requires no such
cynicism about human motives. 'The first principle of economics
is that every agent is actuated solely by self-interest', F.Y.
Edgeworth declared in *Mathematical Psychics* (1881, p.16), and
that is as true as ever. But it is true only in the sense that every
agent is actuated by his own desires. These desires need not be
selfish and the coin in which all preferences can be ordered need

not be cash. There is, in short, nothing inherently odd about what are often termed 'ethical preferences' as elements in the schedule. An economic agent may (or may not) be moved by moral commitments, sympathies, or sense of duty: microeconomics has no view. But, equally, there is nothing special about ethical preferences. They are treated as desires and admitted on the same terms as all other desires. They can be weighed against others and there is nothing in microeconomics to make them inherently heavy or light. The common measure is neutral and indeed so unspecific as to be mysterious. It is merely 'utility' and, in calling it that, we do no more than mutter an ontological spell.

With the schedule in place and the consequences duly computed, action follows. Preferences are, fourthly, *determining*. This is not to make them the only premises of practical reasoning. Action depends also on what Paris believes and how he computes. But in the ideal case, with perfect information and correct computing, preference is automatically transmitted into outcome so as to solve the maximising problem. The agent is simply a throughput. Indeed he is also a throughput in non-ideal cases, merely a more complicated one. There is none of the active judgement which a Kantian account of rational choice would invoke against a Benthamite image of the mind as a balance or scales. It is as if literally true that the heavier pan of the scales determines action. In other words, once the desires of a rational agent have been specified, there is no further call to explain why he acts on them.

Equipped with these four features of preference, we can think further about Athena's offer of wisdom. The uninitiated might deem it a tempting offer (quite apart from the bonus of victory in all battles). But Paris correctly assigned it a value by reference to his current preferences, after comparing wisdom with carnal pleasures in the homogeneous coin of expected net utility and finding that it weighed lighter. This procedure seems strangely blinkered. Would he not have been rational to reckon up the expected utility of becoming wise not to the sensual man he was but to the wise man he would become? Was he not foolish to settle his character by relying on his present sensual tastes? To those beckoning questions the model, aided by its residual

Humean philosophy of mind, returns a firm No. Let us see exactly why and then exploit the answer.

To clear the line, suppose explicitly that Athena was not offering to gratify a taste which he already had. Paris had not been hankering for a wisdom previously unobtainable. Nor was she even offering a new taste for the sake of an old one – Learn to Love Opera and Astonish Your Friends! She was proposing a change of preferences which would come to be welcomed but only in retrospect. Assume, in other words, that Paris, with new preferences, would be glad to have accepted but that Paris, with his current preferences, correctly ranked the offer below Aphrodite's. The crux is thus not one about time preference, delayed gratification, uncertainty, or imperfect information. It is squarely one about change of character.

The firm No has its roots both in the metaphysics of markets and in the epistemology of microeconomic explanation. A market here is a forum where individuals exchange in ways which leave them at least as well satisfied as before. For, questions of power and coercion aside, rational agents never enter a transaction which leaves them worse off overall. The price of goods settles somewhere between the most that a rational buyer will pay and the least that a rational seller will accept (with elegant theorems to narrow the gap); and this fact explains the workings of a free market. In ambitious analyses the institutional aspects of markets are treated in turn as deposits left by previous transactions, in ways aided typically by the theory of games. Modest accounts, which leave the task of accounting for institutions to other social sciences, still insist that everything internal to a free market is a matter of individual choices. Hence there is a deep-seated individualism in microeconomics, which explains economic events and processes by reference to individual decisions. Present decisions can be motivated only by present desires.

Welfare economics too has this order of priority in assessing the efficiency of markets, the productiveness of economies, the welfare of consumers and, at its most ambitious, the merits of social systems. The test is always how well they satisfy preferences, either directly or through intermediate measures of the use of resources. These normative exercises are all of a piece with the descriptive work of positive economics, since, as noted earlier, what ought to be is simply the difference between the ideal and the imperfect actual. Here too it cannot be allowed that markets determine preferences, or not in depth. For, in that case, welfare economics could as well be employed to identify the market arrangements which would create the desires easiest to satisfy fully. This is a possible aim of a normative science but not one to amuse individualists, and microeconomics will not be party to it.

That is not to rule out all influence of markets on preferences. Undeniably new products do give consumers new ideas; new advertisements set new trends; new institutional rules encourage new patterns of preference. But such propellants have to be treated as information acting on more lasting preferences. Otherwise microeconomics would have to wait upon research into the determinants of preference after all and the theory would lose its primacy. The standard theory of rational choice is pivotal, only if there is a domain for which it is true enough that given preferences determine economic workings. In it lie the explanations of the last resort.

On reflection, however, this domain is at best an analytical device. Microeconomists, it seems, are happy enough to let the social system determine preferences, provided that the economic system does not. Yet how are they to distinguish between economic and social systems?[2] The economic presumably includes whatever is produced and how it is produced, exchanged and distributed. This vast network must form part of the social system and have a major impact on the rest of it. Conversely, the social system includes a host of norms, practices, roles and regulations, which can be separated from the economy only by conceptual artifice. It soon comes to look as if the only difference between what is external to economics and what is internal is that the internal relies on a certain amount of psychology, which may depend in its turn on some external system, at least in part.

[2] The line of thought in this paragraph comes from Ian Steedman's paper, 'Economic Theory and Intrinsically NonAutonomous Preferences and Beliefs', *Quaderni della Fondazione G. Feltinelli*, no. 718, 1980. I have also been much helped by his other work in the area and by his useful comments in correspondence.

If so, economics studies either an aspect of the general network, distinguished from other aspects only for analytical convenience, or a part of the general network, whose boundary with other parts depends solely on how academia institutionalises disciplines. In either case individual preferences have none of the special status and motive force which microeconomics requires.

The microeconomist must reply, I think, by appealing to a wider individualism. The Rational Economic Agent is a special case of the Rational Agent who holds a key to all domains of political and social life. If so, rational-agent theories of, for instance, democracy or social exchange are not merely interesting exports from economics. They are also a test of the economic model itself, since it is no longer peculiar to economics that a rational agent does what is best calculated to satisfy his preference schedule. Microeconomics must export or die. That removes the immediate pressure, which arose when the domain meant to be explained as the effects of rational economic action threatened to become the source of individual preferences. But it does so by forming an individualist alliance across the board and thus making the threat a general one. The general threat is that the institutional workings of the social system determine preferences, thus reversing the proposed direction of explanation throughout the social world. Relatedly, the test of success of a social system becomes how well it creates preferences, which it can satisfy – a similar reversal on the ethical front, which individualists must also resist.

Discussion now risks getting out of hand. Issues of individualism vs. holism, of psychologism vs. sociologism and of choice vs. determinism loom. So let me extract a narrow moral from the implicit generality of the economic model. It is that the source of preferences does matter, and so does the manner of their determination. The question is how an appeal to a wider individualism prevents the reversal both of the order of explanation in Positive economics and in the measures of economic success considered in welfare economics. The answer, which I shall now propose, is that it does not prevent it without a revision of the stock notion of rational choice.

Frank Hahn has remarked, 'Economics probably made a mistake, when it adopted the nomenclature of "rational", when all it meant is correct calculations and an orderly personality. The term invites philosophers to invest the whole theory with too much significance.'[3] This seems to me to dismiss a genuine problem too lightly but I grant that so far Paris is rational in no stronger sense. His actions are determined by a complete and consistent set of given, current, homogeneous preferences. The determining is done by following a formula for converting evidence about likely costs and consequences into statements of expected net utility. When all is done by the book, the agent is no more than a throughput. That is why Paris was wholly rational in rejecting Athena's offer of wisdom and why a radical revision would be needed to let him be rational in accepting it.

The obvious point of attack is the givenness of his wants. If Paris had leverage on his own wants, he would at least be less of a throughput. The standard model allows some initial manoeuvre. There are some wants which I have only because I have particular beliefs and which are vulnerable to a change in belief. For instance, I might not want to visit Florida if I did not believe that a Disney World is sited there and would give my children many microwatts of inner glow. There are some wants, whose satisfaction, I may come to realise, frustrates other wants. I might, for example, spot that my passion for garlic is spoiling my love life and rationally choose a course of hypnosis to cure it. In such ways the preference set of a rational agent is not static. But there are strict limits on how far the model can let it vary at his own behest. Wants can be rationally changed only in the service of other wants. Rational action must remain an instrument which furthers ends supplied by an orderly personality. Tinkering is allowed, but only if the agent has a consistent set of dispositional desires to serve as the gauge of improvements.

This condition applies to hierarchical theories of motivation which keep faith with a Humean philosophy of mind. Amartya Sen has suggested that the model could accommodate a distinction between preferences over outcomes and preferences over preferences.[4] Thus a reluctant alcoholic is more complex

---

[3] Hahn and Hollis, *Philosophy and Economic Theory*, p. 12.
[4] See his 'Choice, Orderings and Morality', in S. Körner, ed., *Practical Reason*, Oxford: Basil Blackwell, 1974.

than a simple shepherd. He prefers gin to water but prefers to prefer water to gin. He would be rational to act on the higher-order preference and microeconomics can adopt this kind of thought with thanks. I find the idea promising enough; but it is not as neat as the example suggests. The temptation to say that a rational agent always chooses to act on his higher-order preferences is to be resisted. A reluctant homosexual prefers his own sex and prefers to prefer the other. But, if that is because of implanted guilt, we might well think it his rational choice to set about shedding the guilt. In general there is no reason in the model why preferences over preferences should be granted special weight. Indeed the whole idea of *granting* weight to a desire which, so far, simply *has* weight is, so far, obscure.

On the other hand the use of the current weight of current desires as a measure rules out more than refinements. It makes it hard to see how anyone can rationally act to satisfy a desire which he does not have, even though he foresees that he will have it. Every investment in the future, every delay in gratification, threatens to become irrational. Admittedly the agent can be ascribed a present desire to gratify a future desire. Indeed he will have to be. But there is no reason to expect these indirect desires to be strong or to weigh heavy. If they do, it is a contingent fact about the agent. Nothing yet makes the consistent Epicurean, who firmly pursues the pleasures of the moment, in the least irrational.

If this line of attack is taken to the limit, it becomes irrational to make the effort to boil an egg for eating in a few minutes' time. That line I put aside. But, well short of it, there is still every warrant for thinking Paris irrational, given his current preferences, to opt for wisdom. Why should he acquire this new personality, when it corresponds to nothing, or nothing effective, in his present one? This *nolle prosequi* will disappoint liberals who, like J. S. Mill, hope to persuade people to prefer higher pleasures to lower by pointing out that those who have tried both recommend the higher ones. But the model clearly implies that pushpin is better than poetry for anyone who now enjoys pushpin and is bored by poetry, since the inducement appeals only to a different personality. In general it is, so far, pointless to give someone a reason to have done something, unless it is also a reason to do it. Hence the fact that Paris in his future persona would be glad to have become wise is no reason for him in his present persona to choose accordingly.

The notion of 'an orderly personality' is troublesome. The agent's 'personality' is simply a set of dispositional desires and, I shall contend, ignores crucial aspects of morality and personal identity. But that will come better, if introduced by some further remarks on assigning utilities to the self over a lifetime. There used to be a telling advertisement for a pension scheme which made its pitch with five sketches of the same man at different periods of his life. 1: he is aged 25 and saying cheerfully, 'I have no idea whether my job carries a pension.' 2: at 35 he notes with a slight frown, 'My job has no pension but...' 3: at 45 he is admitting, 'I wish my job had a pension.' 4: at 55 he declares, 'I am deeply worried about retirement.' 5: at 65, white haired and furrowed, he is confessing, 'I really don't know how I shall manage without a pension.' The message is that a pension at 65 matters at 25. It relies on its man identifying at each stage with himself at all other stages. Let us see whether Paris will take the bait.

Let us split Paris' life into the same five stages, with various moments of decision represented by forks in a path. Suppose that the direction taken at each fork depends solely on his choice and that consequences are always clear (thus setting questions of discount for uncertainty aside). Suppose that choice at each stage is governed by a personality different from the previous one in a way to be specified in a moment. Schematically, in short, Paris' life is as laid out in Figure 1.

Paris I makes the legendary judgement, deciding which goddess to succumb to. Aphrodite beckons him along path *a* or *b*, depending on whether, as Paris II, he dies in the fall of Troy (*a*), or makes a discreet escape and lives on in exile (*b*). Hera offers him path *c*, where he lives a dissolute life as Lord of Asia, ending in a cheerful old age with a Bithynian dancer. Athena invites him to become the wise PII** who must choose between a careful career as a philosopher (*d*), and a short life of glory (*e*). Suppose finally that the various changes of personality are enough to see to it that what each Paris chooses is not always what the next Paris is glad to have had chosen.

Age 25	Age 35	Age 45	Age 55	Age 65	Path
		(obit)			a
	PII	PIII →	PIV →	PV	b
PI —	PII* →	PIII* →	PIV* →	PV*	c
	PII**	PIII** →	PIV** →	PV**	d
		PIII*** →	(obit)		e

Figure 1

The puzzle set is partly to assign utilities to each phase and partly to see how they should influence choices. Thus Paris I sets a lower value on wisdom than Paris II** does and cannot put a value on Aphrodite's offer of Helen without knowing whether Paris II will decide to escape the fall of Troy. The 'obvious' solution is to assign to each phase the value which its governing personality would assign and then pick the path with the largest total. But the snag emerges readily in Figure 2.

Decade	1st	2nd	3rd	4th	5th	
Path a	20	0	—	—	—	} (Aphrodite)
b	20	5	5	5	5	}
c	10	10	10	10	10	(Hera)
d	5	15	2	2	10	} (Athena)
e	5	15	20	—	—	}

Figure 2

There are in fact several snags but I shall concentrate on the one involved in shifting perspectives. In some ways the puzzle is like one in Social Choice Theory, where the question is how to distribute utilities among persons with different tastes spread across several generations. There is, for instance, similar trouble with interpersonal comparisons, complicated because in some solutions the later generations will not be born at all. Thus path *c* totals 50 and path *d* 34 but (even granting plausibility to the figures) that is not yet to say that *c* is preferable. Path *d*, with all five stages, cannot easily be compared with *e* which has three (a total of 40 or an average of 13.3?). But such queries are too general for this essay.

The peculiar snag is that there is no obvious point of view from which to discuss solutions at all. Fourteen characters (of a sort) appear in Figure 1 and none is a plausible candidate for what might be dubbed Paris-at-large. The most plausible is Paris I; but only if his rational choice of a path is to be guided solely by his current utility values for each option, and that is precisely the point of view which I am trying to work loose. Also later personalities are characters only of a sort. They are not really like descendants of Paris their ancestor. Children can resent their parents' choices or be grateful for them, whereas Paris II can only regret or take satisfaction in the choices of Paris I. Descendants, basking in the shade of oak trees planted by their grandfather, bless him and not the family-at-large; whereas Paris V, basking in the joys of a philosophical old age, blesses himself. That kind of point cannot be made with the help of Figures 1 and 2, however, since none of the fourteen characters has a past or a future. (If that is not plain, think of Paris I as consisting of ten characters each lasting a year and each subdividing into twelve lasting a month and so on *ad absurdum*.) Paris-at-large has yet to put in an appearance.

The idea is to make it rational for Paris to choose a course of action which is inferior when measured by his present yardstick but which he knows will cease to have been inferior in retrospect. The example is the choice of wisdom over other pleasures. But it should not lead us to approve all choices with this formal feature. Happy morons can be produced by brain surgery and it would be awkward to find that most people would do well to volunteer. So the rational choice of personality is not governed solely by the satisfaction accruing to the later self. It will have to be in some sense a principled choice tied to an idealised conception of the agent's identity.

As noted earlier, however, the usual theory treats principles as preferences and as powerless to move an agent, unless already among his motivations. That creates an impasse. If Paris' current preferences already gave him motive enough to choose wisdom, the problem would not have arisen in the first place. As remarked, the usual theory gives no grounds for making principled preferences to count for more, and with Paris, it seems, they do not. The way out of the impasse, I suggest, is to separate reasons from motives more thoroughly than the usual theory permits. If 'coherent calculation and an orderly personality' can give Paris a motive without giving him a sufficient reason, then the idea of a principled choice can be inserted into the gap.

That adds a further condition to the usual list for rational agency, and we must ask whether it will subvert the microeconomic model as a source of valuable techniques and elegant theorems. The notion of sufficient reason sets problems both substantive and formal. Substantively there are questions about human identity and real interests which land us in ethics, moral psychology, political economy and social theory at large. Formally, the notion needs to be given shape and I shall next do my best.

I want to loosen the usual tie between preferences, actions and outcomes by insisting that a rational agent has rational preferences. Why would that affect the internal ties? It seems merely to restrict the permissible ends to which the rational agent chooses the means. By analogy, why would it affect the rational choice of the best way to travel to Bithynia, if one insisted that Bithynia be a good place to visit? The answer, I think, is that the rational agent is no longer merely a throughput. Paris-at-large has become involved in every decision of his life, in the sense that he is always shaping his identity by his choices. This is not plain in trivial or isolated choices, since they let us take his identity for granted as a going concern. But even here there is a suppressed conditional: only if Bithynia is the rational place to be, can Paris infer that the best way of getting there determines his rational choice of action. An identity is not expressed solely in the choice of ends but shows itself as much in the ordering of means. For example, a chieftain who lives by a code of honour will rank the various ways of disposing of enemies accordingly and terms like 'treachery' will enter directly into the description of the options.

The tempting retort is that a man of honour is instrumentally rational but subject to a different tariff of prices. That, however, begs the persistent question of whether 'utility' can both function as a universal coin and be definite enough to yield price tags. The man of honour prices the manner of actions, whereas the textbook agent prices only their consequences. It is not clear that 'prices' invokes the same metaphor in each case. The man of honour does not first itemise his options and then price them; he itemises them in a language which has prices built into it. This either makes him different from the textbook agent or (as I would maintain myself) shows that the latter is covertly doing the same. At any rate 'utility' cannot be a universal coin, unless a choice apparently between an instrumental and an expressive course of action can always be construed as one between either two instruments or two ways of self-expression. The source of nonsense in Figures 1 and 2, in my view, is a presumption that Paris always faces instrumental choices.

If this is granted, a call for rational preferences subverts the textbook at three points. It makes every choice into a choice (even if suppressed) of what (or who) to become. It denies the moral neutrality of the language of description. It undermines the textbook account of motivation as produced by desires of differing strength. This last point will perhaps cause most objection. A Humean picture of reason as the slave of the passions – of information and calculation as powerless to move an agent unless addressed to an existing desire – has been very widely assumed in the theory of utility. I cannot show such a picture mistaken in a few lines but, at any rate, it is not a *sine qua non* of a theory of rational choice. A principled choice is one which the rational agent makes from belief: in recognising that there is a good reason for him to do something, he makes that reason his own. Kantians claim, and Humeans deny, that such recognition can motivate. If it can, however, that creates no special problems for the theory of choice. The theory will still work, provided that there is a way of ordering options systematically. I cannot see that it matters whether the options are ordered by whether they satisfy preferences or satisfy principles. Nor need the actions change the state of an external world, even if success in reordering one's own preference does usually take time and external support. This is all contentious, I admit, and I do not pretend to prove it with a snap of the fingers. But it is one question whether a Kantian view of the relation of belief to desire in the actions of a rational agent is right, and another whether the theory of choice can live with a Kantian victory. It can, I submit, and for the better.

The other two subversive points are addressed strictly to the textbook account of the model, since, if right, they are already embodied in its actual use. If a morally neutral language for describing actions is impossible, then no one uses one. If every rational choice must involve something about the agent's identity, then every actual judgement covertly presumes that something. Roughly, a Kantian version deals in reasons suited to an autonomous agent, whereas a Humean one calls only for ordered preferences. Where agents desire what befits an autonomous person, the philosophical switch will yield the same judgements. But the door is now open for wider considerations than the textbook account admits. In effect, the textbook presents as neutral and instrumental what is, I claim, neither; and is thus committed to a stand in both moral psychology and, to recall an earlier point, political economy. That lands microeconomists in the sort of debate which they had hoped to avoid.

The risk remains that, in widening the grounds of rational judgement, I have so sullied the clarity of the calculus that chaos results. Certainly the notions of autonomy, identity and expressive rationality form a sort of Bermuda triangle where many a scholar has vanished without trace. So let me cite two matters where the widening seems to have definite advantage and then end by arguing that there is intellectual virtue in living dangerously.

Both matters arise because 'rational' choices can, it seems, sum to an irrational result. One concerns a series of choices presented to the same agent. For instance, a hiker can choose rationally at a series of forks in the path and knowingly end up too far downhill, perhaps because too tired to care that the downhill forks lead only roughly in the right direction. Prudence advises *reculer pour mieux sauter*[5] but immediate preferences override prudence. Hence even prudence requires a standpoint from which the agent can umpire against the run of immediately more urgent desires. That standpoint lies somewhere in the Bermuda triangle.

[5] I borrow this neat tag for the key from Jon Elster's *Ulysses and the Sirens*, Cambridge: Cambridge University Press, 1979, to which I owe a large debt.

The other matter concerns the paradoxes of collective action, notably those related to the Prisoner's Dilemma. Here each actor has a dominant rational choice and the sum of these choices is inferior for all. The fatal choice is dominant for each, given current preferences. If this very fact could count as a reason for each to act against current preferences, that would be of great theoretical interest. But it cannot do so in a Humean philosophy of mind, since it requires a Kantian distinction between reasons and motives. Without pressing for a verdict now, let me at least note that, if a suitable separation of reason and desire helps avoid suboptimal outcomes within the rules of the theory of games, then a promising way of understanding social life formally is enriched.[6]

These seem to me genuine advantages but not ones to be had on the cheap. They require rational economic agents who can stand back from their situation and their dispositions. They must be able to reflect on whether the upshot of their calculations is truly the rational course of action. This is to raise a query about the basis of the calculation. J. S. Mill holds that the free agent is the person who has succeeded in forming his character as he would ideally wish it to be, adding 'and hence it is said with truth that none but a person of confirmed virtue is free' (*System of Logic* VI, 2, iii). The same can be said of truly rational agents, once it is granted that they may find themselves locked into their preferences contrary to their higher interests. Rational action is not only an instrument to satisfy desire but also an expression of the person who has the desire. Hence there is more to the shape of a life than an orderly personality. The extra dimension, which means typically that action has value in its doing as well as in its consequences, affects the merit of the advice which emerges from applying microeconomic theory to human affairs.

That leaves several questions about individualism unresolved. The microeconomic textbook relies on a particularly atomistic and mechanical version, which I have been trying to subvert. Actors need to be more social and less clockwork. But it can sometimes seem as if the only alternative were to make us

[6] The theme is pursued in 'A rational agent's gotta do!' below and at greater depth in 'Penny Pinching and Backward Induction', *The Journal of Philosophy*, 88, 9, 1991.

puppets or creatures of social context. I like that no better: cultural dopes are no advance on psychic robots. There are, however, more tempting individualisms and more human accounts of social context. For instance, the individuals depicted in Mill's *On Liberty* are neither mechanical nor essentially independent of others; and Marx looks forward to an unalienated state of society where each person is fulfilled. These are not (or not only) ethical concerns. They permeate the explanatory work of social science, as each thinker presented it. But I do not mean to imply that liberalism-with-a-social-dimension shades painlessly into socialism-with-a-human-face, and there is no space to say more.[7]

I revert finally to my remark that microeconomics must export or die. The immediate reason was that it could otherwise only be an analytical device to lodge an economy, where individual actions determine outcomes, within a social system which determines individual preferences. Hence the economic model would have to be a special case of a general thesis about social action. Conversely, what is true of social action needs to be imported into microeconomics. It is plainer in sociology and politics that we shape our lives in our choices and hence that explanation must allow for expressive meaning; but it is not truer than in economics. So it is not even a useful device to present economic life as a sum of atomistic choices and social life as a gavotte of structural meanings. The actors express themselves in both and, I submit, the connecting idea is that of rational preference.

There is more to the Judgement of Paris, then, than *The Golden Treasury of Microeconomic Legends* records. Here is how the story continues in *The Book of External Reasons*:

So Paris gave Aphrodite the apple and received her congratulations on his skill at the felicific calculus.

Hera was not amused. 'That was well judged, only if he will escape the Fall of Troy', she complained. 'But we know that he will choose a hero's death then. So, to be consistent, he should have taken a hero's course now and let me make him lord of Asia.'

---

[7] I say more about Mill in 'The Social Liberty Game', in A. Phillipps Griffiths, ed., *Of Liberty*, Cambridge: Cambridge University Press, 1983.

'Not at all', Athena replied. 'Firstly, it is not inconsistent to want now to be Helen's husband for a few years and a hero later. A man might very well pray to the gods, "Make me heroic but not yet!" Secondly, it would be most inconsistent to choose to be a hero as a way of maximising one's windfall profits. To be a hero one must choose heroically. Thirdly, you have offered no external reason for the heroic course, except the muddled thought that old age with a Bithynian dancer is more agreeable than an early death at Troy. Yet I understand your anger. Paris was asked to award the prize to the most beautiful of us and then offered enticing reasons to ignore the beauty of wisdom. Do not blame me. A wise man would not have been moved by such reasons. He would have done what he was asked – as, indeed, Paris would have done, had he accepted my gift of wisdom.'

'But', Hera protested, 'but that is a conclusive thought only if the standpoint of wisdom is uniquely the right standpoint from which to arbitrate between the claims of pleasure, glory and wisdom.'

'Quite so', said Athena with a smile.

CHAPTER 4

The Ant and the Grasshopper

All summer long the Grasshopper consumed and the Ant invested. 'You are acting very irrationally', the Ant warned, 'and you will be sorry when winter comes.' 'I shall be very sorry', replied the Grasshopper with a chirrup, 'but I am not acting irrationally. To be rational is to do what one most values at the time, and I value present delight above its cost in future sorrow. Surely you too would rather sit in the sun and sing?' 'Much rather', said the Ant, 'but to be rational is to do what best promotes one's interests over a lifetime. Future grief has constant weight (where there is no uncertainty about it). So, being rational, I must keep busy investing against winter.'

Winter came and the Grasshopper was hungry. He appealed to the Ant for help. 'I wish I could', said the Ant, 'there is nothing I would like better. But, being rational, I cannot prefer your interests to mine, and you have nothing to offer in return. Are you not sorry you sang all summer?' 'Very sorry', the Grasshopper sighed, 'just as I knew I would be. But now is now – I acted rationally then. It is you who are irrational, in resisting your present desire to help me.'

The Ant reconsidered but found that she had only just enough in store to last her until it was time to start investing again. 'Now is every time', she explained, 'but I can help in one way. Do you know the leaves of the Epicurus plant over there? They are nourishing and delicious. I would eat them myself (and save the trouble of making my own granary), but they make insects very

This fable appears as an appendix to chapter 6 of my book, *The Cunning of Reason*, Cambridge: Cambridge University Press, 1987.

ill after a time and, being rational, I cannot abuse my lifetime's interests. For you, however, the present ecstasy would outweigh the consequences, silly fellow.'

So the Grasshopper sampled an Epicurus leaf and found it excellent, but was soon in agony. 'Is it worth it?' asked the Ant. 'No it isn't', the Grasshopper groaned, 'but it was.' 'Then I have bad news for you – there is an antidote.' 'Quick, quick', begged the Grasshopper. 'It is no use to you', the Ant lamented, 'since taking it makes your present distress far worse, even though it works rapidly thereafter.' 'Bad news indeed! I cannot invest. Farewell!'

The Grasshopper expired, and the Ant lived on into grey old age without ever once doing anything which caused her a moment's overall regret. 'It is hard never to be able to do what one most wants to do', she mused arthritically, 'but then the life of a rational being is a hard life.'

Moral: *It is hard to be wise, but there are many ways to be foolish.*

CHAPTER 5

Moves and motives

When Jack and Jill went up the hill to fetch a pail of water, they were playing a one-shot, two-person game where both emerged as losers. Had they been the cool, clear-headed, rational agents of game theory, they might both have done better. Then again they might not. Game theory is a wondrously austere abstraction from our own tumbledown world of laughter and forgetting, where the heart has its reasons and ignorant armies clash by night. Perhaps something crucial is lost in the abstraction, so that Jack and Jill are an allegory for the just deserts of rational maximisers. In Gary Becker's view 'a person decides to marry when the utility expected from marriage exceeds that expected from remaining single or from additional search for a more suitable mate'.[1] If such a person finds a like-minded mate, one is inclined to say, it will serve them both right. But pause before deciding that Becker has a foolish approach to a trip to the well. Game theory embodies a philosophically enticing claim to portray and advise our enlightened selves and, if social life is not that sort of game, we must go on to say what other sort of game it is.

Social action is action which, in Max Weber's useful phrase, 'takes account of the behaviour of others and is thereby oriented in its course'. To study social action, game theory takes a further leaf from Weber's book and sets up an ideal-type world where all agents are fully rational in an instrumental, 'economic' sense.

Originally published with the title 'Moves and Motives in the Games We Play' in *Analysis*, 50, pp. 49–62. I am grateful to Robin Cubitt, Shaun Hargreaves Heap, Bruce Lyons and Robert Sugden for many helpful comments and discussions.

[1] See his *The Economic Approach to Human Behavior*, Chicago: Chicago University Press, 1976, pp. 3–14, for the full story.

Each Jack (or Jill) has fully ordered preferences, complete information and perfect skill in computing. Preferences are so well ordered that he can always rank any pair of possible outcomes. Information is so complete that he always has a subjective probability distribution for all outcomes, thus taming uncertainties; and everyone knows what anyone knows, since each can reproduce the premises and reasoning of each other agent. Each has the similar aim of (broadly speaking) maximising utility; and each knows also that each has this aim. It is, in short, common knowledge that all agents are rational in the sense just given, a situation which we might mark by calling them 'hyper-rational'.

Philosophers often find this notion of rationality, or hyper-rationality, quite *outré* when it is sprung on them. But, basically, it is the familiar Humean notion abstracted to a limiting case and so not really *outré* at all. I therefore ask for patience while I deploy the idea that social life consists of games played by rational individuals with common knowledge.[2] Having done so, I shall then grant that there is something very odd about an ideal-type world which lacks what I shall term the *grit, dust* and *glue* of our own. But, I shall argue, complaints on this score must be finally directed at the familiar Humean notion. The question will then be how thoroughly to overhaul it.

To lend human interest to austere abstraction, some games have acquired names. There is, for instance, 'Battle of the Sexes', perhaps in honour of James Thurber. In this game Jack and Jill are contemplating an evening at either a bullfight or a concert. Each would prefer to have the other's company, although Jack would rather that both went to the bullfight and Jill favours the concert. Their choices being made separately, there are four possible outcomes, which each ranks as the pay-offs indicate in Game 1.

Thus, if both choose the bullfight, Jill will gain 2 utils and Jack 3 utils, these being the pleasant units of some notional

---

Jack

		Bullfight	Concert
Jill	Bullfight	2, 3	0, 0
	Concert	1, 1	3, 2

Game 1

felicific calculus. (For the moment suspend queries about the quantities and what they might represent; and do not presume that interpersonal comparisons of utility are involved.) Both players gain from choices which coordinate but rank these preferred outcomes differently.

The game has two Nash-equilibria or outcomes where neither player could make a better choice, given the choice by the other. (There are also equilibria where the players choose related 'mixed strategies', like tossing a coin – a complication which I shall ignore.) If Jack knew that Jill was heading for the concert, he would rationally do the same; if Jill knew that he was on his way to the bullfight, she would rationally go too. But neither knows until choices have been made, and the Thurberesque battle is on.

Does either have a reason to pick a particular option? For a one-shot game without communication the answer is no. Any reason for Jack to do one thing would be paralleled by a reason for Jill to do the other, with an inferior outcome for both. That sounds terribly austere. What if he loves her more than she loves him, a fact known to both? Will that not make the concert salient? The answer is again no. Any such difference is already included in the pay-offs. Jack's '2' in the bottom right box is made up of his pleasure in the music, in her company and in relishing her enjoyment and so on. Jill's '2' in the top left box need not be blended similarly. Game theory stands aloof from the details of their separate motivations.

If that sounds too quick, pause to juggle with the pay-offs a little, as in Game 2.

		Jack	
		Bullfight	Concert
Jill	Bullfight	2, 3	0, 0
	Concert	1, 1	4, 2

Game 2

Here, if we may lift the embargo on interpersonal comparisons of utility for a moment, she gets more from a concert with him than he from a bullfight with her; and the *total* utility of the former is more than that of the latter. Now is the concert their rational choice? The answer is still no. Firstly, there is no such thing as *their* rational choice, apart from his rational choice and her rational choice. Secondly, if such properties of outcomes can be motivating, then they feed into the relevant utility numbers along with the other ingredients and cannot work in any special way. The theory has no view on what in particular does or should motivate us. It insists merely that Jack's motives are Jack's and Jill's are Jill's, with each able to be represented as pay-offs to that player. With the utility numbers in place, nothing of strategic significance has changed between Game 1 and Game 2, even supposing that Jill's '4' in the bottom right cell of Game 2 represents more utility than her corresponding '3' in Game 1.

Philosophical doubts begin to stir. But I am sure of my ground, not least because of an arresting bit of argument in an elegant recent survey article on game theory by Binmore and Dasgupta,[3] whose details I shall adapt to Jack and Jill. It is some months later and their relationship has developed. He has become more involved with her, she more nuanced about his place in her tastes and feelings. By now she would be equally delighted to go to a concert with him or (surprisingly, but let it

[3] K. Binmore and P. Dasgupta, 'Game Theory: A Survey', in their edited collection, *Economic Organisations as Games*, Oxford: Basil Blackwell, 1986, pp. 1–45, and especially p. 17 for a discussion of the point about 'trembling hands'.

Jack

	Bullfight	Concert
Bullfight	2, 2	5, 0
Concert	2, 1	5, 5

Jill

Game 3

pass) a bullfight without him. She would be less delighted but equally content to go to a bullfight with him or a concert without him. He, more simply, always prefers her company, so much so that he now most fancies a concert at her side. Here they are in Game 3. (It may save confusion, if I mention that this and later games are not examples of Battle of the Sexes.)

Now surely the concert is the rational choice? Certainly one might think it so for Jack, with the bullfight no longer worth more than a possible '2' and with a musical '5' to tempt him. But, even if that case could be made, it still would not be Jill's rational choice. She is austerely indifferent. If he is going to choose the bullfight, she will score '2' whatever she does. If he is going to choose the concert, she will score '5' whatever she does. She has no reason to opt for the concert, at any rate in the absence of communication.

To prove the point let us introduce an element of what game theorists engagingly call a 'trembling hand'. This is the faint possibility that even a rational player might play a non-equilibrium strategy by mistake, for instance by pressing a wrong button in a fit of hiccoughs and thus starting a nuclear war. Consider Game 4, where Jack just might step under a passing car on the way out of the hotel and be crippled for life – a third course of action, so to speak, even if taken only by accident or clumsiness. 'X' marks the spot.

Since, were that to happen, Jill would rather have gone to the bullfight (in pious memory of old days perhaps), then this is what she will do, however small the risk of its happening. Being otherwise indifferent between her two options, she will be

| | | Jack | | |
		Bullfight	Concert	X
Jill	Bullfight	2, 2	5, 0	-99.9, -1000
	Concert	2, 1	5, 5	-100, -1000

Game 4

swayed by the slightest disturbance of the balance. The bullfight becomes her dominant choice, thus prompting Jack to aim for that equilibrium. The concert is out for both of them.

I call this an arresting bit of argument, because it took me some effort to swallow it. Offhand, it sounds ridiculous. It is bad enough to be told that concert/concert (5, 5) is not compelling in Game 3; and worse to have (2, 2) guaranteed in Game 4. But the argument is formally correct. All motivating elements are already included in the pay-offs. Jill's prospects improve by a tiny fraction, if she chooses the bullfight in Game 4. For a hyper-rational player this cures her previous indifference.

To swallow the argument, however, is only to shift attention to its assumptions. I shall argue next that it requires an ideal-type world crucially unlike our own. There are three groups of assumptions to think about, all of which can conveniently be extracted by noting how the pay-off numbers function.

Firstly, the pay-offs express an assumption that all outcomes are grist to the mill of an agent's preferences. This is strong and silent stuff. It is strong in that Jack can compare not only bullfights with concerts but also guns with butter, death with dishonour, the scratching of his little finger with the destruction of the whole world. It is silent in that 'utility' is a purely notional comparator. Originally it was supposed to register Benthamite pleasure or, in Irving Fisher's phrase, 'a psychic flow of inner satisfaction'. But nowadays it marks only Jack's preference for one outcome over another in a psychologically non-committal way. Although I am using numbers merely as a graphic device rather than a record of quantities of anything, even ordinal comparisons involve complete and consistent self-knowledge of, I am bound to say, a mysterious kind. Let us flag the silence about the psychological character and content of preferences by noting a lack of *grit*, meaning something for the preference order to bite on – passions, reasons or whatever can serve as a real motive to the will. To dispense with all grit is to conjure away any problem in assimilating motivating elements which can include Jack's aesthetic response to the music on the concert programme, his pleasure in Jill's pleasure, his recognition of her as a person whose preferences are to be respected and his moral reflection that concerts avoid some ethical questions set by the cruelties of the bullfight.

Secondly, hyper-rational agents have complete information about themselves and others. There is a complete lack of *dust* in the hyper-rational air. In the limiting case Jack and Jill are so wired into each other's inner states that, were they computers, we would be asking whether they were two computers or one with two interconnected routines. Thus, when I set my chess programme to the 'Self-play' mode, I can pretend that black is playing white, as if Jack had one and Jill the other; but the pretence is possible only because, when Jack really plays Jill, neither is completely transparent. Hyper-rational agents can set no traps (since they would be instantly detected) and can make no mental mistakes. Since only a trembling hand or other random intrusion can prevent the result implicit in the logic of the game, victories are empty and the game pointless. Similarly, hyper-rational agents seal all bargains instantly, without incurring the costs of negotiation, and never engage in conflicts which involve deadweight losses. One's left hand does not dispute with one's right hand over which shall reach for a cooling drink that is meanwhile evaporating.

A 'trembling hand' throws a pinch of real-world dust into the air, thus setting hyper-rational agents to deal with uncertainty. But it clouds their sight by introducing a small random element to which they may respond differently and, although this can give rise to interesting theorems, it can presumably be met with mixed (probabilistic) strategies. Something more drastic is needed to make the players separate persons, mentally opaque to each other, like real Jacks and Jills. That finally requires a moral psychology in which agents are not, so to speak, patients, as I shall argue presently. For the moment, let us simply register an inviting gap. We have assumed so far that Jack and Jill hold the same theory of motivation, so that each can be sure how the other will act, given the preferences of each and the information available to both. What theory is that? Presumably it is the one implicit in the basic definition of rational choice. But what if this theory of motivation can be challenged? Then there is room for a new kind of doubt about what other players will do. As soon as this doubt is possible, however, it infects the certainties which have been giving us pause. For instance in Game 3 Jack was sure that Jill was indifferent between bullfight and concert, and sure in Game 4 that she would choose the bullfight. But, if he cannot count on her deliberations proceeding as the standard theory assumes and prescribes, then his rational choice becomes indeterminate.

To flesh the point out, notice, thirdly, that there is no *glue* in the hyper-rational world. The standard concept of rationality is thoroughly instrumental, with rational agents always ready to switch strategy for the sake of a marginal gain in their own overall utility. This sets an intriguing problem of what Derek Parfit aptly terms 'bias to the near',[4] which is troublesome even for a solitary agent planning the future and poses a radical threat to Jack's relations with Jill. Notoriously Jack will sometimes do better for himself, and he and Jill will both fare better, if he can overcome the built-in bias to whatever best satisfies his current preferences (and she to hers). But, although this might incline him to an indirect strategy which suspends 'self-interest', the suspension is only for tactical reasons and only for as long as those reasons hold. Any commitments therefore bind him only *pro tempore*: promises are made to be broken as soon as it pays. To make them durable, he needs to hold a *moral* theory as part of the theory of motivation which he has in his head and Jill needs to know what it is. To provide for durable commitments, game theory needs a moral psychology

[4] In his *Reasons and Persons*, Oxford: Oxford University Press, 1984.

seemingly at odds with its standard assumptions about motivation.

Here lies water so deep that game theorists may hesitate. Some refuse to have anything to do with it, arguing, for example, that it is tempting only if we demand that individually rational choices shall not sum to Pareto-inferior (or 'collectively irrational') outcomes. Otherwise there is nothing to fret about if rational agents cut off their noses, thus spiting their collective and several faces. But others would indeed be tempted by a redefinition of rationality which made it rational to honour commitments even when a forward-looking calculation of consequences was against it. Then the question becomes what moral theory to ascribe to rational agents without undermining the whole basis of game theory. The current favourite is some version of contractarian ethics. But whether it will truly do the job is deep water indeed.[5]

The issue comes to a head in Game 5, where Jill has preferences typical of a Prisoner's Dilemma and scores more from choosing the bullfight both if Jack does too and if he chooses the concert. Jack, knowing this, chooses the bullfight and they spite their faces with a vengeance. (The minus signs are there to make the point graphic, even if raising a query which I shall not linger on.) They spend a rotten evening, reflecting how much both would rather that both had opted for the concert. They could do with something to distance themselves radically from the utility numbers. But, so far at least, a hyper-rational world without grit, dust or glue has them in thrall.

To save time, I shall jump straight to the eventual question: What kind of grit, dust or glue would get them to the concert? An obvious diagnosis is that Jack and Jill are too instrumental for their own good. But this way of putting it suggests that it would pay them, instrumentally speaking, to be less instrumental. If so, the snags are prone to recur at the second order. So I shall cast around further afield by trying out two more radical challenges to the Humean philosophy of mind assumed so far,

---

[5] The water is tested in 'Honour among thieves' below.

Jack

Bullfight   Concert

	Bullfight	Concert
Bullfight	-2, -2	6, -3
Concert	-3, -3	5, 5

Jill

Game 5

one broadly Wittgensteinian, the other broadly Kantian. By 'Humean' here I mean partly the role given to desire (or preferences) as the motor of action, with belief (or information) relegated to being the slave of the passions, on the ground that 'reason alone can never be a motive to any action of the will' (*Treatise*, Book II, Part III, Section 3). This will be the target of a Kantian riposte presently. But I also mean the wider picture of action as an effect whose cause is a mental state composed of desires and beliefs. Wittgensteinians will have none of that.

When game theory abstracts from social life to a 2 × 2 matrix, it skins off all particular social context so as to isolate a universal core. All social embodiments of the same matrix are game-theoretically equivalent. It does not matter whether the agents are persons or, for instance, firms or nations, nor whether the options are ways of spending an evening or ways of conquering the world. This gives the approach its power but also leaves it vulnerable. Supposedly Jack and Jill have been a mere illustration for the benefit of those who are not quite at home with pure abstractions. In fact, I submit, an implicit and specific social context has been doing a great deal of work. Jack and Jill already have some kind of relationship relevant even to their one-shot games and exemplifying not the 2 × 2 matrix but a common pattern of such relationships located in what might be called a culture or form of life. The matrix is a monochrome snapshot of a colourful, dynamic situation reached by a trajectory and fraught with expectations. If this matters, and especially if it matters how the situation came about, then numerically identical exemplifications of the game need not be equivalent after all.

The players might be Britons on holiday in Spain. Then again, they might not. Who cares? Well, even if they are strangers to each other, it matters who they are and why they are there. Normative expectations surround the meeting even of strangers, depending on whether they are tourists or natives and what background expectations each brings to their cultural or sexual encounter. Each dresses, moves and speaks as if flying a string of flags for the other to decode. These signals may be conscious or unconscious, easy or hard to read, but they are certainly visible to an informed eye. Each discloses something about class, status, income, occupation, gender, nationality, character, attitudes and so on, thus staking out normative ground. Their options have been listed as 'bullfight' and 'concert' but these are very curt specifications of options varyingly saturated with many species of meaning. Game theory seems at first sight to declare this all irrelevant, since the pattern of the pay-offs and common knowledge that the players are rational is enough to go on. But perhaps it latently includes some typified reckoning of the context and character of the players, some generalised minimal elements of grit and glue. In that case the matrix is not as austere as it seemed.

Look again at the components of the pay-off numbers. Each number is a homogenised sum of assorted satisfactions, for instance Jack's tastes, his pleasure or pain in Jill's responses, which may include his pleasure in her pleasure in his pleasures, his sense of what is proper or right and so on. Round each component hover subjunctive conditionals, to do with what difference it would make if something in the situation were different. For example, if Jill became queasier about bullfighting, that would lower Jack's utility for bullfights, unless he became less enamoured of Jill. Such conditionals do not operate in a human or cultural vacuum. Their context is highly relevant as soon as either player needs to take them into account. Suppose, for the sake of argument, that the 3 utils, which Jack gets from their both going to the bullfight in the original Game 1 includes − 1 because Jill is edgy about its cruelty (offset by her finding it exciting, and reinforced by her regret that he is missing a dose of higher culture). There is a hard question about how he knows that ' — 1' is a reliable figure and it leads us to ask how *she* knows. The whole matrix is shot through with huge assumptions about the power of introspection. As soon as introspection is challenged, the conditionals cease being merely secondary. The mental states, which were supposed to sit still to be photographed for the matrix, are replete with guesses about likely responses to variations in the world where the players interact.

This line leads to the idea that Jack and Jill are playing 'games' of another character altogether. There will no longer be some single point which all games have in common, like the maximising of an individual's pay-off. Instead there will be only criss-crossing family resemblances, sharing only the loose family tie that all are constituted and regulated by rules governing the way to go on. Interplay becomes, in some sense, prior to play, rather as tennis is not the meeting of persons who have separately chanced upon the same individual and solitary pastime, but a collective activity which constitutes the purpose of individual shots. This is Wittgenstein territory and, by saying so, I hope to be excused an exposition. Instead I shall pick out two large implications and raise one large query.

The first implication is that indeed we cannot always isolate a pay-off matrix common to games with different contexts. The mating game which Jack and Jill play and the diplomatic game which arms negotiators play cannot both be fully captured by, say, the Prisoner's Dilemma. For, even though one might plausibly wish to say of each set of players that they are stuck with self-defeating dominant strategies, it now matters how they came to be stuck. This is what I had in mind when speaking of a snapshot of a situation reached by a trajectory and fraught with expectations. 'Trajectory' is a metaphor for the forward integration of context and moves. The feasible moves are permissible options for how to go on and their significance is a function of the context, conceived as rules of that particular game. That is one reason why introspection has become suspect. There is no reason to credit a chess player with an adequate knowledge of what he is doing, just because he makes introspective claims to himself. We must first have reason to be sure that he understands the public game properly. If game theorists reply that even in one-shot games players can be credited with external information, then I retort that such information is, crucially, intrinsic to the descriptions under which players consider their situation.

Secondly 'expectations' in games from a Wittgensteinian family are not (or not only) predictions, as in game theory. *Normative* expectations are involved. For instance, Jack and Jill will have *entitled* each other to expect typical responses and their interaction is charged with a moral vocabulary. Even in what looks like a genuinely one-shot game, where they have met as strangers intersecting only for a single evening, they bring conventions to their brief encounter. Otherwise they will not succeed in interacting, even though they occupy the same place at the same time. The normative expectations surrounding a one-night stand are not those of a disarmament conference. Hence the figures in Game 3 may not signify indifference on the part of the row-player in all other contexts. The convention for dealing with indifference might differ between dating, courting and disarmament.

The standard game theorist can, of course, protest. If Jill turns out not to be 'indifferent', then the utilities in the pay-offs have been wrongly ascribed. But this is not compelling, if the complaint was that the pay-off numbers are overloaded because they are an attempt to represent as a single net sum what remain complex hypotheticals with normative components. Meanwhile the contextualising of games suggests fresh ideas about the relation of game-theory to morality. One favourite way of getting Jack and Jill into the right box together, and out of a Nash-equilibrium which is inferior for both, is to have them make one another promises. Yet, as noted, promises given for instrumental reasons by agents who look only forward are made to be broken whenever it pays. Perhaps this snag does not bite where a game is the extrusion of a normative context governing both moves and motives.

That thought, however, also introduces my large query. In one reading of Wittgenstein, the inner mental states of Humean moral psychology are so radically externalised that moves and motives can be identified solely through the context, as if to know the rules fully were thereby to know how to go on. I shall take it, however, that the players are to be left some latitude and that the rules are to be construed in a more constructivist way. The model game is not bellringing, where the aim of each is exhausted by the collective aim of ringing Steadman Triples, for instance, but tennis or chess, where each has a distinct aim. But then we have a large query about the relation of players to rules. Specifically, are we to see the kind of moral commitment, which might serve Jack and Jill well, as a demand by the context or as an interpretation by the players? Whereas the latter answer seems to reinstate the snag by restoring Jack and Jill their individuality, the former seems to swallow them up.

Anyone struck by this dilemma might care for a Kantian line. Some features of the context are re-internalised but as demands of a Reason which is the slave of neither the context nor the passions. Ideally rational agents, playing a game where moral choices must be made, will choose from 'the moral point of view' – the universal, impartial, impersonal standpoint which Kant advocated. What started as instrumental hyper-rationality now tries to emerge as moral autonomy. Even the fact that Jack and Jill both do better for themselves becomes an incidental, if gratifying, by-product of the fact that each has chosen what is right. The relation of players to rules is that autonomous players follow the guidance of external reasons in their internal deliberations.

This line requires an explicitly two-tier moral psychology, whose lower tier is still broadly Humean and whose upper tier is firmly not. The lower tier is one of hypothetical imperatives, where a rational agent can proceed by calculating the most effective means to satisfy desires. Lower-tier precommitments can be rational, as when Ulysses had himself bound to the mast so as to hear the sirens and survive. But they are instrumental devices and psychologically artificial. If the cord binding Ulysses is internal, in that it consists only of a promise given to himself, then he can always untie the knot, and will untie it as soon as inclination or prudence demands. By contrast the imperatives of the upper tier are categorical. They are addressed to an autonomous Ulysses, forbid him to treat other persons as means to his ends and guide him independently of his sentiments or calculations. Motivation on the upper tier is netted into a community of autonomous persons, a kingdom of ends or *Rechtsstaat*, so that moral precommitment becomes binding for as long as autonomy lasts. Rules become full-bloodedly normative, provided that they satisfy these moral conditions, because they constitute the special and universal form of life which a moral agent embodies.

I shall not try to justify a Kantian ethics here. But I do want to suggest that game theorists, whose moral psychology cannot cope with a Wittgensteinian revolution, might find succour in Kant. The crux concerns the possibility of drawing up pay-off tables which are neutral between socially different contexts. The Wittgensteinian objection is that there is no neutral currency of satisfactions for assessing actions which belong to different practices. Underlying it is a suggestion that to be rational is to follow an appropriate rule appropriately, rather than weighing options as if in the pans of an omnicompetent pair of scales. To accept it would be catastrophic for game theory, as it destroys the whole basis of utility theory. At the same time, however, it threatens to inject so much grit, dust and glue that agents lose all distance from their situation and become cultural dopes. That can hardly be the right reading of Wittgenstein but, whatever is, game theory needs to hang on to agents who have a rational will operating at a distance from context. Can Wittgensteinians somehow oblige?

Meanwhile, Kantian moral theory is less catastrophic. It assigns an agent's 'ethical preferences' to an upper tier, provided that they are genuinely moral as certified by their passing the universalisability test, and decrees calculating from a moral standpoint. This certainly distances Jack and Jill from their situation. It thereby offers game theory a two-tier motivational structure, in which preferences over preferences operate differently from preferences over outcomes. This seems to me a promising advance. At the same time, however, there are snags. Any inflexible maxim like 'Do what others would most prefer' is liable to recreate the original problems with, so to speak, the colours reversed. There are Prisoner's Dilemmas for altruists as well as for egoists. Also a maxim commanding unselfishness can paralyse everyone, if everyone follows it. (Try cooking dinner for a group of relentless altruists with different tastes.) More seriously still, even if some choices do need to be placed morally off limits, others involve moral or upper-tier judgements which are sensitive to consequences, including what other players are likely to do upon reflection. Otherwise ethics loses touch with the domain of rational interaction, when, for instance, the Good Samaritan is deciding how grand a room at the inn to rent for the man who fell among thieves. The morally rational agent can do without the will of a rhinoceros. Thus there is no simple Kantian magic on offer. We certainly need a glue resistant to bias to the near; but one less rigid than superglue.[6]

The test question is what the rational choices are in Game 5, where Jill's apparently dominant choice steered Jack, and hence both of them, to an outcome inferior for both. On the one hand the 'collectively rational' outcome is the concert (5, 5) and it is tempting to make it accessible. On the other hand received opinion about the one-shot Prisoner's Dilemma is that defection is the rational choice, and I am convinced by it. So we need to go carefully in suggesting that context can undo dominance.

Revert to the nursery rhyme and envisage the game which will face Jack and Jill, when their parents find the broken china pail and ask who is to blame for this naughtiness. If both own up, each will lose a month's pocket money but honour and justice will have been so well served that both emerge with credit. If neither owns up, they will not be believed, will still have to pay and will emerge in disgrace. If Jill alone owns up, she will forfeit two months' pocket money but without dishonour, whereas Jack will feel simply terrible. If Jack alone owns up, however, Jill, being nastier and naughtier than he, will be thoroughly pleased with herself. Quantifying notionally, we get Game 6.

Although Game 6 has the same numbering as Game 5, the labels are different. The crucial '6' in the top right box now records Jill's 'preference' for a ride on Jack's honesty. But it

---

[6] A successful outcome to liberal attempts to construe justice as a form of procedural fairness might meet the case. But that is a long story and no happy ending is in sight.

Jack

Dishonesty   Honesty

		Dishonesty	Honesty
Jill	Dishonesty	-2, -2	6, -3
	Honesty	-3, -3	5, 5

Game 6

suppresses some upper-tier questions about trajectory and expectations. How is that outcome to be described? It is one which is, for instance, unfair, exploitative and lands Jack with the misplaced opprobrium of leading his sister astray. Is this the description under which '6' is the utility figure correctly recorded for Jill? If not, is it, nonetheless, the description which should be used by a rational agent deciding whether she has better reason to be honest or dishonest? When Jill reflects that 'if Jack fails to own up, I am rational not to own up' and also reflects that 'if Jack owns up, I am rational not to own up', are these reflections truly parallel?

Such questions prompt a challenge to the assumptions which connect individual pay-offs to reasons for action. A direct connection requires agents who are, in the ideal-type case, transparent maximising machines. But there are other ways to conceive of persons and, correspondingly, other ways to read the table of utilities. Kantians conceive persons as ends-in-themselves, with whom a truly rational agent will deal by seeking the impersonally right outcome. Others conceive persons as bearers of locally established norms and practices, who will do whatever best accords with the prevailing rules. A neat way of contrasting these alternatives might be to invoke Bernard Williams's distinction between 'thin' concepts, like 'good', 'right' or 'fair', and 'thick' concepts, like 'honourable', 'kind' or 'considerate'. Although that would soon invite more problems, when we asked whether concepts like 'honest' or 'reasonable' are thick or thin, these strike me as fertile questions about the 'persons' whose games are to be illuminated by a theory of games.[7]

Amid these deepening complexities game theorists may lose patience with philosophers and withdraw into an ideal-type world where utilities are unambiguous reports of commensurable preferences and motivation stems directly from them after discounting for risk. But, if so, I would be sorry. Game theory relies on a double abstraction from our world of laughter and forgetting. It first idealises persons as rational economic individuals and then idealises their interaction for a limiting case, where there is no grit, dust or glue. The second idealisation is clearly prescriptive and, supposedly, can be made usefully so by injecting measured amounts of grit, dust and glue and then reworking the prescriptions. But, in bringing the ideal-type nearer to earth, the theory unsettles the first step, because it needs agents distanced from their preferences. That calls for a philosophy of mind where expected utilities do not form a logical bond between moves and motives. The heart has its reasons, but not the kind which expected utility theory knows all about. The head has its reasons too, but not always the kind that can notionally be priced in utils. We are looking for a philosophical psychology where persons have *grit* in their motives, *dust* in the spaces between them and *glue* in their relationships.

Yet Jack and Jill are still playing games. The metaphor remains illuminating. There are often pails of water to fetch, which one person cannot carry alone and two cannot manage without a concern for the common good. If game theory cannot see them safely home with its standard assumptions, I hope that philosophy can help find some better ones.

[7] Bernard Williams, *Ethics and the Limits of Philosophy*, London: Fontana Books, 1985, especially pp. 129 and 140. I have pursued the questions in *The Cunning of Reason*, Cambridge: Cambridge University Press, 1987, chapters 5 and 6, and in 'The Shape of a Life', in J. Altham and R. Harrison, eds., *World, Mind and Ethics*, Cambridge: Cambridge University Press, 1995.

CHAPTER 6

A rational agent's gotta do what a rational agent's gotta do!

A. I have just completed a course in game theory and I feel rotten!

B. Why?

A. In learning to be a rational agent, I have ceased to be a reasonable person.

B. Nonsense! A rational agent is simply a very reasonable person.

A. I'm afraid not. Let me show you the difference. Suppose we set out for a walk along the scenic Enlightenment Trail with its six historic pubs. We agree that, as we reach each pub, we will take it in turns to decide whether the walk ends there or continues. If we get past the first five, the walk will definitely end at *The Triumph of Reason*. Here is a map of the route, with the pubs in the right order and our individual rankings of them as stopping places shown in the brackets. '5' means top, '0' means bottom and my ranking is given first in each bracket. I have the first choice.

B. Yes, I see. The first pub is at the leftmost node. It is that rotten hole *The Rational Choice*, ranked fifth by you and bottom by me. *The Triumph of Reason*, at the rightmost node, is your second favourite and my delight. So that is where our walk will end.

A. No, not if you and I know each other to be rational agents.

A shorter version of this dialogue appeared in *The Royal Economic Society Newsletter*, 1993. It was sparked by a research project on the Foundations of Rational Choice Theory, conducted with Robin Cubitt, Shaun Hargreaves Heap, Judith Mehta, Chris Starmer and Robert Sugden, whom I thank for many lively discussions of the topic. For a more thorough treatment see my 'Penny Pinching and Backward Induction', *Journal of Philosophy*, 88, 9, 1991, pp. 473–88.

In that case the walk ends at *The Rational Choice.*

B.   Don't be ridiculous!

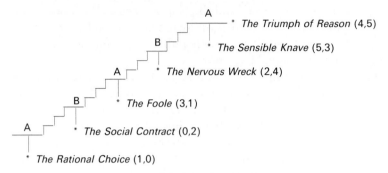

The Enlightenment Trail

A.   I mean it. We shall not reach *The Triumph of Reason* (4,5), because I would say 'halt' at *The Sensible Knave* (5,3). You, foreseeing this, would halt at *The Nervous Wreck* (2,4), which I would preempt by halting at *The Foole* (3,1). You would therefore stop the walk at *The Social Contract* (0,2), which is less to my taste than *The Rational Choice* (1,0). Hence *The Rational Choice* is indeed the rational choice. Sad, isn't it?

B.   Game theory seems to have made you horribly selfish.

A.   No, that is not the trouble. Our rankings may be selfish but they need not be. They merely register how we each rank the pubs as stopping places, giving no clue to our reasons. The trouble is caused solely because, with preferences given, a rational agent's gotta do what a rational agent's gotta do.

B.   It strikes me that the options at each turn are being too narrowly described. Try thinking in terms of policies rather than pubs. If you chose a policy of cooperation, you would end at a pub you prefer to *The Rational Choice*, provided that I did the same. You can expect me to do so, because it offers me a better pub too, provided that I read your initial pass as applying a policy of cooperation. We can thus make it to *The Triumph of Reason* as rational agents.

A.   I would have several cooperative policies to choose from. 'Cooperate to the end' is not the most rational, since

'Cooperate until we reach *The Sensible Knave*' is better for me. That makes your best policy 'Cooperate until we reach *The Nervous Wreck*', and the trouble recurs. Each of us soon spots that 'Cooperate until we reach pub n' is less good than 'Cooperate until we reach pub $n - 2$', and we are back where we started.

B. Then cheer up! There is a basic flaw in your reasoning. I would halt at *The Nervous Wreck* (2,4), only if I could validly infer that you would halt at *The Sensible Knave* (5,3). That inference would need the premise that you were a rational agent and thus sure to opt for the outcome which you prefer. But, if your reasoning is right, you would have shown yourself not to be a rational agent by letting us get beyond the first pub. So I would not be irrational in letting us past *The Nervous Wreck*, and you, therefore, need not stop the walk at *The Rational Choice*.

A. Wait a moment! If I let us pass the first pub, would you let us pass the second?

B. Probably. I would reckon that, since you were not a rational agent, there would be at least a sporting chance of your letting us pass the third.

A. In that case it could be rational for me not to halt at the first pub. So you would be wrong to infer that I was not a rational agent after all.

B. Awkward.

A. More than awkward. If you are dealing with a rational agent, then you stop the walk at your first chance, for reasons already given. But a rational agent, foreseeing this, would not give you the chance. So an opening pass by me would be rational if it was read as irrational, and irrational if it was read as rational. You would have no coherent way to read it.

B. Then I would be left unsure whether you were rational or not. Of course I cannot draw even that conclusion without querying the assumption that we each know the other to be a rational agent. But that assumption seems to imply that questions of what happens if we pass the first pub cannot even arise, since we cannot pass the first pub. So let us rewrite the starting conditions so that I begin by *believing*, instead of knowing, that you are rational. Then I can revise this belief, if you let us reach the second pub.

A. And, since that would make you unsure what to do, it also undermines my reasoning at the first pub? If I do not know what you would choose, then I have no uniquely rational choice?

B. Yes, we would have to work with probabilities.

A. No, there is no basis for them. In rational choice theory with a single agent, probabilities are given independently. Robinson Crusoe can calculate that by making a net he can probably catch more fish, even if he has to allow for the fish being made nervous by the strange new shape in the water. But he cannot calculate a probability which depends on the probability that Man Friday will do such and such, if Man Friday's probable choice depends on Crusoe's probability assignments.

B. Why not?

A. When choosing whether to pass the first pub, I need to judge how likely you are to pass the second. You would need to judge how likely it is that I acted rationally. I acted rationally only if I judged correctly that you are likely to pass the second. But you are unlikely to do so, if you judge that I acted rationally – in which case I would not have judged correctly. There is no coherent way of working with strategically interlocked probabilities. Now do you see why I regret taking up game theory?

B. Well, I see that probabilities cannot be fully strategic. If the reasons which lead you to assign probability p to my doing something make the probability of my doing it $(1 - p)$, we are stuck, except perhaps for $p - 1/2$. So let's try injecting an independent element. Just suppose we do somehow reach the middle of the walk. (If it helps, suppose there are a hundred pubs on the Enlightenment Trail and we have reached the fortieth). Then I say to myself, 'A seems a reliable sort of fellow; he has passed many pubs, so he will probably pass the next.' If you reason similarly, we shall get on fine. The independent element is the sheer regularity of your previous behaviour. It puts a stop to the regress by injecting an unrationalised probability, thus giving a basis for an inductive inference. As Hume so rightly says, Reason alone cannot be a motive to any action of the will and all our reasonings rest in the end on custom.

A. So it is rational for us to regard some of one another's behaviour as automatic?

B. Yes, since we can then interact to mutual advantage.

A. But it is not automatic. If we pass pubs, we do so not because we have stopped thinking but because we have reason to pass them. This is plain if one looks ahead to the end of the series. Each of us is still motivated to stop as soon as he foresees an outcome which he likes less by continuing. So *The Triumph of Reason* is still out of reach, because I like it less than *The Sensible Knave*. Hence we both know that your induction from mere regularity will fail presently. When? That is, of course, a tricky question but even to raise it is to presuppose that our behaviour is not automatic.

B. Not even *as if* automatic?

A. Only *as if* automatic in so far as it is guided by reasons which give the same result as mere custom would. But where reason and custom diverge, reason will prevail.

B. Then we are stuck. The standard theory attempts to find a fully rationalisable strategy but it turns out to be self-stultifying. When I offer an extraneous anchor, you insist on rationalising it. We are at an impasse.

A. Not yet. I trace the trouble to the role played by our individual orders of preference in guiding our rational choices. They are drawn up in advance, are known to both parties and are the fixed motivating elements throughout. That is, ultimately, why a rational agent's gotta do what a rational agent's gotta do. Reasonable persons, on the other hand, stand back from their preferences, if offered a good reason not to be their slave. I propose that we construct a philosophy of action which allows such distancing and the sort of reflection which can guide us to *The Triumph of Reason*.

B. Don't we already have one? When I complained earlier that game theory had made you selfish, you replied that your preference order need not be a selfish one. So there is already scope, presumably, for taking another person's preferences into account when arriving at one's own.

A.   Yes and no. Yes, the fact that you deem *The Rational Choice* a rotten hole can lead me to demote it in my list of preferred outcomes (provided that we are not both so altruistic that neither can arrive at a preference order at all!). But, no, once the guiding preference orders have been established, they cannot be overridden without a fresh philosophy of action. So far, if it falls to me to make the closing choice between *The Sensible Knave* and *The Triumph of Reason*, and if my preference is for *The Sensible Knave* then that is what I shall choose, regardless of how I came to have that preference. You can count on it; and the trouble starts at once.

B.   What difference could being 'reasonable' make then?

A.   You asked us to suppose that we could 'somehow' reach the middle of the Enlightenment Trail. How? Rational agents cannot. But reasonable people, I surmise, will each identify a fair compromise between the preferences of each and then make the choices which contribute to that outcome. The difference is not that reasonable people are more sympathetic to one another's preferences than rational agents, since, as noted, a rational agent's preferences can include elements of sympathy. The difference is that reasonable persons consider their own preferences impartially, when making a reasonable choice of action.

B.   But can they?

A.   That is two questions. Firstly, to make it possible, we need a philosophy of action where the agent can distance himself from his preferences – a Kantian account of how reason can override inclination perhaps. The second question is why anyone can be trusted to act in this impartial way.

B.   Yes; for instance, why on earth should I trust you to give *The Sensible Knave* a miss, if we get that far?

A.   Because we have got that far. In effect we shall have exchanged promises. In not halting at the first pub, I make you an implicit offer to pass at my next turn and you accept it by not halting at the second pub, thus implicitly offering to pass at your next turn.

B. Need it be implicit?

A. No. But game theorists tend to think that words are, as they put it, 'cheap talk' and make no difference, because rational agents always do whatever is rational in any case. Promises are therefore made if and only if it is rational to make them, and then kept if and only if it is rational to keep them. Hence promising changes nothing. I want to challenge this attitude by suggesting that reasonable people can make promises which are to be relied on and can do so by their actions as well as their words.

B. An implicit promise seems to me too vague. Would it or would it not commit you to pressing on to the end? You might feel that you had kept your promise by halting at *The Sensible Knave* (5, 3), as this would give me a better outcome than *The Foole* (3, 1).

A. Murky, I agree. But perhaps there is a genuine question about whether *The Triumph of Reason* (4, 5) is, impartially speaking, better than *The Sensible Knave* (5, 3). Perhaps (5, 3) produces more total satisfaction than (4, 5). Interpersonal comparisons of utility...

B. Don't duck the issue! Assume that (4, 5) is a more reasonable outcome than (5, 3) and explain why you, as a reasonable person, can be trusted to live up to it. What makes a reasonable person an unswerving Kantian?

A. In general, nothing. In this particular case, with a single walk which ends as soon as either party decrees, Kantians get to *The Triumph of Reason*. But with a series of walks I think reasonable persons would follow a policy of Tit-for-Tat, which punished defections, perhaps tempered by allowing the other player one lapse. Kantians, presumably, would play cooperatively on every walk, even if taken advantage of on every previous walk. That would be unreasonably stupid.

B. So reasonable persons stand back not only from their preferences but also from their policies? That threatens to start a new regress, when I ask myself what is to guide my choice between, say, a Kantian policy and one of Tit-for-Tat.

A. I'll think about it.

B. In the meantime, you face the original problem again, if the series of walks is of known finite length: the final walk will end at *The Rational Choice*, because both players know that defection will go unpunished; so, therefore, will the penultimate walk; and this loose end unravels the whole series.

A. Ah, but a reasonable person will continue to the end in the final walk. The crucial point is that, whereas rational agents look only forwards, reasonable persons can look back too and reflect that conditional promises have been made, whose conditions have been fulfilled. Admittedly, rational agents, like rule-utilitarians, can adopt a policy of looking back to promises made earlier. But their reason for doing so is a forward-looking one and so ceases to operate when it no longer suits.

B. Fine. So let's make an explicit mutual promise to have supper at *The Triumph of Reason* tonight. Yet how sure can I be that you will not give in to temptation if and when we reach *The Sensible Knave*?

A. You can be quite sure that a reasonable person would resist. Of course, you cannot be quite sure that I am one of them. But the Enlightenment Ale at *The Triumph of Reason* is like nectar. Isn't it worth the risk to get past *The Rational Choice*?

B. Not until you tear up your *Summa cum laude* from your game theory course.

II

Roles and reasons

CHAPTER 7

Of masks and men

'There's no art to find the mind's construction in the face', King Duncan reflects sadly in Act I of *Macbeth* on hearing that the traitorous Thane of Cawdor has died confessing his treasons. As if to demonstrate the point, he confers the title on the trusted Macbeth and thus sets his own murder in train. The problem of Other Minds has defeated him twice in succession. In so far as the problem is a practical one, philosophers can only sympathise. But finding the mind's construction is not only a matter of discerning motives. As Marcel Mauss makes plain in his breath-taking disquisition on the self as 'a category of the human mind,'[1] it involves the concepts and categories with which we shape our experience, order our aims, see meaning in events and understand ourselves. That makes the reading of our neighbours' faces hard enough – indeed it makes it hard to read our own. But it can make the reading of distant faces seem beyond all art, as we wrestle with the diversity of other cultures at other places and times. The mind's construction is built around an understanding of self, and that is elusive partly because it changes with time and place, partly because we do not grasp it properly even amongst ourselves.

This essay first appeared in M. Carrithers, S. Collins and S. Lukes, eds., *The Category of the Person*, Cambridge: Cambridge University Press, 1985, pp. 217–33. It has benefited from helpful comments by Steven Lukes and also by Steven Collins, whose inspiring essay 'Categories, Concepts or Predicaments?' (pp. 46–83 in that volume) has given me great pleasure and profit. I have also learnt much of relevance from Richard Gordon.
[1] M. Mauss, 'A Category of the Human Mind: the Notion of Person; the Notion of Self', originally printed in French in *The Journal of the Royal Anthropological Institute*, 68, 1938, and reprinted in his *Sociologie et anthropologie*, Paris: PUF, 1950. I shall be quoting from the translation by W. D. Halls for the Carrithers, Collins and Lukes volume *The Category of the Person*, cited above, pp. 1–25.

That suggests two lines of address, the historical and the analytic. Historically we can say at least something about changing conceptions of what it is to be a person. For instance, Homeric culture scarcely conceived the self outside social roles and lacked a single, generic word applying to each and every human being. Reformation Protestants, on the contrary, thought of everyone as a soul or spiritual self distinct from its social and bodily life. Those two cultures lie on a path which leads to our own day and, in telling the historical tale, we shall benefit from tracing the growth of understanding or else from realising that our own ideas are parochial. By contrast, the analytic approach picks on the conceptual puzzle in self-knowledge. It views human nature as a single, timeless enigma which has troubled all thinkers in all places. What troubled the Pueblo Indians, the Greek tragedians, the ancient Chinese sages and the fathers of social science still continues to trouble us. The living and the dead all contribute to the same debate. The dead, annoyingly, cannot attend in person; but they supply evidence by artifact and in writing, which living interpreters kindly shell out of its archaic language and historical period. Thus rejuvenated, all who have ever tackled the topic become candidates for this year's prize in mental philosophy.

The two approaches are not in collision but there is a tension between them, which every student of the social sciences will recognise. It is palpable in Mauss's magnificent study and I shall start by picking it out. Then, being a philosopher by trade, I shall fret with some analytical loose ends and ask what is to be done with them. The search for answers will involve his historical account too, since not even a philosopher can suppose the mind's construction a purely timeless affair.

Mauss ranges from the Pueblo to the Romans, from medieval Christianity to the individualism of today, showing the different forms which the idea of self has taken. His lecture is in part a chronicle, stretching from the first use of ceremonial masks in symbolic dances to the private sense of our own uniqueness, which each of us now has. But it is offered as an 'example of the work of the French school of sociology', belonging to a social history of the categories of the human mind and to a project of explaining them one by one. This gives it a Durkheimian concern with social structures and externally generated norms. Yet the note struck is not one of glum social determinism. There is also a moral concern to improve our self-understanding, as in Durkheim. The concept of a person, Mauss says in his opening paragraph, 'originated and slowly developed over many centuries and through numerous vicissitudes, so that even today it is still imprecise, delicate, fragile, one requiring further elaboration'. Thus a tension among history, sociology and philosophy is built deep into the whole enquiry. It is a symptomatic and fertile tension, as I hope to show, after summarising Mauss's theme.

Mauss states his principle for investigating categories of the mind thus: 'we describe particular forms of them in certain civilisations and by means of this comparison try to discover in what consists their unstable nature and their reasons for being as they are'. His chronicle starts with the Pueblos and the clan. 'On the one hand the clan is conceived of as being made up of a *certain number of persons*, in reality of "characters" [*personnages*]. On the other hand, the role of all of them is really to act out, each in so far as it concerns him, the prefigured totality of the life of the clan' (his italics). In other words, we start with something which we can hardly recognise as a concept of a person at all. Among the Pueblo it is membership of a clan, together with sets of roles within the clan, which constitutes persons. It is the life of the clan which constitutes agency; and personhood is symbolised by the ceremonial masks which an actor wears in sacred dramas. Yet roles, masks, titles and property also set family apart from clan and a man thinks of himself as surviving death and reappearing on Earth as one of his descendants. By the same token he must think of himself as his own ancestor. So there is, to our eyes, a second concept of person already there; but also one we can scarcely recognise. This phase of human history is summed up by remarking that 'a whole, immense group of societies has arrived at the notion of "role" [*personnage*], of the role played by the individual in sacred dramas, just as he plays a role in family life'.

The Latin persona takes a step further. It sets off as 'a mask, a tragic mask, a ritual mask and the ancestral mask' but soon becomes 'a fundamental fact of law'. The route is from masks to

privileges of those with a right to the masks, to *patres* who
represent their ancestors, to anyone endowed with ancestors, a
cognomen and family property. Hence we arrive at a notion of a
person as a possessor of rights, a group from which only slaves
are excluded. At the same time the Stoics, aided by later Greek
ideas about a person as a kind of private *prosopon*, have
contributed a notion of the person as a moral fact, which comes
to inject a concept of moral conscience into the juridical concept
of a right.

But, Mauss continues, there was no 'firm metaphysical
foundation' until the Christians supplied one. 'Our own notion
of the human person is still basically the Christian one.' The
Council of Nicaea marks a milestone with its *'Unitas in tres
personas, una natura in duas naturas'* (unity in three persons, one
person in two natures). Mauss finds in this pronouncement on
the dual nature of Christ the metaphysics of substance and
mode, body and soul, consciousness and action. That may be a
daring leap; but a person presently becomes a 'rational substance,
indivisible and individual'. Cassiodorus is cited in proof, but he
failed to make of it 'what it is today, a consciousness and a
category'. That was the achievement of long years of labour by
the philosophers; and Mauss's essay ends *au grand galop* with
Descartes, Kant and Fichte. The category of self emerges, to
replace the mere concept of self which went before, and each
person now has his own self or ego, in keeping with the various
Declarations of Rights.

I shall want to say more presently about the category of self as
a philosophical achievement and as a psychological innovation.
But that is enough about Mauss's historical chronicle, which he
sums up thus: 'From a simple masquerade to the mask, from a
"role" [*personnage*] to a "person" [*personne*] to a name, to an
individual, from the latter to a being possessing metaphysical
and moral value, from a moral consciousness to a sacred being,
from the latter to a fundamental form of thought and action –
the course is accomplished.' Nor is the journey ended. Our
modern category of self is 'formulated only for us, among us' and
may evolve in its turn as we learn 'to perfect our thought and to
express it better'.

Apart from its own evident fascination, this saga poses large problems of method. As promised, I pose one which brings out the tension among history, sociology and philosophy. It lies broadly in the way to conceptualise self and role. More precisely, it lies in Mauss's apparent suggestion that the story leads from a start in pure role without self to a finish in pure self without role. This is not, I hasten to add, a wholly fair digest of the central theme, as will be stressed in a moment. But certainly the current notion of a person as an individual ego is not the Pueblos' notion, nor the Greeks', nor the Romans', nor the medievals'. It is undeniably true that something 'originated and slowly developed over many centuries', the something being, roughly, a sharp distinction of self from role. At the same time, however, something else has remained unchanged. Mauss notes firmly that all languages in all societies have had ways for speakers to refer to themselves and that 'the "self" [*Moi*] is everywhere present'. For, he continues, 'there has never existed a human being who has not been aware, not only of his body but also of his individuality, both spiritual and physical'. In every culture, then, whatever its place in the chronicle, there has been a constant element, a sense of self, present as much in American Indian masks as in Hamlet's soliloquy, Descartes's *Meditations* or the existentialist's *je suis mes actes*. It seems to me that Mauss is right on both counts. Yet the threat of sheer incoherence is palpable.

Mauss himself skirts the danger. He draws a line between, on the one hand, linguistic anthropology and psychology, where the *sense* of self is universal but largely a matter of grammar and self-reference; and, on the other hand, law and morality, where a *concept* of self has been evolving. The distinction of disciplines here does not convince me and I shall not dwell on it. But I am struck by his distinction between the universal *sense* of self, the evolving *concept* of self and, as we reach Kant, the recent *category* of self. This trinity will engage us later, when more has emerged about the changing self and the unchanging self. We shall do best, I fancy, if we start with *role*.

Even if the notion of role arises with masks worn in sacred dramas, it cannot be as simply divorced from that of self as the image of the mask suggests in our secular age. Today, it has, I suppose, two main uses. One is in analysing social institutions and practices, where it can be formally defined as the dynamic aspect of a social position. The other is in analysing more intimate reaches of social life, where it borrows from the theatre, making a dramaturgical analogy with *dramatis personae* or characters in a play. Both uses, it seems to me, embody the oldest perplexity about the self. For, although the institutional use might seem to dispense with selves and the theatrical use to be fully modern in insisting on them, each soon admits to ambiguity.

Institutionally, roles set structure in motion. For example, British society has positions for priests, grocers, mothers and prime ministers, recognised by law and public opinion, prepared for by education and practice, and filled in authorised ways. Each has normative expectations or duties attached, which are sparked by social interaction. It is possible to regard these dynamics as automatic and to try to explain social change as an automatic response to an overall conflict in roles. But nothing in the idea of structural roles requires it and I do not myself find it plausible to make actors the creatures of social structure. For instance, there is a fairly well-specified role of local councillor but it is not thereby a predetermined one. What is well specified is a set of imperatives and, to go with them, a set of legitimating languages which govern the proper interplay with sundry role-partners. As civic leaders, councillors are required to advance the good of the community with due regard for economy, justice, humanity and local prosperity; and all citizens at large may demand these virtues of them. As party representatives, they must satisfy party members that they are carrying out the manifesto and keeping the party faith. In city hall committees, they interact with civil servants in a language of rational solutions to technical problems. In each of these aspects (and there are several others) the role has specific ends and negotiable means, so that the role-bearers are both enabled and constrained in striving for consistency. They have a duty to innovate in interpreting a loose brief and by, so to speak, inventing the orders which they are obliged to obey. Hence some distinction between person and office is built into the role itself; and I believe that this is true of institutional roles in general. Even on the premises of a structural role theory, it soon becomes plain that the incumbents of a seemingly impersonal system are in fact less marionettes than stewards.

Conversely it would be false to think that the dramaturgical notion of role yields a clear picture of actors as individuals. The relation of actors to the characters they play does not yield an easy distinction of men from masks. We may be inclined to view actors as donning and doffing masks like hats but that is not the only way to conceptualise theatre. Acting can also be regarded less as impersonating someone than as personifying them. This may seem implausible for village hall theatricals, where no one forgets that Hamlet is really Mr Bunn the baker, but it rings true for professional acting and is almost irresistible for the special case, which the dramaturgical analogy is supposed to illuminate, that of human beings playing themselves in the drama of their own lives. Here the self cannot be the mask alone, as the point of the analogy is to deny that we are merely beings-for-others; nor can it be the man alone, without destroying the analogy; so it must be some fusion of man and mask, which therefore reinstates the initial perplexity. Meanwhile plays have scripts, plots and conventions, which constrain and enable the players in their interpretation of character, just as norms enable and constrain the incumbent of a social position. There is no one-sided truth about theatre either.

With self and role so entwined, it cannot be right to think of self emerging as butterfly from a caterpillar of role and chrysalis of *persona*. Consider, for instance, the tragedies which ancient Greek dramatists wove from older legends and sacred mimes. They would clearly belong in date to the caterpillar period, and, witness the carved masks which prevented facial expression and let one actor play many parts, there are no modern 'individuals' in them. Conflicts are always role-conflicts. Yet the puzzle of self and role is fully there. For example, the characters in Sophocles' *Antigone* are trapped in their societal roles. Antigone must decide whether to bury her brother Polynices, who lies dead outside the walls of Thebes after his treasonable attack on the city. Family duty commands burial but she is also subject to the king's edict forbidding burial for a traitor. The king is Kreon and his edict embodies hallowed custom; but he is also her uncle, head of her house, and bound by family duty. Antigone decides to follow what she takes to be the higher law and buries her brother; Kreon does what he takes to be his greater duty and has her walled up alive. This is a tragedy without individualism or private moralities. Yet it is not a 'tragedy' as newspapers now use the term to report blows of fate, like the flattening of a toddler by a runaway steam roller. Antigone and Kreon *choose* the path which dooms them, yet choose as persons who are their masks, not as individuals who play their parts. There is an anguished fusion of self and role, which reduces neither to the other. I find this fusion very hard to grasp, I confess, but not because it belongs to an antique world which we have lost. The trappings are antique but the puzzle is wholly modern.

If Greek tragedy could work modern marvels with a fifth-century notion of a person, what exactly has changed since? When Antigone uses the first person singular, she displays more than a grammatical *sense* of self; she has at least a *concept* of self; but, Mauss would no doubt say, she lacks a *category* of self. Since, I agree, something has changed, let us see whether the divide comes between the concept and the category. The suggestion is that Greek thought has the sense and concept of self but is not individualistic enough for self to be a category. It is only with legal ideas about rights, Christian ideas about the soul, and Cartesian ideas about the ego that our modern, categorial self is born. It is then licked into shape by Kant and bequeathed as the individualism which Durkheim held to be the sacred form of the modern age. The suggestion is interesting enough but, I find, hard to make out. How, historically, does the concept of self turn into the category?

Mauss does not explain. But, as member of 'the French school of sociology', he was committed to Durkheim's programme of reworking Kantian themes in functionalist terms, whose rationale is pithily expounded at the start of *The Elementary Forms of the Religious Life*.[2] So his answer could be a sociological analogue of

---

[2] London: George Allen and Unwin, 1915.

the Transcendental Unity of Apperception.[3] At any rate, Kant will be central to any convincing answer and I shall next trace another route to him, one which starts with the seventeenth-century 'way of ideas'.

Descartes opened this chapter in philosophy by grounding our knowledge of the world in the 'I' of the cogito (and in the being of a God who is no deceiver). This ego was a monadic spirit communing directly with God and, be it noted, owing nothing to social location. It was a *res cogitans*, a mind meditating reflexively on what was present to it and thus coming to know a metaphysical reality. Thanks to Descartes and then to Locke, it came to seem beyond dispute that all rested with the mind's contents and an enduring self aware of them. These mental contents acquired the generic name of ideas and, as analysed by Locke and Berkeley in particular, presently became the momentary, private, atomic perceptual phenomena now familiar to every English-speaking first-year philosophy student. Such fleeting fragments of experience could not apparently constitute or guarantee the solid, persisting world of physical objects and the way of ideas set a threatening problem.

A tempting solution was to make the mind itself the ground of continuity. But that thought fell foul of Hume's sceptical empiricism. His *Treatise of Human Nature* set out to base all other sciences on what could be established by the science of Man, which rested in turn on the impressions and ideas directly given to the mind. As he confessed gracefully in the closing appendix, however, there was a radical snag. The world's furniture, at least in the doctrine of the vulgar, consisted of lasting existences, whose states over time were connected by real bonds. The mind, on the other hand, was aware only of a series of impressions and ideas. How then did we know of lasting objects and real connections? Hume admitted himself stumped. 'In short there are two principles which I cannot render consistent, nor is it in my power to renounce either of them, viz. *that all our distinct perceptions are distinct existences and that the mind never perceives any real connection among distinct existences*' (Appendix, his italics). A lasting

---

[3] See Steven Collins's excellent essay 'Categories, Concepts or Predicaments?', cited above.

self might have done the trick by making the real connection lie in the fact that a continuous series of data could be presented to the same observer. But Hume, turning his sceptic's eye inward, could find no lasting self. 'When I turn my reflection on myself, I can never perceive this *self* without some one or more perceptions; nor can I ever perceive anything but the perceptions. It is the composition of these, therefore, which forms the self.' His inner bundle was quite unfitted to cement distinct existences into enduring things.

A way out of this scandalous impasse was offered by Kant. The continuity and identity of the mind could indeed be used to underwrite the world of things causally related in Newtonian space, provided that it could be established transcendentally. The proposal was grandly termed the 'Transcendental Unity of Apperception'. It relied on a far-reaching novelty, transcendental argument, which let epistemology take over work assigned by Descartes to God. 'Self' does not in fact feature on Kant's list of the categories but it could be claimed to merit categorial status for its work in unifying our judgements. The 'I' stands outside experience but is present in all our orderings of experience. Thus Mauss calls it 'the precondition of consciousness and science', arguing thence to individualism as the form of modern social thought.

There seems to be a confusion here, however, between the two forms of individualism, which Durkheim had picked out. On the one hand there is 'the individualism of Kant and Rousseau, that of the *spiritualistes*, that...[of]...the Declaration of the Rights of Man'.[4] This had Durkheim's blessing and he looked to it as 'henceforth the only system of beliefs which can ensure the unity of the country'. On the other hand there was the 'egoistic cult of self' wished on us by 'the narrow utilitarianism and utilitarian egoism of Spencer and the economists'. If we were speaking of the sacred form of modern social thought, I would be inclined to suggest that the honours were equally divided between them (excluding other contenders). But 'the precondition of con-

---

[4] See 'Individualism and the Intellectuals', translated by S. and J. Lukes with a preface by S. Lukes, *Political Studies*, 17, 1969, pp. 14–30, especially, for the remarks quoted in this paragraph, pp. 20–3.

sciousness and science' sounds more like a scientific form of modern social thought. In that case we should, I think, look to the epistemological origins of egoism.

At any rate, despite Kant (and Fichte), English empiricists soldiered on with the mixture of enlightenment and despair bequeathed by Hume. They did not adopt a categorial self or deal in transcendental arguments. The Principle of the Association of Ideas continued to ground mental philosophy and scientific inference. Hopes were pinned on an empirical psychology to complete Hume's science of Man. These endeavours also drew on another kind of atomism, expressed by Hobbes and especially important for social and political thinking. The unit of analysis here was man, conceived as a self-interested, rational, essentially presocial animal. Rationality lay in the shrewd calculation of individual advantage, with conflicts of interest reconciled in principle through a notional social contract. Within this individualist framework, varieties in institutions were accounted for by variations in desires and in distributions of power, given the basic disadvantages of a state of nature. Themes from Hobbes and Hume came uneasily together in Utilitarianism, which offered both a moral science of economics and a scientific ethics of welfare. Utilitarianism is a complex and unstable total theory but it lent itself to popularisation. It summed up a view of human beings as rational economic agents, which is, I think, the form of individualism with the greater claim to have influenced modern social theory.

I do not suggest that individualism is a single or precise thesis. Broadly an individualist is, I suppose, anyone who gives analytical priority to single agents (or their states). The priority may be ontological, epistemological or metaphysical; it may be ethical, political or social. A systematic trawl for individualists nets a very mixed cran of fish, as Steven Lukes notes in his rich essay on the topic.[5] But my business now is with social theory and here I take the typical modern individualism to be the one which we owe to nineteenth-century liberals and utilitarians. As a thesis about actual human behaviour it is a basic blend of

---

[5] 'Methodological Individualism Reconsidered', *British Journal of Sociology*, 19, 1968. See also Lukes, *Individualism*, Oxford: Blackwell, 1973.

economics and psychology, well caught in F. Y. Edgeworth's dictum that 'the first principle of economics is that every agent is actuated by self-interest'.[6] When we look for its origins, we find Hobbes and Hume, rather than Kant.

Hobbes and Hume differ over the concept of a person. Hume, as just noted, can find nothing but a bundle of perceptions from which to compose the self. Social theorists descended from him treat an agent as a set of ordered preferences which action aims to satisfy. Those of Hobbesian persuasion add a presocial atom, whose preferences they are. Hobbes's atoms have a primary urge to self-preservation and are moved by a restless desire for power after power which ceaseth only in death. That is to build a conflict of interests into the foundations of social life and it generates the Hobbesian problem of order. No such conflict follows from Hume's account however – indeed he held that we have a natural sympathy for our fellows among our dispositions. Individualist social theory is heir to both and that makes it hard to decide what concept of a person is involved in it. But these differences matter less for present purposes than the central point upon which they agree. For they agree in making the identity of a person independent of roles and social positions.

On any such account the social system of positions and roles belongs among the externalities or parameters within which individuals decide and manoeuvre. Norms and rules provide standardised reasons for action by rational agents seeking to maximise satisfaction. Some norms will, no doubt, have been internalised, thus becoming a direct source of motives for action, since obedience then brings its own reward. Others remain external and supply only legitimating reasons, in the sense of public justifications for doing what the agent wants to do from other and private motives. But, even when internalised, roles remain secondary, since the currency of the model is the psychological coin of inner satisfaction and not obedience *per se*. In other words role-distance is built deep into the analysis of social action and role-playing is always instrumental, even when it is gratifying in itself rather than merely convenient. This is

[6] *Mathematical Psychics: An Essay on the Application of Mathematics to the Moral Sciences*, London: Kegan Paul, 1881, p. 16.

explicit in Hobbes, where the individualist distinction of self from role is patent. It is implicit in Hume, where sentiment and not duty moves the individual.

The upshot is to make social action hard, indeed impossible, to understand. Consider, for instance, Erving Goffman with his picture of actors as individuals, living on the seamy underside of society and working the system for their own ends. Their attitude to rules, norms and roles is (largely) instrumental and their real motives are (usually) the pursuit of perceived private advantage. The key to understanding what an actor is up to in Goffman's scene is therefore to spot the man behind the mask; and the theoretical crux is whether there can be such a man. Goffman is oddly silent about the self. There are occasional remarks: 'A self is a repertoire of behaviour appropriate to a different set of contingencies';[7] 'by "personal identity" I mean the organic continuity imputed to each individual, this established through distinguishing marks such as name and appearance'[8]; 'the self is the code that makes sense out of almost all the individual's activities and provides a basis for organising them'.[9] But, as far as I know, he never explains what organises the repertoire, supplies continuity of motive or establishes the code. The Hobbesian answer would be that it is the actor himself, which is to make him an utterly mysterious we-know-not-what. The Humean answer would be that there is nothing beyond the repertoire or bundle of coded preferences, which is to lose the actor altogether. I am not sure which nasty horn of this dilemma Goffman would choose.

The dilemma can be generalised. Individualism relies on a 'self' in each actor, which gives shape to his real motives and, in combination with others, accounts for the dynamics of a social system. Yet this self is threatened in two directions. If it reduces to a Humean bundle of perceptions, which are then traced to socialisation and hence to the system itself, it vanishes into the system which it was meant to explain. If it is a Hobbesian core, so private and so much at a distance from its public, legitimating

[7] *The Presentation of Self in Everyday Life*, New York: Doubleday, 1959.
[8] *Relations in Public*, Harmondsworth: Penguin, 1971, chapter 5, p. 189.
[9] *Relations in Public*, Appendix, p. 366.

masks that the real man is impenetrable, it vanishes from scientific enquiry. The puzzle is how to avoid this two-way vanishing trick. What sort of self do we need?

In hope of an answer, I revert to Greek tragedy, with its acute role-conflicts. When an actor is trapped in conflicting roles, the self is exposed. Examples are less common in everyday life, because of inbuilt orderings. For instance a mother, who must steal to feed her starving children, is not thoroughly caught between roles of mother and law-abiding citizen, because her role as mother has a socially recognised priority. She is not being forced to choose between two roles which define her being equally. Greek tragedy, however, specialises in this ultimate kind of choice. Antigone's roles of sister and subject lay equal demands on her. Agamemnon has no appeal to socially recognised priorities in deciding whether to sacrifice his daughter to gain a fair wind for his fleet. Each must resolve not merely what to do but who to be. In trying to grasp this fusion of identity and role, we can hope to understand more about the category of self.

It is tempting to suppose that the ethical fix occurs only because Greek tragedy lacks an ego. The typical modern presumption is that there is a self distinct from both roles, who must choose between them. This presumption, however, far from easing the dilemma, makes it impossible. Consider Sartre's ascription of Bad Faith to anyone who performs the duties of an office just because he holds the office. That suggests a contrast between a person who shuffles off his responsibilities onto his roles and a person who makes choices which are authentically his own. But that is not how Sartre tackles moral dilemmas. For instance, his account of the problem facing a young man, who must decide after the fall of France in 1940 whether to stay with his mother or to join the French forces abroad, certainly insists that there is no hiding behind moral authorities. But the moral authorities are not just those of church or society. They are also those of independent conscience and inner feeling. So it is left utterly unclear what possible test of authenticity remains. There is no self *en soi* and *pour soi* to stand apart from all roles. 'In life a man commits himself, draws his own portrait, and there is nothing but that portrait.'[10] If this were what the category of self comes to, we would not have advanced beyond the Greeks at all. Telling Antigone to choose authentically, to be true to herself or to draw her own portrait would amount to saying that it matters not one whit what she does. Hence, it seems, there has to be a self to be true to, an inner being to sit for the portrait.

But snags persist, when we ask further about this inner being. So far we have tried two versions, neither appealing. In the Hobbesian she is to look to her self-preservation and in the Humean to the order of her preferences. Both try to convict her of a terrible confusion about the claims of duty and both make the confusion worse. The generic source is that both require a rational actor always to have a *further* reason for doing what office gives only a role-governed reason to do. This further reason is typically that conforming will be for her good. Here 'good', like 'utility', is to be defined neutrally so as not to prejudice the relation between prudence and morality. In short, and with a similar caveat about neutrality, she is to weigh the claims of role and any other considerations in the scales of expected utility. Can we straighten her out accordingly?

The answer is surely No. But the grounds of it are less clear. It certainly would not do to suggest that she try weighing duty against utility, since the utility of burying her brother is not decidable independently of the role she adopts. For Antigone-as-sister it weighs heavy; for Antigone-as-subject it weighs less. But I posed the dilemma as one where utility held the scales. The trouble is that the metaphor cannot be cashed in, unless we can answer the question 'utility for whom'? That makes it plain, I think, that the self will need to be more than a schedule of preferences, since preferences now must be attached to something. If we attach them to Antigone in her different roles, we are back with the previous snag that they vary systematically with the role. So it might look a better idea to attach them to an atomic self. But, granted that her tragic choice is one which will delineate this blank self, nothing is achieved thereby. This

[10] *Existentialism and Humanism*, London: Methuen & Co., 1973, p. 42. The discussion of the young man's dilemma is on pp. 35–6.

ultimate self would not be applying a measure but creating one and that would leave us still stuck with my complaint about Sartre. Considerations of utility thus fail to be neutral and the addition of a pure self does nothing to help. If Antigone is to have any sort of assessable choice, we must work with what Sophocles provides. There is no missing piece.

Pure self seems to me an illusion; but a plausible illusion when conjured up against limiting cases at the other extreme. Durkheim says at the end of the *Rules*, 'Individual human natures are merely the indeterminate material which the social factor moulds and transforms'.[11] The obvious retort is to postulate a pure self independent of the social factor. But there is no call for one, granted that even a structural role-theory need not make role-playing automatic. So a self robust enough not to be absorbed into the system need not be so pure that it vanishes into darkest privacy. This is the moral I want to draw from the conceptual frame of Greek tragedy. *Antigone* offers us implicitly a 'category' of self to secure a precarious space between social factor and inner world.

Now we can turn to Kant, rather than to Hobbes and Hume. There is a social analogue of the task which Kant gives the self in securing a world of persisting, causally related objects amid a mass of experienced phenomena. Analogously the system of social positions and role-playing actors is not given in experience. Each of us knows of it by understanding the interactions which we are caught up in. To understand, we must bring concepts to bear, with the mind, as Kant says about understanding the physical world, acting not as a pupil but as a judge. The social analogue of reflective consciousness is intelligent agency. We identify the positions and roles of the social world by acting intelligently within them. Intelligence depends on continuity of the self, by analogy with the unity of the self required to weave phenomena into physical objects. For meaningful social phenomena, the apperception is that of a social agent.

Antigone's actions are *hers* not because of the sameness of the private will of the pure self behind them but because they are

---

[11] *The Rules of Sociological Method*, New York: The Free Press, 1964, chapter 5.

done by the same social actor. What actor is she? *Who* buried Polynices? The answer demanded by the tragedy is that Kreon's royal niece did it, being the same person as Polynices' sister. It adds nothing to this answer to invoke a pure self as a gloss on what is meant by 'same person'. That Antigone is the same social actor is both necessary and sufficient.

We ascribe to actors both a personal and a social identity. The difference seems at first great. Offhand my personal identity is unique and immutable – what makes me myself is peculiar to me and, without it, I would cease to exist – whereas my social identity is a general description, which others could exemplify. It seems that I could not have been born 2,000 years ago, as that would have been someone else, but I could have been an engine driver and still be me. This is, however, only a trick of the example, which works because 2,000 years is a long time from now and an engine driver a shortish social distance from a philosopher. Presumably I would have been the same person if conceived ten minutes earlier but not if brought up in contemporary New Guinea. Self is the unifying agency among my social actions and it can survive only mild dislocation in both time and social space. Just as a personal identity is not to be confused with personality, so social identity is not to be confused with social placement; for both there is a uniqueness.[12]

That much is consistent with the notion of a person in Greek tragedy, which therefore seems to me to have a category of self implicit in it. What then is modern? It is, I think, the idea that we construct our own social identity. Without Roman law and medieval Christianity, I doubt if the idea would have come to make sense. It needs notions of individual persona and private spiritual substance. With them behind us, we can picture social actors as individuals who paint their own social portraits, for whom there is nothing social but the portrait. Yet the idea still verges on the unintelligible. It comes easily to us, I suggest, only because we do not suppose that people construct all of their own personal identity. A *substantia individua rationalis*, to use the

[12] For more on social identity and personal identity see my *Models of Man*, 1977, chapter 8, or *The Philosophy of Social Science*, 1994, chapter 8, especially pp. 176–80, both published by Cambridge University Press.

medieval Christian term, acts as anchor for our idea of personality as a variable, open to self-programming through aversive therapy, biorhythms, colonic irrigation, dianetics, encounter groups and on through the alphabet to yoga and zen. Something similar but more social is also needed to anchor our choice of roles and of interpretations for the roles which we choose. This gives more scope for the construction of self than there is in Greek tragedy but a great deal less than individualism would have us believe.

That is as far as I can take the topic here. Analytically, I have suggested that social forms can never shape human beings completely, because social forms owe their own shape to the fact that human beings are social agents with ideas about social forms. I have denied, however, that persons are natural first and social afterwards. That still leaves plenty of elbow room and the moral I draw from Mauss is finally philosophical. It is that human beings have slowly been learning to express what has all along underlain their universal sense of self. The Pueblo expressed it by regarding himself both as a clansman absorbed into his clan and as identical with his own ancestor, the ancient Greek by recognising choice as an aspect of institutional role, the Roman by making a cognomen a source of personal rights, the medieval Christian by ascribing social duties to the soul. We ourselves are inclined to make the self more private but, even so, we hold on to an idea of identity as, in part, what is expressed in relations with others. Each view contains an unresolved tension and our own is no exception. Not all steps are forward. So I do not think it perverse to treat the dead as candidates for this year's prize in mental philosophy. I wish only that it was plainer how the prize should be awarded.

CHAPTER 8

Honour among thieves

Old-world ethics set Reason to discern a meaning in human life which pointed beyond it. Platonists sought the form of the Good and the Right, to which a moral life should conform. Aristotelians hoped to attune the good life to moral rhythms in the larger universe where human nature belonged. New-world ethics dispensed with all such external sources of meaning. In the Enlightenment main line, moral progress was entrusted to science as a matter of furthering goals internal to human well-being. As Helvetius put it, 'ethics is the agriculture of the mind'. Utilitarianism proceeded accordingly. Even Kantian agriculture gave Reason a task which was transcendental, rather than transcendent. In one way or another, ethics was to be rationally grounded without appeal to God or to Nature other than human nature. That was the only course, if, as Dilthey declared later, 'life does not mean anything other than itself. There is nothing which points to a meaning beyond it.'

Life can still mean something beyond the individual, however, if culture or community can bind us into a moral whole prior to its parts. But the Cartesian origins of the Enlightenment work against that thought. The *cogito* revealed an individual ego, ontologically as independent of other people as it is of the physical world. When the Enlightenment set about a science of society, it began with a science of mind, where minds were individual and society a set of relations between individuals. That favoured a moral psychology where the only reasons which

© The British Academy, 1990, reproduced by permission from *Proceedings of the British Academy*, vol. LXXV, *Lectures and Memoirs*. I am grateful to John Dunn, Timothy O'Hagan and Quentin Skinner for their very helpful comments on the original draft.

can move individuals are those internal to their own character and concerns. It went nicely with a secular and individualist theory of the social contract, thus making it a central problem of ethics to reason an enlightened egoist into disinterested cooperation.

Today's post-moderns are at one with yesterday's Romantics in despairing of this whole approach. In the words of Burke's thunderous verdict on the French Revolution, 'the age of chivalry is gone. That of sophisters, economists and calculators has succeded; and the glory of Europe has departed for ever.' Yet such gloom may be premature. Contractarian ethics is flourishing at present and its exponents are full of ingenious ways of proving that it is rational to be moral. The economist emerges as someone who knows the price of everything and hence the value of everything too. When an individualist psychology is properly construed, we allegedly find that indeed it pays to be good. 'There's glory for you', we might exclaim, provided that there is a knock-down argument involved. I propose to ask whether it is truly rational to be moral from an individualist and contractarian point of view, and, if not, where exactly a corrective should be applied.

All this is spoken from a great philosophical height. The line which I wish to discuss, however, is precise and down-to-earth. So, shifting abruptly from the sublime to the particular, I shall lead off with a vignette of that epitome of modernity, markets and the good life – the antique dealer. Whether fairly or not, I shall suppose antique dealers to be enlightenedly self-interested persons, whose life has no meaning outside itself and some of whose activities, as revealed in the Sunday newspapers, set an interesting problem for contractarian ethics.

Antique dealers know many tricks. One is to form a 'ring' which gets together secretly before an auction and agrees how high to bid for items in the sale. These items, if secured, are regarded as the property of the ring, which then meets afterwards to share them out among the members, usually at a private, closed auction of its own. Each member emerges not with quite what he would have acquired at the public sale, if left to himself, but with an acceptable bundle at bargain prices. Each will make more money than he would have done without the ring, the losers being the outsiders who were trying to sell their possessions on an open market. Since the arrangement is profitable and illegal, it suggests that there is honour among thieves because honour pays.

Such rings are instructive for contractarian ethics. They are formed through rational individual choice. If all involved comply with their promise, all do better than they would otherwise have done. Yet it is not necessarily rational to comply in full. So members who do comply seem to have accepted a *moral* obligation, thus proving that, overall or at least sometimes, it is rational to be moral. But, at the same time, suspicion lingers that, whatever precisely the mutually profitable relation involved, it is not moral obligation nor a moral source of reasons for action. I shall start by giving contractarian ethics a run for its money and then focus the suspicion for the sake of a wider view of morality and rational action.

Think of the dealers as the rational agents of standard decision theory or rational choice theory, playing a game in the sense defined by the theory of games. The game is in three stages, the first ending with agreement to form the ring, the second with the resulting pile of booty from the public auction and the third with its private distribution among the players. Each stage has various feasible outcomes and each player has a complete and consistent order of preference over them. For instance, it may be that Alf will finish up with the ikon, Bert with the samovar and Charles with the Tampion clock; or Alf with the samovar, Bert with the clock and Charles with the ikon; or an outsider may acquire some of these treasures at the second stage; and so on. The feasible outcomes change between stages, in particular because those of the third stage depend on what is agreed at the first and what happens at the second. Throughout, each dealer follows a strategy of getting more for less, governed by how much he would prefer a given outcome on the one hand and how unlikely he is to get it on the other. (I word this vaguely because nothing turns on niceties of maximising or satisficing, of maximax, maximin or other variants of the approach.)

The expected utility involved in each dealer's calculations is his own. He wishes the others neither good nor ill. He cooperates if and only if he expects to be better off thereby (or at least no worse off) himself. He is moved by considerations conventionally described as moral, but only in so far as it pays him to take them into account. The rationality, which marks each player and which each knows the others to embody, is strictly instrumental, with no other office than to serve and obey the demand of preferences. Thus each dealer, reflecting on his own increased profits, finds it instrumentally rational to join the ring and the first stage sets no puzzles.

The next stage is more challenging. Alf very much wants the Tampion clock for himself. The ring has agreed a limit of £1,000 and he knows that he could resell it for £2,000. There is a risk both that an outsider will bid more than £1,000 and that, even if the ring gets it, it will not fall to him at stage three. He could, however, find a crony outside the ring to bid for it at the public auction. With his fellow dealers holding back, it would be a sure thing at a bit over £1,000 and, if he is careful, no one will know that he is involved. He has of course made a pact of honour not to do this sort of thing, but that makes it the more profitable to do it. Shall he make the free-riding choice? The challenging answer is, 'morally speaking, no; instrumentally speaking, yes; overall, no'.

The challenge to an ambitious contractarian ethics is to show that in joining the ring Alf acquires a sufficient reason to comply with its rules even on occasions when it would raise his pay-off not to. By 'ambitious' I mean that 'morally speaking' is to be construed without reference to reasons for compliance independent of all contracts whatever. Older social contract theories of ethics and politics are not as ambitious as this. Locke, for example, presents the contract as our best way to fulfil God's purpose in setting us on earth and expects us to bear this in mind when framing and acting out its provisions. An ambitious theory dispenses with all independent guidance, whether divine or derived from natural rights or implicit *a priori* in the concept of morality. What it leaves in is not altogether clear, because even the idea that the contracting parties are rational individual agents presupposes a contestable moral psychology, as we shall see. But the broad impetus is to exhibit moral reasons as arising wholly from human activity, useful for human purposes and rationally motivating on that score alone.

To give ambition a sporting chance, take the game theory notion of a pay-off as giving a neutral sense in which one outcome may be *better than* another *for* a person or group. 'Instrumentally speaking' it is better for Alf to make sure of the clock by stealth. But what exactly is meant by the suggestion that 'morally speaking' it may not be? It seems not to be true that *all* members of the ring do better if the clock is secured by the ring, since Alf does worse. It seems not to be enough that *most* members do better, in that each then has a prospect of acquiring it afterwards. How exactly do we tell the tale so that Alf is not only pulled in two directions but will do better to let the clock reach stage three, instead of diverting it earlier on the quiet? The central idea is that, if the proverbial 'honour among thieves' is to mean exactly what it says, then it is rational for Alf to do the honourable thing, even when it seems to have less expected utility than the dishonourable. This needs to be demonstrable but not too easily.

It would be too easy to prove it by adding some hidden costs. Alf would be taking risks in cornering the clock. There is a risk of blackmail by his crony. There is a risk of being identified, when he comes to resell it. If the others find out, there is a risk in using dark alleyways and a certainty of being excluded from future rings. We might argue that the balance of risk against extra profit favours keeping faith. But this is too easy because it relies solely on fear. Perhaps, as Hobbes contends, a group of people can cooperate to secure the advantages of commodious living, only if there is a common power to keep all in awe. Yet this is not the ideal answer, because the policing needed to keep the risks of defection high is a dead-weight loss. A ring which operates successfully on trust will be cheaper and, from a collective point of view, more effective. Conversely, an ambitious contractarian theory must try to show that even a modest background threat of violence is a sign that some members are not properly rational.

It would also be too easy to give Alf the pangs of a bad conscience, thus raising the costs of free-riding from the inside.

Self's	Outcome	
Preference	Self　　+	Others
1st	Defect	Comply
2nd	Comply	Comply
3rd	Defect	Defect
4th	Comply	Defect

Figure 1

An ambitious theory will allow this only if it is *rational* for Alf to let his conscience worry him. Otherwise too much work is being done either by a brute fact of Alf's particular psychology or, worse, by a moral concept slipped in from outside. But this may be only a preliminary objection. The thought that Alf can decide whether to be moved by feelings of guilt invites the further suggestion that he can perhaps choose his dispositions – a matter to return to. For the moment, however, it is too easy to burden Alf with a conscience and too unlikely that all thieves have much of one.

Approached through the theory of games, the root problem is set by the Prisoner's Dilemma, arising where each dealer can 'comply' or 'defect' and has the order of preference over the four combinations for 'self' and 'others'.

Each reasons that, since it is better for him to defect if others comply, and better for him to defect if others defect, it is better for him to defect *whatever others do*. With all reasoning like this, all defect and the ring collapses to their mutual disadvantage. This is the so-called 'dominance thesis'; and the snag of raising Alf's costs is that the problem vanishes if the outcome described by the top line becomes so unlikely or so expensive that it no longer ranks as his first preference. If there is to be genuine honour among rational thieves, Alf has to think his way round the dominance thesis, not forget about it. To finagle so that the game turns out to be one where his top preference is for mutual compliance, as, for instance, in Figure 2, would be disingenuous.

A tempting move is to recall that we are looking at only one round among several in one stage of a game with other stages or even, having an eye to past and future rings, in a series of such games. This lets Alf reckon with the reactions of other players in

Self's	Outcome	
Preference	Self +	Others
1st	Comply	Comply
2nd	Defect	Comply
3rd	Defect	Defect
4th	Comply	Defect

Figure 2

later rounds. For instance, in a supergame of indefinite length, it may pay to comply in the first round and then play tit-for-tat. It can also pay to invest in the kind of reputation which will induce others to play in ways which suit one. Such considerations might make it rational for Alf to override preferences which, for any single round or game, are correctly described by the Prisoner's Dilemma format.

In my view this is still too easy. As a general move, it works by putting enough of a long-term price on the free-rider outcome to demote it from first place in the short run. For, given the minimal rational-choice idea of what motivates a rational agent, this is the only way in which it can work. I shall therefore refuse to be tempted, at least until more is said on the topic of motivation. Meanwhile it is not a convincing move in the present case, where the dealers are not fully transparent and Alf can get away with cornering the clock. If he has read *The Prince*, he will have noted Machiavelli's advice that the prince will do best by maintaining a reputation for keeping faith, while secretly breaking faith when occasion suits. An ambitious contractarian ethics, especially if addressed to an everyday world where we are not fully transparent, must tackle Machiavelli head on. This means, among other things, not assuming an established social order in which supergames can be played with reliable information about institutional arrangements and future costs and benefits.

More promising, perhaps, is a notion of pre-commitment. Alf, foreseeing that, faced with a Prisoner's Dilemma, he will defect, commits himself in a way which avoids the dilemma. This is the strategy of the alcoholic who, in a sober moment, locks the cellar and gets rid of the key. But how? Alf could warn the other dealers to keep an eye on him or make himself somehow transparent to them. But this is, in effect, to take a more Hobbesian view of the necessary form of the original contract by establishing more of a power to keep all in awe. It amounts to conceding that there can be honour among thieves only if they give up all chance to get away with dishonour; or, to put it more simply, that there cannot be *honour* among rational thieves.

Alternatively he could place the key out of his own psychological reach by, for instance, changing his dispositions, so that he is no longer disposed to steal a march on anyone who will play fair with him. But, as yet, we see neither how he could nor why he should. As with self-deception, he must consciously monkey with his own motivations and then pretend to forget doing so. It is not clear how this can be done. It is not clear that, while he remains a rational agent, it cannot therefore later be undone. It is still unclear why it would be rational for him to do it.

Someone may suspect that my example is by now doing too much work. Contractarian ethics is a serious attempt to work through the ethical implications of denying all meaning to human life external to human life itself, and yet to emerge with an account of how there can be moral reasons for action. To focus the attempt on honour among thieves, one might complain, is to include an obvious booby trap. If thieves' 'honour' were the genuine article, they would of course not be thieves. Conversely, if thieves were all mankind's epitome, it would be no surprise to find the problem insoluble; but the lesson is only that human nature should not be assumed to have an inbuilt bias to personal gain.

I stand by the example, however, which I chose in order to press contractarian thinking on two fronts, one psychological and one social. Psychologically, its familiar current versions rely on an instrumental notion of rationality, which relies in turn on the Humean view that only desire can motivate action. These components together put an embargo on discussing the rationality of an agent's ends. A rational agent can have any set of reflectively consistent ends, provided that they translate into preferences, or desires for situations to come about, which can then motivate a choice guided by rational calculation. In that case the generic problem arises not in ethics but because individually rational choices can sum to collectively irrational results. A collectively irrational outcome is Pareto-inferior, in that another feasible outcome would have been better for some and worse for none. The critical question is then whether it would have been rational for each agent to choose what, when summed, would have yielded a Pareto-superior outcome. The answer might turn out to be no. But the defeat for reason would be very serious and, in my view, would leave philosophers to shuffle the post-modern deckchairs as their ship goes down.

Modern Enlightenment ethics depends on finding a way of saying yes which also shows how a rational agent can indeed act in the manner needed. A promising key lies in the suggestion that to consider a situation from a moral point of view is to stand aside from one's own gains and losses and ask what an ideal, impersonal, impartial observer would make of it. Nothing transcendent is involved, because the moral point of view is not external to all human life on an ambitious contractarian account. So, when this ideal observer points out to Alf that the ring will collapse if everyone rides free, thus leaving every member worse off, it ought to do the trick. The example is fair because it emphasises that Alf has no independent desire to be moral. He will contribute to the collectively better outcome if and only if given sufficient reason. But reasons can motivate Alf only if they persuade him that his existing desires will be furthered by acting as they propose. So far, reference to the collective good *can* move him, because the collective good includes his own, but *will not*, because it is trumped by there being better reason for him to defect.

The moral psychology involved follows Hume's precept that 'reason alone cannot be a motive to any action of the will'. It takes the form of distinguishing sharply between beliefs and desires and then insisting that only desires can motivate. This all goes nicely with the idea that whether a choice is rational depends finally on the given preferences of the agent. But it seems to me fatal for an ambitious contractarian ethics, which wants it to be rational for Alf to do the honourable thing but does not allow a given desire to do it. Alf can perhaps *acquire* a desire to do the honourable thing, but only if it would be rational to acquire it in terms of his overall given desire to be better off.

One possible escape is to reject this underlying moral psychology. The sharp line between desire and belief is very disputable. For instance, a desire to do the honourable thing has a large cognitive content and can be felt only by an agent with a battery of honour-concepts. If it can be 'felt' at all, it must be possible for belief to be a motive to the will. After all, there is supposedly no restriction on the preferences of a rational agent beyond a reflective consistency. The modern Humean will presumably reply that, since Alf can believe that diverting the clock is dishonourable but still desire to do it, the distinction between belief and desire stands. But now comes a dilemma. If desires with cognitive content are ever allowed in, then the gate is open for desires to do whatever is the moral or rational thing; and the rival Kantian has no further trouble in explaining how the categorical imperative can motivate. If, on the other hand, Alf can be moved only by simple desires without cognitive content, the whole apparatus of instrumental rationality collapses. The pivotal desire throughout has been a desire to be better off. This desire most certainly has a cognitive content, or, rather, is too blank to motivate until given one. Either way reason can be a motive to the will.[1]

Although this reopens the game, it does not show that Alf would indeed be rational to do the honourable thing. It does suggest, however, that rational agents cannot be conceived as universal dummies with an amorphous desire to do whatever is better for them. Thus encouraged I turn to what I earlier called the social front, in order to press contractarian thinking from another quarter.

Traditionally, social contract theories of moral or political obligation work from a state of nature and trace the emergence

---

[1]　The last two paragraphs are very compressed. I have argued the case more fully in *The Cunning of Reason*, 1988, chapters 4 and 5, and in 'The Shape of a Life', in J. Altham and R. Harrison, eds., *World, Mind and Ethics*, 1995, pp. 170–84, both published by Cambridge University Press.

of norms among its rational inhabitants. The account is presented historically, but that is presumably a device, being quite implausible as history and open to the crushing retort that the makers of the contract must *already* have had the necessary concepts and institutions. Modern versions are presented analytically by abstracting a group of rational agents from their context and, having placed them behind a thick or thin veil of ignorance, asking what institutions they would design. But the older approach then gets its revenge, if, as is currently alleged,[2] the abstraction yields a modern, socially concerned, Western-style democracy only by slipping in an historically specific shared conception of the good. The lesson seems to be that universal dummies moved only by a desire for things to go well for them are not made human enough to work with just by dubbing them rational.

At any rate that is why I have picked a specific kind of norm, honour, and agents with a specific idea of what is better for them, a larger and cheaper bundle of clocks, ikons and samovars. Dishonour involves both shame and guilt. But, being thieves, they put a negotiable price on both, feeling ashamed only when caught out by others and feeling guilty only when too greedy for their own good. The contractarian problem is then to convince them that free-riding does not pay the rational thief. In this precise form it is no more soluble than when posed abstractly. But the source of trouble is more instructive. It lies, I submit, in the distinction of ends from means. Ends are specified in terms of possession of objects representing future profit and hence utility. Honour comes in as one of the possible means of acquisition, to be judged strictly in relation to the ends. This is a strangely tactical notion of honour.

Honour is a strategic concept in the sense that it governs the value to be placed on an activity, both on the doing and on the having done. The honour-value of a clock acquired by cheating is not its profit margin. Alf's diverted clock is worth £900 net to

---

[2] Especially by some critics of John Rawls's *A Theory of Justice*, Oxford: Oxford University Press, 1971. He has granted the point in his *Political Liberalism*, New York: Columbia University Press, 1993, although one could doubt whether this was necessary or wise.

his bank balance and zero to his honour. The way of cornering it was ingenious in a thief but stupid in a man of honour. There is a surface symmetry here, with the virtues of theft being the vices of honour and honourable reasons to do something being pecuniary reasons to avoid it. But the symmetry is not deep, because one angle of vision depends on separating means and ends, the other on fusing them. Social relationships, which are instrumental from one angle, are, to introduce a new word, 'expressive' from the other, thus, I shall argue next, limiting the scope of a wholly instrumental view of rationality.

A contractarian ethics tries to persuade rational agents that it will pay them to switch from an instrumental to an expressive angle of vision, when dealing with other similarly rational agents. It does not aim to turn them into saints, if that means returning good for evil, honour for dishonour. The rational policy is to act justly to the just, and unjustly to the unjust, thus improving on a world where

> The rain, it raineth every day
> upon the just and unjust fella.
> The former suffers most because
> the unjust hath the just's umbrella.

In a wholly just world, everyone's umbrella is safe. In a wholly unjust one the umbrella market collapses and we all get wet. But, since this rationale is instrumental at heart, it depends on making free-riding not worth the risk, because rational individuals are, or let themselves become, too transparent to fool others. Whatever merit this may have for a world of separate individuals, it seems to me to fail where there are hidden cartels, like the antique dealers' ring, which can make suckers of just persons who are excluded.

The ring's advantage is that its members can cover for each other, thus sharing the cost and effort of looking honest to outsiders. This lets it ride free on the legal property arrangements which outsiders practise. Meanwhile, the members treat each other in the honourable way in which they pretend to treat the rest of the world. By making a distinction between insiders and outsiders, they have made possible an instrumentally very rational policy of acting justly to the unjust insiders and unjustly to the just outsiders. So long as they can get away with it, they have outplayed contractarian ethics at its own game.

Contractarians must reply, I think, that the ring is unstable, because each member, being still a thief at heart, will undermine it. Witness Alf's temptation to divert the clock on the quiet, thieves cannot manage the switch from instrumental to expressive rationality. Where the underlying motive remains personal gain, it cannot be suspended thoroughly enough to stop members of a ring of honour from snapping up undetected bargains at the margin. This reply seems to me to be finally right. But it also seems to me to sabotage contractarian ethics, because it works only if, unlike Alf, rational persons are not finally motivated by personal gain. If that sounds obvious in those terms, notice that 'personal gain' is short-hand for a Humean economist's phrase like 'the satisfaction of the agent's own preferences'. What motivates is not some specific content, like profit, or disposition, like greed, but the fact that the preference is the agent's own. Any consistent set of preferences or desires can motivate a rational agent so far.

It is time we asked exactly what Alf is up to. In what precise way is he 'better off' by getting the clock cheap? What is he going to do with the proceeds? They are plainly not for the benefit of the public at large, whom he has cheated throughout, nor for the benefit of his colleagues, whom he cheated at the second stage. They might be for the benefit of the community centre round the corner from Alf's home. But this would make life instrumentally better for *him* only if either it eases a bad conscience, which it is not rational to have, or it pays off in his relations with his neighbours. We still ask what kind of pay-off. In other words, where does the line between outsiders and insiders finally fall?

It may be that, in the last resort, Alf is the only insider. It is conceivable, I suppose, that Alf's relations with his wife, children, friends and neighbours are fully contractual and wholly instrumental. But, if so, Alf is trapped by appearances, which do not signify what they symbolise. Suppose that he wants the love of a wife who loves him for himself, or the affection of friends who warm to his unselfish affection for them, or the regard of neighbours who respect his public-spirited character. These things are not for sale. He can buy the appearance of them; but that is only the outward aspect of an inward reality which he cannot buy. Deceit will get him the appearance, but he is culturally fooled or inwardly self-deceived if he takes it for the reality.

Instrumental rationality cannot be unpacked solely in terms of preference. To judge one action more instrumentally rational than another, it is not enough to know that the agent prefers its expected consequences. We also need the measure of value being applied, including the end allegedly better served. The end in this case is whatever Alf cares most about, what he seeks not for the reason that it furthers a more distant or wider end. The relation between Alf and what he most cares about is intimate, with his deepest concerns to be seen as an extension and expression of himself. They are not means to his flourishing but its constituents. Otherwise, unintelligibly, he will be trapped in instrumental relations with himself. So, if it is Mrs Alf's birthday and she is among his deepest concerns, there is no question of why it pays him to give her a birthday present. In making her happy he expresses the relation between them.

The circle round Alf, which marks the boundary between insiders and outsiders, can be shrunk or expanded. It may fall between family and others, between friends and acquaintances, between neighbours and strangers. Where it falls may vary with context, so that friends become mere acquaintances, when matters of business are involved. Although I have no philosophical view on the proper boundary, I will just mention its limits. One is, as noted, that it may include only Alf himself. Here I voice the suspicion that no one can be an island and a person. His most intimate relations cannot be solely of possession. He needs to be related to other people who know him as he is, not merely as he wishes to seem. The other is that it must include all humanity or even all sentient beings, if Alf is truly to flourish in some moral sense. This is the expressive contrary of the contractarian attempt to unite reason and morality through an enlightened construal of instrumental relations. Meanwhile, let us suppose, for the sake of argument, that Alf's circle has an intermediate boundary and includes enough people to form a group which has his allegiance for no instrumental reason. He helps his friends and neighbours because they are his friends and neighbours, thus expressing who he is and where he belongs.

Honour is an intermediate relation which defines a group and gives its members the expressive reasons for action which go with dealings among insiders. One calls them personal reasons, with a stress on the first person singular and plural. What *my* honour demands of *me*, it may not demand of you even if we both belong to the group. But differing particular demands are governed by *our* honour, which claims mine and yours. This is not to say that, if you are an outsider for me, I can treat you dishonourably, since honour codes vary on that score. A soldier's honour traditionally includes duties of respect to some women, although often not to those of inferior classes or nations. Witness this example or that of the Mafia, reasons of honour are not beyond criticism and I shall pursue this matter presently. But they stand in instructive contrast to instrumental reasons.

It is tempting to mark the contrast with Weber's distinction between *Zweckrationalität* and *Wertrationalität*. But, although his '*zweckrational*' equates nicely with 'instrumental', he says that action is *wertrational* when its goal is so dominant for the actor that it drives out all calculation of means and consequences, as with acts of heroism and self-sacrifice. This suggests Colonel Blimp facing stiffly into the past, while a canny enemy slaughters his troops by stealth. But, as Weber himself points out when discussing politics as a vocation, it is a mistake to oppose principle to consequences in this bone-headed way.[3] The principled politician needs to calculate consequences finely, knowing that policies rarely work out as planned, partly because the world is fluid and complex, and partly because opponents are not idle. Calculation is in the service of principle, however, and its use is in judging whether an outcome is realistically the best to aim at. Similarly men of honour must work out what their honourable course of action is (or which honourable course

---

[3] 'Politics as a Vocation', in H. H. Gerth and C. Wright Mills, eds., *From Max Weber: Essays in Sociology*, London: Routledge & Kegan Paul, 1948, pp. 77–128.

is better). There is no reason why the choice has to be obvious.
Honour sets measures of value, for the journeying as much as the
destinations, but it does not turn unflinching fools into heroes.
Recalling Machiavelli's advice to the prince in pursuit of glory,
that he must emulate the fox as well as the lion, we might say
that honour is not peculiar to the rhinoceros.

Less cryptically, honour is a game but in a sense closer to
Wittgenstein than to game theory. It is not a game where
rational players measure strategies by their expected pay-off in a
currency external to the game. For the game of honour, the
measures are internal to the rules of honourable conduct, which
are of two kinds. Constitutive rules define the essential relationships
between the players and set their purpose. Those of chivalry, for
instance, define what it is to be a gallant knight or, presumably,
a damsel in distress. Regulative rules facilitate progress within
the constitutive framework, covering, for instance, the proper
way to court a damsel or defend her honour. In general,
regulative rules are an aid to solving problems of action set by
the rules constituting the game. Neither kind of rule merely
constrains the players. The one enables them to play the game at
all; the other enables them to play it well.

Although occasionally only one strategy is possible, the usual
case is that a player has several and is in search of a best one. An
important feature of rules is that they guide each player's
expectations about what other players are likely to do. This is a
crucial factor in game theory, where rational choices are often
interdependent. For example, the highway can be simply
modelled as a coordination game, where it is rational for me to
drive on the left if and only if I expect you to do the same. But
game theory deals only with games where rational choices are
instrumentally rational and so where 'expect' means 'predict'.
In Wittgensteinian games there is scope for *normative* expectations,
which *entitle* players to count on others behaving in accordance
with the constitutive rules. These kinds of expectations are
conceptually distinct and, if the normative were dominant
wherever they applied, we could put Wittgensteinian teeth into
the notion of expressive rationality.

But the games of social life are not so self-contained. I doubt if they ever were, even for my artificial example of the age of chivalry. At any rate they plainly are not in a modern world, where norms and reference groups are fragmentary, shifting and command only partial allegiance. Let me give a light-hearted illustration. British Rail used to sport notices in the lavatories of their trains saying 'Gentlemen Lift The Seat'. Try parsing this locution. Construed in the present indicative, like 'cats purr' or 'bears hibernate', it gives information about animal habits and licenses predictions. But, to grasp the illocutionary aim, we need the subjunctive – 'if you were a gentleman, you would lift the seat' – backed by the optative – 'would that you were a gentleman!' – to yield an imperative: 'lift the seat!'. The currency is one of normative expectations among travellers aspiring to be gentlemen. But presumably the perlocutionary force was lacking in a socially mobile modern world. Perhaps the notice was doomed to fail as soon as it became necessary. At any rate it has now disappeared, the normative expectations having been defeated by the free-rider problem.

The antiques game, too, is not self-contained. But it matters exactly why not. The obvious diagnosis is that, although the members enter a constitutive relation, they do so for mutual advantage and retain aims which govern what it is rational to do in a standardly game-theoretic sense. Not everyone who professes to be a gentleman is one; and the thieves remain individuals throughout. Analogously, an individualist theory of the social or moral contract, which views a civil society as an association of atoms with personal ends, cannot make loyalty rational when it pays to step out of the game. There is a more Wittgensteinian diagnosis, however. Although the members have entered a constitutive relation, they have not abandoned other constitutive relationships. They are playing several games, which pull in different directions. Since other games matter more to them, they play the antiques game instrumentally, when there is a conflict. But defection is instrumentally rational here, only because it is a good move from the standpoint of a more significant game. This diagnosis differs from the other in that it need not endorse an individualist view of games or of players. It is consistent with a theory of the social contract, like Rousseau's, which takes the contract as constitutive of the players themselves.

Notice that Rousseau's citizens retain a private will, which may be different from, or contrary to, the general will which each has as a citizen. 'His private interest may speak with a very different voice from that of the public interest.' Hence 'he might seek to enjoy the rights of a citizen without doing the duties of a subject'. That is Alf in a nutshell, with the dealers' ring being a 'faction' and not an expression of the General Will. Rousseau's way of dealing with free-riders is drastic and I am not working round to endorsing it. But his contrast between individuals and citizens goes irresistibly with that between instrumental and expressive reasons. Like the honourable or principled thing to do, the public interest may be hard to discern. The search for it motivates the citizen, however, because that is the condition of being a citizen. In this way of taking the social contract, it sets up the widest game, the one in which players are themselves and act from expressive reasons, which are not instrumental in some yet wider game.

Here we seem to have reached Wittgenstein's famous thought that 'What has to be accepted, the given, is, so to speak, *forms of life*' (*Philosophical Investigations* II, p. 226), with one's community being the form of life with moral authority. At any rate this is the stopping point for what is currently termed a 'situated' ethics and it works by blocking questions of what it is rational or moral to accept as 'given'. But, if one wants to be able to challenge the moral authority of communities which function effectively by subjecting some kinds of persons to the accepted power of others, the stopper has been applied too soon. For instance the Mafia flourishes in the modern world thanks to rules of allegiance, which once served to unite Sicilian families against foreign oppression and still give its members a sense of who they are and where they belong. Islamic communities are held together by sets of beliefs and practices which, in their fundamentalist forms, keep women in fierce subjection. I would not wish to issue a moral *carte blanche* just because we are dealing with, so to speak, forms of life.

It may be tempting to try starting with groups smaller than a community and more self-contained, as a source of non-instrumental reasons, for instance family, friends and immediate neighbours. If basic rights and duties are those which go with membership of these molecules (or 'little platoons' as Burke might call them), then we might have a workable test for distinguishing between just and unjust communities. The snag of miniaturising and personalising 'the given', however, is that there are no definite miniature forms. The family, for instance, is a favourite modern candidate for the molecules which can be chained as an account of the just society or moral community. But 'the family' is no ideal Platonic form. Some copybook nuclear families of two parents and 2.3 children are a human disaster; some one-parent families are a model of human flourishing; and other varieties of the family group are legion. Yet I do not wish to be dogmatic. It may be that there is some basic, small-scale human relationship, which, while having the authority accorded to single individuals by the idea of individual rights, also has members with basic duties towards each other.

But the difficulty of finding one goes deep, because, in a world where 'life does not mean anything other than itself', rights and duties point to different ideas of what a person is. If we are by nature separate individuals, then rights seem plausibly to be understood as a strategic device to ensure the benefits of mutual cooperation, and duties as then added as the logical way to secure the device. Contractarian ethics seems to me an ingenious attempt to work from an agent-relative to an agent-neutral account of moral reasons in this way. But it has failed to cope with Alf's antics, because it cannot reason him out of securing the benefits as cheaply as he can. A Kantian ethics might have done so, by starting with universal duties and refusing to deal in mutual advantages at all. But, Kant being a contractarian only in politics and not in ethics, that is beyond a contractarian's grasp.

Meanwhile 'duties' can also suggest a *tertium quid* between agent-relative and agent-neutral ethics. If we are by nature not separate individuals but persons essentially located in some of our social relationships, then our duties may be an expression of who we are and where we belong. That, of course, is just what causes the trouble with the loyal *mafioso* or the community whose characteristic action-guiding concepts draw distinctions of class, race, gender or, in general, power, which fall foul of the United Nations declaration of rights. As noted, it is a trouble which crops up for small or large groupings alike. Nonetheless Alf's antics do show, I hope, that a rational agent's ultimate reference group cannot be himself alone. He needs some group to identify with in relationships whose flourishing is a measure of his flourishing.

In finding Alf an identity, we abandon the individualism of current contract theories. That seems to me no hardship. The dislocated free-rider is like someone who wins a prize by cheating. He has the gold cup but not what it signifies; he has gained it but not won it. He is the master who tries to compel the love of his slaves. Moral pretence can fool many of the people much of the time, but it cannot reproduce what it imitates. Where morality requires that one treats another person's interests as one's own, short cuts, which give the appearance without the substance, are literally self-defeating. Hence an individualism which supposes that there is rational self-interest prior to all human relationships is untenable. The social or moral contract which constitutes a form of life also constitutes the persons for whom this is the most intimate relationship.

On the other hand, that does not rule out a contractarian theory like Rousseau's, resting (in a liberal interpretation) on a more social and sociable individualism where a citizen's duties come before an individual's rights. Here the choice to create the new association is made by individuals but, since it produces 'a remarkable change in man', is to be judged rational *ex post*, not *ex ante*. Citizens realise with hindsight that the choice has been self-creating and, if a General Will results, expressively rational. I am not sure whether a liberal interpretation can be sustained but the attempt seems to me worth making.

In any case, there is surely scope for thinking in terms of a liberal republic, where people are citizens before they are consumers and take their duties more seriously than their opportunities. As with our thieves, however, this can mean being expressively loyal to one another for the sake of robbing outsiders, thus raising a general objection to any situated ethics, which thinks in terms of separate communities each constituted by its own rules. Now the problem set by asking 'Why should *I* be moral?' arises again for international dealings. A contractarian ethics where the individuals are nation-states will need to decide whether rich nations have reason to view the troubles of poor ones with an impartial eye. I broach the question so late in this chapter only to register a dilemma. If the answer is no, then it threatens to be no again, when one asks whether a nation-state itself constitutes a single community. Why should one sub-culture pay to support another in a plural society? If the answer is yes, then we shall need to take a Kantian sighting on a kingdom of ends, thus stretching the Wittgensteinian notion of games and institutions to breaking point. This dilemma spells trouble for any ethics which relies on constituting individuals as members of historical groups, while treating forms of life as 'the given'.

In upshot rational ethics in a world where 'life does not mean anything other than itself' depends on there being good reasons for action whose measure of rationality is not instrumental. Otherwise honour among thieves is thoroughly awkward. Either it pays Alf to deal honourably with his cronies or it does not. If it does, it is because a cartel is exploiting outsiders and that can hardly be the morality which modern ethics should recommend. If it does not, it is because someone with Gyges' ring can do better still for himself – a serious matter in a mobile modern society of strangers, where such rings of invisibility are easily come by. The diagnosis must be that the relationship among thieves cannot be honour. *Ersatz* relations do not bind morally. But that leaves the question of when expressive relations do and do not bind. Not all honour codes which give meaning to people's lives are thereby to be commended. Some, for instance, chain social inferiors into subjection. To say so, however, we need a distinction between good and bad reasons for action which can apply to expressive choices. I appeal for help.

Meanwhile these awkward antique dealers are a moral fable for our times. Does it pay to be good in an enterprise culture, where relationships are instrumental and their analysis contractarian? Apparently it does, because markets flourish to mutual benefit where there is trust, and fail without it. The snag, however, is that very enterprising persons do better still by forming rings which exploit the less enterprising. Their benefits are not in fool's gold, since bank balances genuinely increase. Money buys commodious living. It buys the trappings of culture too. So a proof that glittering prizes are not always gold needs to cut deeper. It must connect culture and meaning to a moral concept of a person which makes neighbours of us all. Here we are dealing in moral antiques – a part of the trade where there is no substitute for the genuine article.[4]

---

[4] The theme of this essay was prompted in part by reading David Gauthier's *Morals by Agreement*, Oxford: Oxford University Press, 1986. For an admiring but firmly critical view of his attempt to make contractarian ethics the genuine article, see my essay, 'The Agriculture of the Mind', in D. Gauthier and R. Sugden, eds., *Rationality, Justice and the Social Contract*, Hemel Hempstead: Harvester Wheatsheaf, 1993, pp. 40–52.

CHAPTER 9

Dirty hands

13 February 1692 is still remembered in the Western Highlands of Scotland. At 5 a.m. a blizzard was raging down the valley of Glencoe but there were soldiers about. They were two companies of the Argylls under Captain Robert Campbell of Glenlyon, peaceably billeted on the MacDonalds of Glencoe for the past two weeks. The MacDonalds, who had newly sworn allegiance to King William of Orange, had treated them well. Sacred bonds of hospitality had been forged – a reassuring sign that enmities were fading between MacDonalds and Campbells and between Highland supporters of the Stuarts and the new Edinburgh government of 1688. But that was illusion. Captain Campbell had received secret instructions the previous day. 'Sir, You are hereby ordered to fall upon the rebels, the MacDonalds of Glencoe, and to put all to the sword under seventy ...This you are to put in execution at five of the clock precisely ... This is by the King's special command, for the good and safety of the country, that these miscreants be cut off root and branch ...' At five of the clock precisely the Argylls turned on their hosts. Almost forty MacDonalds were killed on the spot and many more, who scrambled away up the bleak walls of the glen, died of exposure in the blizzard. Crofts were burnt, cattle and goods carried off. That was the infamous Massacre of Glencoe. I shall start from here and gradually

This essay first appeared in *The British Journal of Political Studies*, 12, 1982, pp. 385–98. My warm thanks go also to Professor J. R. Jones of the University of East Anglia for historical advice and helpful comment, and to Patricia Hollis, then leader of Norwich City Council, and A. R. H. Glover, its Chief Executive, for experienced comment on the twists of civic virtue.

follow the moral questions which arise into the arena of politics at large.[1]

The slaughter was smallish beer by local standards of carnage and pillage. Indeed the MacDonalds themselves had massacred as many Campbells within living memory. They had few friends even among the Highland clans and fewer among Lowlanders and English. Yet the outrage was immense at the time and still potent enough now to bring the Dirty Hands problem graphically to life. The immediate reason for outrage was coolly summed up by Sir Thomas Livingstone, who, himself deeply involved as Commander-in-Chief of the king's army in Scotland, remarked, 'It's not that anybody thinks that the thieving tribe did not deserve to be destroyed, but that it should have been done by such as were quartered amongst them makes a great noise.' I shall say a little about this aspect of the noise and then turn to the wider reasons, which have to do finally with the moral identity of political agents and an unresolved crux in the ethics of statecraft.

Campbell and his soldiers had committed 'murder under trust'. That was the judgement of the Scottish Parliament, recorded in its 1695 *Address to the King Touching the Murder of the Glencoe Men*, and it referred to the abuse of hospitality and breach of honour. The penalty for murder under trust (not in fact pursued on this occasion) was to be hung, drawn and quartered. The offence was perfectly plain both in the *Laws and Ordinances Touching Military Discipline*, and in the code of honour practised among the Highland clans. So, both as soldiers and as Highlanders, the killers stood condemned. Admittedly the murder had been done under explicit higher orders. But the Parliament would have none of this, declaring roundly that, because the laws of God and Nature are above those of men, no instructions or orders could justify breaking them. There is often, I grant, a hard question of whether an order is morally permissible. Indeed, that is very much part of the Dirty Hands problem. But, since I am not defending Captain Campbell, I shall assume that murder under trust falls well outside what is

[1] John Prebble, *Glencoe*, London: Secker and Warburg, 1966, and Harmondsworth: Penguin Books, 1968, gives a well-evidenced and reflective account, which I have followed gratefully.

permitted by any modern, secular version of the laws of God and Nature. That particular order, let us agree, should not have been given nor, once given, obeyed.

This also disposes of Major Robert Duncanson, who signed the order, and of Lieutenant-Colonel James Hamilton, second-in-command of the nearby garrison at Fort William, at whose bidding it was executed. But it does so only for the specific matter of murder under trust and without touching the ethics of the larger strategy which led to the tactical outrage. The larger strategy was to wipe out the MacDonalds of Glencoe as a savage example to all waverers, and here responsibilities and reckonings are cloudier. The tactical plan seems to have been Hamilton's but his superior, Colonel John Hill, the commander at Fort William, knew of it. Also Hamilton could not act without Hill's orders and, indeed, had them. But Hill had delayed giving the order for several anguished days and, when he did utter, he did so obliquely by telling Hamilton to act on 'the orders you have received from the Commander-in-Chief'. I shall return to Colonel Hill's moral predicament later.

The Commander-in-Chief's orders were not flatly to commit murder under trust. Livingstone had written to Hamilton, 'Sir, here is a fair occasion for you to show that your garrison is of some use ... I desire you would begin with Glencoe, and spare nothing which belongs to him, but do not trouble the Government with prisoners.' As the final phrase hints, however, discreet foul play was not ruled out. The pretext for assaulting the MacDonalds was that they had not sworn allegiance to King William by 1 January 1692. That it was a pretext is plain, since MacIain, their chief, had presented himself to Colonel Hill at Fort William on 30 December in order to take the oath and had been unable to do so until 6 January through no fault of his own. This fact was well known to all involved. So, whatever tactics Hamilton decided on, he was not going to have to answer moral questions from headquarters.

The buck does not stop with the Commander-in-Chief, however. He too was following orders. The decision to make an example of the MacDonalds of Glencoe belongs to Sir John Dalrymple, Secretary of State for Scotland. 'It is a great work of charity to be exact in rooting out the damnable sept, the worst in all the Highlands', he had written to Livingstone on 16 January. 'It must be quietly done, otherwise they will make shift for both men and their cattle.' He also wrote directly to Hill at Fort William on the same day, 'Pray, when anything concerning Glencoe is resolved, let it be secret and sudden, otherwise the men will shift you, and better not meddle with them than not do it to purpose.' Like the rest, Dalrymple knew that the MacDonalds had sworn allegiance and was undeterred. ('I am glad that Glencoe did not come within the time prescribed.') Moreover, it was he who worded the highest official directive for the business – 'If M'Kean of Glencoe and that tribe can be separated from the rest, it will be a proper vindication of the public justice to extirpate that sept of thieves.' This directive did not bear his authority, however. It comes from the official document signed at head and foot on 16 January 1692 by King William himself.

The dirty hands thus included the king's. (Be it noted that the Royal Commission, which reported in 1695, held that 'extirpate' truly meant that the MacDonalds 'were only to be proceeded against in the way of public justice, and in no other way' – a truly fine example of how a word can be resprayed during a cover-up.) I have set out the chain of command in some detail, so as to distinguish its political and military elements. The military ones I shall treat as a simple reminder that the state controls force and backs its moral judgements with violence. In granting that soldiers should not commit murder under trust, I did not say that they had all or only the moral duties of civilians. If they do not, however, any special licence derives from political authority and the dirty hands which concern me are those engaged in politics.

By the same token, the question which I am extracting from the Glencoe massacre is not the general one of when, if ever, the ends justify the means. Certainly we could raise that question. On the one hand, the massacre did its job in bringing the rest of the rebellious clans to heel. 'They come from all parts to submit to the King's mercy', Hill was soon reporting, as other chieftains flocked in to avoid being, as they put it, 'Glencoed'. Fairer play or peaceful means might perhaps have had the same effect but more slowly and at greater cost in lives and money. Also, more regiments would have had to be tied up in Scotland, when the king wanted them urgently in the Spanish Netherlands. On the other hand, Glencoe had its price. The new allegiances, prompted by fear, were tactical and no government cares to rule through a reputation for savagery and dishonour. National unity in the wake of 1688 was going to be precarious and future trouble in the Highlands could be foreseen. The utilitarian balance is thus tricky, since it would be hard to prove that no alternative strategy would have had likely consequences as satisfactory. But, granted that the government was legitimate and national unity a proper aim, there is a utilitarian case for making a bloody example and even for adding a stench of foul play *pour encourager les autres*.

But are these the general terms in which to discuss the Dirty Hands problem? I think not for two reasons. One is that it contrasts principle and consequence in a most misleading way. It is common, I admit, to think that politics is a dirty game because even good people are forced to abandon their principles for the sake of getting at least something done. This view is taken especially by those who uphold an ethic of duty so absolute that consequences are hardly to be considered. 'Love your enemies, do good to them that hate you, bless them that curse you, and pray for them that despitefully use you' is an example which springs to mind. By such a test all counting of costs is a betrayal of principle. But nothing in the idea of duty itself demands this unswerving disregard for the resulting mayhem on earth or guarantees that a cosmic justice will pick up the pieces in heaven. Most ethics of duty are more elastic, recognising that there is often doubt which of conflicting principles to apply and what precise course of action a given principle requires. The Grand Inquisitor in *The Brothers Karamazov* is faced with deciding what to do when Christ returns to earth and threatens to lead the people into the ways of the Sermon on the Mount. The consequences are too terrible to contemplate and the Grand Inquisitor decides that Christ must again be put to death. That is a decision taken for reasons of Christian principle, however, and not after abandoning principles altogether.

Conversely, an ethic which judges by consequences must still assess them from a point of view. Utilitarianism, for instance, specifies a yardstick of the greatest happiness (or good). Such yardsticks are like enough to requirements of duty to scotch a charge of betraying principle. If politicians have a specially urgent care for costs and consequences, that implies nothing about lack of principle. In politics, it will be argued later, the best is the enemy of the good. For the moment I insist only that to forgo the best is not to abandon principle in pursuing the good.

The other reason for not seeing the question as a general one of ends and means is that it would miss the crucial interplay between private life and public office. If a private traveller had found shelter with the MacDonalds and, after two weeks' hospitality, had shot his hosts and stolen their cattle, there could be no excuse. Or, to be precise, any excuse would need to be premised on some previous and terrible breach of honour by the host himself, which gave the traveller a personal right or duty. In finding that Campbell and his men had committed murder under trust, the Scottish Parliament placed them on a private footing and disallowed a plea of acting under orders. But that is not to disallow the plea across the board. Soldiers are sometimes morally required to carry out orders which bind them only because they are soldiers. The topic would still come out cosily, if soldiers were morally required to do only what private persons were not morally forbidden to do. But I shall be arguing that life is not so cosy and, in that case, it is important to pose the problem as one about the duties of office.

It also matters that soldiers hold political office. This is not obvious, because we are used to discussing constitutions which separate political and military offices. For Glencoe, indeed, I grant that Captain Campbell's moral position as a soldier differed from that of Dalrymple as Secretary of State. I grant also that the difference is not solely that Dalrymple gave the orders and Campbell obeyed them. But both were officers of the crown and this sets them apart from officers of merchant banks, the Catholic church, the MacDonald clan or any other body without the state's authority. By the political theory coming to be accepted at the time the king's authority (under God) derived from the people and he and his servants spoke as *vox populi*. Today the monarch is a mere voice and God is of erratic political standing; but the state's servants still wield the authority of the people. They are *our* agents and their dirty hands are *ours*. I do not mean that the citizens are always to blame for all the sins of their uncivil servants, since, I assume, offices can be abused or the state apparatus lose its claim to legitimacy. But, even where the government truly represents the people, there may be dirty work for it to do; and then its dirty work is ours. That is what groups a secretary of state, who orders a massacre, together with a soldier, who executes one, and sets both apart from a company director, who orders a lie, and a salesman, who tells it.[2]

Are there, then, officers of state who have a moral duty to do for us what we would be morally wrong to do for ourselves? Those inclined to say yes cannot do better than quote Machiavelli:

Princes who have done great things have held good faith of little account ... It is necessary to be a fox ... A wise lord cannot nor ought he to keep faith when such observances may be turned against him ... Nor will there ever be wanting to a Prince legitimate reasons to excuse this non-observance. (*The Prince*, chapter 18)

Machiavelli argues that the Prince must exercise his duty to act for the good of his people in a world full of 'wolves' and of 'snares'. So he cannot himself practise the virtues of a good citizen without betraying the interests of his subjects. Yet he must be seen to uphold those virtues, since no state can flourish unless its citizens display them. A wise prince therefore preserves a moral front by seeming to keep faith and seeming to act with honour, while secretly breaking faith and ignoring honour when occasion demands. There is dirty work to be done for the glory of the principality and a virtuous prince cannot discharge his duties without doing it. He should get his hands dirty and wear clean gloves.

This advice cannot easily be paraded in public. The Prince is never short of legitimate reasons for dishonour, but only if he never has to admit to acting dishonourably. That is why Sir Thomas Dalrymple was so put out when his plan for extirpating

---

[2] For an illuminating discussion see Michael Walzer, 'Political Action: The Problem of Dirty Hands', *Philosophy and Public Affairs*, 3, 1973, pp. 160–80.

the MacDonalds was carried out by murder under trust. A trumped-up battle at hopeless odds would have been as morally suspect but far more legitimate. It is also why the king was no doubt relieved when his Royal Commission glossed 'extirpate' as 'proceed against in the way of public justice'. If we are almost as scandalised by the cover-up as by the massacre, that proves only that it was botched. The first duty of a fox is not to be caught foxing.

Opposite Machiavelli we may set the simpler view that political leaders should be citizens squared. Thomas Jefferson (if an abrupt change of context may be allowed) stated it roundly in a letter to Don Valentine de Feronda in 1809, 'I never did or countenanced, in public life, a single act inconsistent with the strictest good faith; having never believed there was one code of morality for a public and another for a private man.' By this account the statesman should be guided solely by private virtues in public life. If he ought to keep faith with his neighbours, he ought to keep faith in his public dealings too. Machiavelli's view of virtue in princes cannot be extended to people at large, because a princely fox can operate only if people at large are not like him. But there is no such difficulty about supposing that everyone, prince and citizen alike, should practise the virtues of private life. The vision of a society governed by people whose integrity is that of private citizens and who shoulder the burdens of office as they would those of home is an attractive one. It has a simple and a subtle version.

The simple one equates the integrity of the individual with unswerving obedience to conscience or to curt moral imperatives in all situations. If thou shalt not lie, then thou shalt not lie in office and thou shalt not order others to lie. This is the stuff of martyrs, and it has its obvious appeal. For example, I clearly cannot acquire a duty to murder people just by taking a job as a hit man for the Mafia[3] and it is tempting to add that the same

[3] As Thomas Nagel says in his fine paper 'Ruthlessness in Public Life', in S. Hampshire, ed., *Public and Private Morality*, Cambridge: Cambridge University Press, 1978. J. R. Jones has pointed out that there might be grounds for another view in the early days of the Mafia, when the extended family was a last unit of resistance to alien rule. I have also learnt much from Bernard Williams's paper, 'Politics and Moral Character', in the same volume.

goes for the Prince's hit man. But there are several reasons for thinking that the statesman should not practise the moral consistency of a saint. The integrity of the martyr is saved at his own expense, whereas the statesman's refusal to compromise is paid for by his people. The martyr concedes nothing to the differing moral opinions of his neighbours, whereas the statesman represents both the martyr and his neighbours. Hence the martyr yields nothing for the sake of constructing the moral consensus without which the statesman cannot work. The martyr goes to the stake himself and that we admire. But, let loose with political power, he sends others to the stake with an equal will and, in shutting his eyes to the moral nuances of political life without thereby abolishing them, he licenses very foul play, provided that it is conducted outside the limits of his simple moral lexicon. This seems to me the result of flatly denying all the presumptions which make the Dirty Hands problem both urgent and difficult.[4] But the saint is not the only alternative to the fox; and the statesman, conceived of as citizen squared, need not wear his integrity on his sleeve.

The subtle version has a more nuanced view of principle and of the nature of integrity in private life. It endorses what was said earlier against drawing sharp contrasts between an ethics of duty and an ethics of expediency. Integrity, therefore, is not a stark affair of flying the flag of principle, going down with the ship and damning the consequences. For instance, the story goes that Churchill was told during the afternoon of 14 November 1940 that there was to be a massive air raid on Coventry that night.[5] A word of warning would have saved hundreds of lives. Yet no warning was sent. For, if the Luftwaffe found themselves expected, they would deduce that their Enigma cypher had been broken; and that was a consequence worth more in the war effort than hundreds of lives in Coventry. It might seem that

[4] The case against a simplistic view of integrity in politics is well put by Max Weber in 'Politics as a Vocation', in H. H. Gerth and C. Wright Mills, eds., *From Max Weber: Essays in Sociology*, London: Routledge and Kegan Paul, 1948, pp. 77–128.

[5] According to R.V. Jones in *Most Secret War: British Scientific Intelligence 1939–45*, London: Hamish Hamilton, 1978, Churchill was given no such information. But those who deciphered the German signals had certainly informed the War Office; so the case stands, even if Churchill is not the focus of it.

Churchill had sacrificed his integrity to the war effort. But, on reflection, would it not have been self-indulgence to give the word? Did integrity not demand the keeping of a wider faith? That, at any rate, is how the subtle version would have us see it. The citizen squared must treat the demands of office as a legitimate claim on his private integrity; yet, in doing so, he concedes nothing to Machiavelli.

This subtler version will often result in Machiavellian advice but there is still a difference. It shows itself when we ask whose integrity is at stake. Machiavelli makes it that of the Prince, since there is no more final answer to the question 'Who is the Prince?' The citizen squared, by contrast, is an individual first and a Prince (or prime minister) afterwards. The identity of an individual does not change with office and we are all individuals. On Machiavelli's account, therefore, the Dirty Hands problem is ultimate, since the morality of princes has a different origin from the morality of citizens. On the citizen-squared view the units of moral accounting are always individuals, whatever special dilemmas face individuals who hold public office. But that is an abstract difference so far and, to put flesh on it, I return to Colonel John Hill.

Hill's task as governor at Fort William was not simply a military one. He was charged, it is true, with keeping the king's peace and extending it among hostile clans. But he was not obliged to use powder and shot. Indeed it would have been rash to rely on force of arms, since his troops were a raw and ragged lot, stricken with disease and unfit for much campaigning. So his main efforts had been civilian, working on the clans by diplomacy and exploiting their disunity by veiled threats. By 1692 he had hopes of pacifying all within his reach. To judge from his reports, he brought a moral fervour to this task, seeing it as God's work, befitting a former Cromwellian officer, who had helped pacify the Highlands in just such a way thirty years before. He was also, however, a link in the military chain of command and the massacre at Glencoe could not go ahead without his order. Although he had been by-passed in the planning, he knew what was afoot and disapproved both tactically and morally. Being a man of integrity, one might think, he would refuse or resign (as two of his junior officers did). But, after a week of inner debate, he in fact instructed his second-in-command to carry out 'the orders you have received from the Commander-in-Chief'. Nonetheless the Royal Commission in 1695 declared themselves 'unanimous that he was clear and free from the slaughter' since he had done nothing 'till such times as, knowing that his Lieutenant-Colonel had received orders, he, to save his honour and authority, gave a general order to Hamilton to take four hundred men and to put in due execution the orders which others had given him'. He later used this salvaged authority to temper the wind to the surviving MacDonalds and to press on with his civilian efforts.

We may think that the Commission let him off lightly. But his dilemma was real and his solution not flatly outrageous. There was real conflict between his military and civilian roles as governor (in so far as they would have been distinct to a man of the time). His civilian diplomacy had enmeshed him in relations of honour with the clans and, friendless though the MacDonalds were, murder under trust was dishonourable. Besides, it was Hill himself who had received MacIain's offer of allegiance just within the time limit and he had written to his superiors on the MacDonalds' behalf. A diplomat has been defined, with nice ambiguity, as an honest man sent to lie abroad for the good of his country; and I daresay that a little lying abroad was morally tolerable in a civilian governor. But it would not stretch to conniving at his military orders from London. He was faced, like Pontius Pilate, with irreconcilable duties. Which horn of the dilemma did integrity require?

The citizen-squared view would have it that integrity is not a matter of identifying with one role or the other but of remaining true to one's own self. Since Hill thought the massacre wicked, this suggests that he should have refused his consent. (Certainly we are unmoved by his subsequent plea that 'if any censure the severity of man's justice, yet the justice of God is to be revered. For there was much blood on these people's hands.') But, whatever Hill ought to have done, this approach assumes that we can put moral constraints on individuals, distinct from all normative constraints on holders of office. I shall argue next that this misconstrues the relation of self to role, the nature of moral choice and hence the Dirty Hands problem.

Remember that Hill was a Christian. I grant that it cannot be right to think of him as therefore having a third role. That would complicate matters to no purpose, since, instead of having to choose between two duties, he would now have to choose among three. Sometimes, no doubt, principles can be viewed as roles: but only when they are external to the agent. For instance a secret Catholic after 1688 might need to reckon on his duties as a (notional) Protestant. But that artificial situation was not Hill's, who was straightforwardly a Christian and not a man distanced from the religious code of his time and place. But, just because being a Christian is not a third role, it does not follow that it is a predicate of individuals. The right conclusion, I submit, is that Hill's choice lay between the duties of a Christian civilian governor and those of a Christian military governor. I have three reasons.

Firstly, the holding of office can change the basis of moral decision. For instance, I have a special duty to my own children, and, when their school catches fire, am morally entitled or even required to save them first (at least if no extra lives are lost thereby). But, if I were the fireman sent to put out the blaze, then I should treat my children exactly like all others. It is morally corrupt to use the powers of office to further personal relationships. This difference between private and public persons could be expressed by saying that private individuals acquire new moral duties with office. But it is neater and clearer to say that office holders have moral duties which private persons do not.

Secondly, the attempt to place universal moral requirements on everyone, whether in office or not, fails to resolve the moral dilemmas of office. Such requirements are too broad. Churchill could not have decided whether to warn the people of Coventry by reflecting that he had a general duty of benevolence. On the other hand, if general principles are treated as elastic, so that they can be massaged into specific shape for specific situations, then office becomes a specific situation. For instance, if 'Thou shalt not kill' does not rule out the killing of enemies in uniform or grossly handicapped infants, then the office of soldier or doctor is morally special.

Thirdly, it is fallacious to argue that, where roles conflict, there must be a place to stand which is prior to all roles in order to umpire the conflict. Role-conflict is rarely a collision between clear imperatives, since roles are not fully scripted. Like all state officials, Hill was licensed to use violence. His civilian licence was covert and presumably did not extend as far as his overt military licence allowed. But there were limits even to the military licence and part of his problem was where they lay. For the rest, he was trying to reconcile some wielding of the state's violence with civilian duties, which shaded into relations of Highland honour and hospitality. In none of these relations did he engage with the MacDonalds as man to man. Each aspect of his situation was structured and the structuring cannot be peeled away to expose the true human situation beneath. There is no true human situation other than the web of social relations. There was no place for him to stand prior to that of a Christian governor.

The obvious objection is that this seems to make persons the creatures of their roles and hence to ignore the fact that they can always resign. So there surely is a moral standpoint outside the role? No, I reply, that is not obvious at all. To make roles inescapable is not to make the actors creatures of them, except on a highly structural and deterministic version of role theory, which I would reject.[6] Nor can the actor escape by resigning. Consider, for example, those German judges appointed under the Weimar Republic, who found themselves still in office under the Nazis and set to administer growingly anti-Semitic laws. Some resigned but others, reckoning that they would merely be replaced by ardent Nazis, stayed on, grimly trying to do some slight good. Whether or not they made the right choice, they were certainly right about the responsibility. Those who resigned escaped the office but not the responsibility. If, for the sake of argument, it was wrong to resign, then that shows how honour can be smirched by resigning as well as by soldiering on. Once a

---

[6] See 'Of masks and men' above.

dilemma has been posed for a person in office, integrity does not demand that he keep his hands clean by stepping aside. It is too late for clean hands, whatever he does.

Hill's position is not unlike Pontius Pilate's. Faced with a lynch mob of his Jewish subjects demanding the death of Jesus, Pilate took water and washed his hands before the multitude, saying, 'I am innocent of the blood of this just person: see ye to it' (Matthew 27:24). No water washes as clean as that; but we should not therefore rush to condemn Pilate's choice. Despite the terrible press which he has had, it is not obvious to me that integrity required him to protect a just man at the cost of a riot. Integrity does not offer a separate lever. The question is what it was right for the Roman governor of Judaea to do and, once that question is answered, integrity demands simply that the governor go ahead and do it.

The citizen-squared view differs finally from the Machiavellian in bidding the man in office do what he would do, were he not in office. This demand is incoherent, since the problem would not exist for him, were he not in office. It is simply a final invitation to indulgence, as if integrity were measured by the smug but mistaken comfort of a clean conscience. The Royal Commission declared that Hill had saved his honour and authority. That finding may have been more convenient than true. I insist, however, that Hill had no easy way to save his honour and that 'honour' here is a moral term connected essentially with role and office. If he would have been wrong to refuse the order, he could not have saved his personal honour by resigning.

My general question has been whether there are two sources of morality, one grounding the duties of persons in office, the other those of private individuals. The citizen-squared view says no, since there are in the end only the universal duties of individuals. But, in refined form, this answer is reached after allowing that the demands of office make a difference. For there are codes of duty for office-holders – for instance the British Army's *Laws and Ordinances Touching Military Discipline* at the time of Glencoe – which affect what a moral person should do. The citizen-squared view insists, however, that such codes are not in themselves morally binding on individuals. There is always a further moral question of whether the office-holder should do what the local code requires. Sometimes he should not. But, when he should, it is likely enough that he will be doing something which he should not have done, were he not in office. In giving this answer, the citizen-squared view tries to abstract from the particular situation in two ways. It abstracts from the local laws and observances to a universal moral ordinance implicit in every role. It abstracts also from every role and office to a universal individual prior to every decision. I object to both moves.

That might sound like support for a moral relativism. But that is not my intention. It is important, I grant, to allow for the contemporary context of Hill's dilemma. The distinctions, which I have been making between civil and military, social and individual, public and private, were not as well entrenched then as now. Hill belonged to a Covenanting tradition, which made conscience the arbiter of a man's duty to God and which gave the kirk a temporal authority. During the civil war, for instance, it had been common for reprobates (meaning royalist officers, papists, episcopalians and other such) to be hanged or slaughtered summarily as enemies of God; and some massacres were ordered by ministers of the kirk. So there is force in saying that Hill would not have seen his situation in quite the way in which I have painted it. This might seem to imply that Hill faced a moral dilemma only because he was caught between two interpretations of what he took to be God's will. But that would suggest that a man who feels no moral conflict in carrying out orders is not morally to blame for the results – a view which licenses atrocities by the brutish or the fanatical. To stem the implication, I insist that there is always a question of whether orders should be obeyed. Yet the answer to it depends partly on local circumstances. Hill had made use of the local Highland code of honour in establishing trust with the MacDonalds and the fact that he helped break the code comes into the moral reckoning. He was required to do what was right, given those social relations; or, in other words, neither, absurdly, what would be right, whether or not he was so placed, nor, as an opposite corrective, merely what he happened to believe was right.

Similarly, we cannot abstract from social agents to presocial, moral individuals. I may have made the Princely view sound as if a Prince were necessarily a social actor, whereas his subjects were individuals. In that case it would be plausible to suggest that there are two moralities, one social and the other individual. But there is no need to put it like that. The Prince's subjects are not individuals but citizens; and the difference in the moral demands of public and private life attaches to different social positions. Here too a relativism is tempting, since the moral duties of citizens seem to vary with the idea of community marking their place and time. Machiavelli had one idea of community in mind, Thomas Jefferson another. But we can require social actors to stand back from their local conventions without having to find them a vantage point outside all roles. Moral questions are about how we should live out social relations with others and, I submit, answers involve nothing more private than a citizen.

Someone may complain that questions couched in these terms are liable to be unanswerable; that if Agamemnon is to decide between his fleet and his daughter, he needs a neutral perch. But I do not see where such a perch might possibly be; nor, for reasons given earlier, do I grasp why it would help to have one. It may be that Agamemnon's dilemma has no escape, in that it is true of him both that he ought to sacrifice his daughter and that he ought not. That is a plausible guess at the nature of tragedy. If it is correct, however, it is so in the eyes of heaven as much as in the thinking of Homeric Greece.

Although local circumstances matter, it should still be possible to generalise the Dirty Hands problem and I shall end with some summarising remarks about politics at large. They concern the art of the morally permissible in an arena where there is no one more private than a citizen. I shall make them under the headings of authority, violence and compromise.

Political actors, duly appointed within a legitimate state, have an authority deriving finally from the People. Currently that means from you and me. No doubt they can abuse that authority. No doubt it is sometimes unclear whether they truly have it. But sometimes they have it and, on the Princely view, must sometimes use it for dirty work. When their hands get dirty, so do ours. The extent of the dirt is hard for us to gauge because our agents' duty is to conceal it from us. This is in part because we value the comfort of hypocrisy but more because they have failed, if we know. Machiavelli's Prince must seem to keep faith and today's secret services must seem to play fair. The idea is disturbing yet, once Machiavelli's starting point is granted, there is no escape. The starting point is simply that there are wolves about who do not wish the good of the people and who do not keep faith; and that they can be thwarted only by marshalling the apparatus of legitimacy against them; and that the apparatus has to be used dishonestly. Our fascination with the grubby yet genuine integrity of secret-service agents is evidence that we grudgingly accept this much, although our preference for fiction as the source of fascination is a sign that we cherish our hypocrisies.

All this recognises that the state, in claiming a monopoly of legitimate force, relies on a covert violence. But the case extends far beyond bloodshed. Milder Glencoes are regularly conducted in the course of slum clearance, compulsory purchase, industrial closure, the siting of airports, road building or the management of exchange rates. They occur whenever the state's agents use our authority to massage the law for the public good. The massage may be a matter of secret breach or of biased interpretation. Often, I hasten to add, there is no warrant for foul play and the dirty hands belong straightforwardly to guilty people. But we order, or at least license, our agents to pursue policies which cannot be translated into action, if honesty and openness are required too. The casualties of urban renewal, for instance, are greater if the plans are made public in advance. The resulting blight then has to be remedied by wider destruction of property and community. Yet secrecy demands firm lies in the face of questions. Thus, the family promised safety today will be 'Glencoed' tomorrow. This too is violence, even if the weapon is not a musket but a clearance order.

It is hard to resist the thought that dirty hands, where 'legitimate' (in quotes), must be a sign of defective institutions. Can there not be laws and policies which good people can

apply without dishonesty? It is no real answer that good people
must deal with evil people, because evil people can be honestly
exposed and brought honestly to book. Why precisely, then,
must good people apply principle so deviously that dishonesty
becomes a virtue? The answer lies finally in the harmless
platitude that politics is the art of compromise. Politicians must
keep a kind of faith with several groups who lay conflicting
claims of loyalty upon them. In our system local councillors, for
instance, must answer doctrinally to party workers in the
language of the manifesto, must care pragmatically for the
interests of constituents with words of common sense, must
administer with the aid of officials in an Enlightenment language
of reason, must manoeuvre humanely among pressure groups
each with its own single criterion of what matters; and so forth.
Each claim is legitimate; each sets a test for what is best, which
they will not fully meet. Confronted with this plurality of aims
and values, they must plead that the best is the enemy of the
good. If they aim for the best, as defined by some single
criterion, they will fail to deliver even the good. To deliver even
the good requires a deviousness, whose justification by principle
can only be oblique. Theirs is the integrity of the trimmer; and
I reject the harsh contempt for trimmers as lacking all integrity.

Even the good man in politics has no fast guide to the best
and is tied into a system which practises violence in many
forms. That is why I have dwelt on Colonel Hill's predicament
over Glencoe, rather than on Captain Campbell who supervised
the massacre or on the Secretary of State who turned the first
wheel. Hill's appointment at Fort William gave him the
People's authority. That it was an authority backed by violence
is symbolised by his military rank and the military character of
his post. That even civilian authority is backed by violence
shows in the continuity between his military and civilian duties.
That he was a good man I presume from his conscientious
efforts to act in a Christian manner. That the best may be
unattainable is shown by his moral dilemma. He was caught in
a chain of command which had the People at one end and the
soldiers at the other. His dilemma was that of inescapable
responsibility under partial constraint and his hands were dirty

from the start. That, I maintain, is the nature of the game.

But Hill played his part. Am I saying that he played it well? To be exact, I am not – I doubt that he saved his honour by partly sparing his authority. But that is to be exact about murder under trust. For the rest of the programme of purification, there is no shirking all responsibility for the violence and I do not see that honour required his refusing appointment as Governor. Politics is for foxes, and we really cannot complain if those we appoint to be devious then do what is asked of them. Complaints are in order when the fox loses his foxy integrity. But, in the nature of the case, there is no public measure of that moment.

A chapter on the art of the morally permissible cannot end tidily. If there were a clear line to mark the limits of deviousness, there would finally be no Dirty Hands problem. There would be a definite answer to the question, for instance, of whether an American President should conduct a nuclear arms strategy in the interests solely of his own people or regard South America as a backyard to intervene in when it suits. Political decisions would still be tricky in practice but in theory they would set only the moral problems of all decisions. That would be reassuring; and so my plea for foxes is correspondingly alarming. Nor do I see how to restore calm by proving that only wolves suffer, when foxes practise their art well. For that is how the political arena emerges, when Hill's dilemma is generalised. It is an arena where the best is the enemy of the good, where we license our agents to pursue the good and where they can succeed, only if they operate partly beyond our ken and our control. Can some critic please find me a more comfortable conclusion?

CHAPTER 10

Friends, Romans and Consumers

At the end of the 1980s, as Eastern Europe buried its Caesars without praising them and Western Europe set about merging its nations, thoughts turned to the meaning of citizenship. What was this elusive relation? What had it been in a more settled world and what would, could and should it become? To judge from the Western chorus then hailing the victory of capitalism over communism, to be a citizen is to be legally protected in the private enjoyment of what one gains in the market place. To judge from the words of the local victors themselves, communism would be replaced with a neighbourhood socialism of ordinary citizens. Meanwhile, other forces had smouldered on since 1917. They were those of nationhood and, deep in its shadow, anti-Semitism, of bourgeois aspiration or *Bürgertum* and of religion. So, although slices of the Berlin Wall were for sale in velvet pouches in the shops of New York, there were other portents. Neo-Nazis were parading in Leipzig, Christmas carols were being broadcast in Bucharest and the fundamentalist wing of Islam was rallying its faithful.

Since the most fragile of these contenders was neighbourhood socialism, persons of liberal instinct were worried. The need to rethink the idea of citizenship in a liberal democracy was, and is,

This essay, as its opening suggests, dates to 1990. Versions, improved by the comments of those attending the 1990 Colston Symposium on Political Philosophy at Bristol, appeared in *Ethics*, 102, 1991, pp. 27–41, and in D. E. Milligan and W. Watts Miller, eds., *Liberalism: Citizenship and Autonomy*, Aldershot: Avebury Press, 1992. For the present version I have added a touch of hindsight and thinned out parts of the argument more fully covered in 'Honour among thieves'.

urgent. My title picks out three candidates for its key. 'Friends' have a small-scale, personal tie, resistant both to the commands of the state and to cost-benefit calculation. 'Romans' belong to a *civitas*, whose spring is public duty and whose sentiment is republican or nationalist. 'Consumers', striking a modern note in the funeral oration for dead Caesars, are individuals related through contracts made to mutual advantage. I mean to enquire which, if any, of these relationships holds the key to civil society in a world where old ties have lost their magic.

To focus this daunting question, we might recall a British attempt to tackle the idea of citizenship. In December 1988, the British Parliament launched a Commission on Citizenship, under the patronage of the Speaker of the House of Commons and prompted by a lack of communal enterprise in the enterprise culture. There seemed to many observers, including Mrs Thatcher, then Prime Minister, and Douglas Hurd, her Home Secretary, to be a dangerous malaise, taking the form of public apathy among the respectable and a rash of antisocial behaviour among the lower orders. A plausible diagnosis, connecting the two groups, was that enterprise can undermine the very culture which it needs if it is to flourish. The call to enterprise bids each of us pursue our private good. The famous invisible hand works only if enough of us include a contribution to the quality of communal life in our idea of the good. 'Culture' is one name for the public ethos which reinforces this virtuous habit and thus, by restraining self-interest, also enables individuals to do better for themselves than they would in a merely selfish society. But what is true for all is not true for each, and the dominant logic of the free-rider problem erodes the benefits of cooperation. Although this threat to citizenship has been of concern since the industrial revolution, it had waxed in the 1980s, stimulated by libertarian thinking about the virtues of markets and private enterprise.

The Speaker's Commission, in a 1989 draft of its report, declared its aim to be 'to consider how best to encourage, develop and recognise Active Citizenship...provisionally defined as the positive involvement of the individual, group or organisation

in the wider community'.[1] The preamble described its approach
as seeking 'an enhanced vision of citizenship', so as to add a
fourth dimension to a notion of citizenship which currently
involved 'political, civil and social entitlements and duties
within a framework of law'. This fourth dimension 'would
involve the ideal of public good and civic virtue which finds its
expression in the largely voluntary contribution to society of
citizens acting either as individuals or in association with one
another'. The need was deemed to arise for three main reasons:
that too great an emphasis on the self-reliant individual acting
in competition can undermine social cohesion; that associations
are needed to mediate between central government and the
individual; and that the delivery of social rights at a level
appropriate to a civilised and modern democracy may be
threatened by expanding needs, slow economic growth and a
shortage of skilled wage-earners.

This all sounded like a well-rounded expression of open-minded
concern, until one noticed its oddity. The 'fourth dimension',
summarised as 'the citizen acting in a voluntary capacity', was
presented as an extra and novel dimension. Yet how could any
notion of democratic citizenship ever have done without it? In
describing the existing notion as one of 'entitlements and duties
within a framework of abstract law', what did the Commission
suppose currently animated citizens? The implicit answer, I
think, was that citizens are self-regarding individuals, who are
prone to count their entitlements as benefits and their duties as
costs. They incur the costs because minimal duties are enforced
by law and because there is overall benefit in citizenship, defined
as 'a status bestowed on those who are full members of a
community'. (This definition comes from T. H. Marshall,
whom the Commission quoted with approval in both draft and
final reports.) In that case, however, individuals, seeking to
minimise the cost of their bestowed citizenship, do well to avoid

---

[1] The final report, *Encouraging Citizenship: Report of the Commission on Citizenship*, London:
HMSO, 1990, was content 'to propose practical ways in which our participatory
arrangements can be strengthened' and muted all grander ambitions. That may have
been because public criticism of the draft proved unanswerable without conceding too
much to opponents of Thatcherism. At any rate, the braver draft report better
captures the public concern which created the Commission.

voluntary public activity; and one could wonder why Britain had a public life at all.

In fact, of course, there has long been plenty of activity 'in a voluntary capacity', mediating stoutly between central government and the individual. The Commission overlooked it because it was oddly silent about *local* government. By contrasting government (paid?) and the individual (voluntary?) it underplayed the unpaid activity of many thousands of citizens who contribute to a thriving tradition of local government. Here is a busy public arena where, for instance, women can and do take part in a proportion to their numbers far higher than in Parliament. Here rests the basis of Britain's claim to be a plural democracy, in so far as pluralism has to do with sources of authority distinct from that of central government. Even if one were to pretend that local politics do not count as 'voluntary activity', plenty of individuals who take part in it are also engaged in their communities in other ways. From this standpoint, the 'fourth dimension' described as an addition is simply a necessary component of what has long existed.

CONSUMERS

The point suggests that the Commission's view of its task was a symptom of the problem addressed, rather than a step towards its solution. The problem itself is urgent, if one agrees that social cohesion has become fragile of late, that mediation between government and individual has become harder, and that the delivery of social rights is under threat. The connecting thought here is that citizens have increasingly come to think of themselves as the 'Consumers' of my title or, to put it abstractly, in terms which presuppose that the basic political relation among us is contractual and that the political community factors as an association of private individuals whose public contributions are instrumental.

That makes the communal aspect of citizenship a public good, in the economists' sense that benefits cannot be confined to those who contribute to the costs. The resulting free-rider problem has a standard remedy of state intervention 'not to overrule the judgement of individuals but to give effect to it', as J. S. Mill remarks smoothly in what is perhaps still the best formulation of the difficulty.[2] But this remedy has always had the snag that, although the use of law may secure the grudging payment of contributions, a cheerful public ethos is what is really needed – the original problem over again. Furthermore the recent libertarian revival is hostile to enforcing anything smacking of a moral view of good citizenship, because moral choices should be left to the individual and cannot be made compulsory without robbing them of their moral value and undermining individual responsibility.

There have been other attempted remedies, however, notably those prescribed by Mrs Thatcher, when Prime Minister, and Douglas Hurd, when her Home Secretary. Mrs Thatcher's started from her oft-quoted conviction that 'there is no such thing as society' and her insistence that collective social arrangements are illegitimate and doomed to fail, if they fetter the individual will. In May 1988 she set out her general line on freedom and moral responsibility in a celebrated address to the General Assembly of the Church of Scotland, which became known as 'the Sermon on the Mound'. Christianity, she said, is about 'spiritual redemption and not social reform'. It tells us to render unto God the things which are God's; for the things which are Caesar's, it commands us simply to obey the law and use our talents to create wealth. Having quoted St Paul ('If a man will not work, he shall not eat'), she remarked that 'abundance rather than poverty has a legitimacy which derives from the nature of Creation'. The wealthy will, she hoped, be spiritually moved to mercy and generosity but that is their (spiritual) business, and 'any set of social and economic arrangements which is not founded on the acceptance of individual responsibility will do nothing but harm'.

With her strong sense of original sin, she was not suggesting that the problem would simply go away, if left to individual voluntary initiative. 'Making money and owning things could become selfish activities', she warned. Her line was only that

[2] J. S. Mill, *Principles of Political Economy*, seventh edition, London, 1871, Book V, chapter 11, especially section 12.

compulsion makes matters worse. Persuasion can be tried, however, and she went on to prescribe a spiritual cocktail of family values, a democratic ethos honouring individual responsibility, education in our Judaic-Christian tradition and patriotic celebration of our national identity. She then spun the threads together in the words of the hymn *I vow to thee my country*, noting its mention of a second unseen country of the spirit: 'soul by soul and silently her shining bounds increase'. 'Not group by group or party by party or even church by church', the Prime Minister added, 'but soul by soul, and every one counts.'

Her sermon thus divorced the material and spiritual sides of our lives, making us economic individuals for purposes of government and leaving mercy and generosity to our private consciences. Good works depend on the prior creation of wealth, for, as she once pointed out to the House of Commons, no one would have heard of the Good Samaritan, had he not had money. Although citizenship, construed as supererogatory contributions to the good of others, will not necessarily flourish if left to individuals, there is no alternative.

This strikes me as a very unpromising way to try harnessing self-help to the communal wagon. In effect, it takes citizenship as a status bestowed only on those who, like the Good Samaritan, have made a success of their individual responsibilities. Losers, who have not made the grade, are owed nothing. Winners, meanwhile, have made it by helping themselves; and why should they not continue to do so? A straw in the wind at the time was the 1989 Mintel survey of young opinion, *Youth Lifestyle*. It reported 'a new consumption and success ethic among the young', which led 31 per cent of the respondents to list 'money' among the top five ingredients of happiness, whereas only 17 per cent listed 'love': 'an "I-want-it-now" generation' was Mintel's summing up. Another straw was the failure of income tax cuts for the better off to show up in rising donations to charity. The corner which the wind was blowing from was memorably pin-pointed by a successful builder, interviewed on television and asked what lesson he drew from the previous ten years. His pithy reply was, 'Sod the little man!'

In chapter XXXI of *Leviathan*, Thomas Hobbes tempers his

dour picture of the Natural Condition of Mankind as Concerning their Felicity, and Misery (chapter XIII) by observing that for a full knowledge of our civic duties, we must know the laws of God, which enjoin 'equity, justice, mercy, humility, and the rest of the moral virtues'. Yes, but I cannot see why these optional extras should come into play. The contractarian core of economic individualism says nothing about God and apparently recommends only such virtues as it pays to practise. Success in an enterprise culture does not come from mercy and humility, nor in any obvious way from equity, justice and the rest. So why will the successful have any reason to reverse the attitude which gained them success? It may be said, as in recent contractarian theory, that individuals do best to act as maximisers constrained by a moral point of view, when dealing with others similarly rational. But, unless this amounts to more than advising the strong to deal justly with the strong, it is all too consistent with the strategy summed up as 'Sod the little man!'

That does not dispose of contractarian ethics, but it will serve to introduce Douglas Hurd's idea of citizenship, as presented in articles and speeches, while he was Home Secretary. In that office he was alarmed by the growth in petty crime both among the dispossessed and among the vandals and lager louts on the lower slopes of the enterprise culture. Being no more enthused by the growing white collar financial crime higher up, he set about reviving an older conservatism, which he hoped to marry to the new libertarian variety. 'The government is not about to adopt Thomas Hobbes as its patron saint', he assured readers of the *New Statesman*.[3] Instead he took his bearings from Edmund Burke and this quotation from *Reflections on the Revolution in France*:

No cold relation is a zealous citizen...To be attracted to the subdivision, to love the little platoon we belong to in society, is the first principle (the germ as it were) of public affections. It is the first link in the series by which we proceed towards the love of our country and of mankind.

Here in 'the little platoon' of family and neighbourhood, our strongest loyalties still reside, Hurd affirmed, *en route* to his own similar-sounding conclusion:

[3] The quotations which follow are from his article, 'Citizenship in the Tory Democracy', *New Statesman*, 27 April 1988.

Those qualities of enterprise and initiative, which are essential for the generation of material wealth, are also needed to build a family, a neighbourhood or a nation, which is able to draw on the respect, loyalty and affection of its members.

Hurd's citizens were not Mrs Thatcher's atomic individuals: 'Men and women are social beings', who find it natural to be sociable and to express 'affection and allegiance for many collective organisations – from a soccer club to a choral society or even a political party'. This temperament shows itself in 'the English tradition of voluntary work' – Justices of the Peace, school governors, neighbourhood watch coordinators and 'the thousands of people who give their time freely to the huge and thriving number of British charities'. (Notice the omission of persons active in local politics.) Witness these examples, the tradition is diverse, plural, innovative and runs counter to the obsession on the left with 'a society dominated by the relationship between the individual and the state'. It thrives wherever power is kept out of the hands of the corporatist battalions and given to the little voluntary platoons. 'Private property is the natural bulwark of liberty because it ensures that economic power is not concentrated in the hands of the state.'

The obstacle to voluntary activity is thus located in the bureaucratic state and its corporatist battalions, which are 'emphatically not what Burke meant by "the little platoons"'. Unfortunately, however, neither are neighbourhood groups of self-made persons with families. The little platoons of Burke's eighteenth-century England belonged to the battalions and regiments of a hierarchical society and were disbanded, along with this whole rural army, in the industrial revolution. Can they be re-formed through the qualities of initiative and enterprise essential for the generation of material wealth? I doubt it. Our new men seem to me too like those described by Tocqueville in *Democracy in America*:

Each of them, living apart, is a stranger to the fate of the rest...his children and his private friends constitute to him the whole of mankind; as for the rest of his fellow citizens, he is close to them, but he sees them not, he touches them, but he feels them not; he exists but in himself and for himself alone; and if his kindred still remain to him, he may be said to have lost his country.

In short the problem remains why the qualities needed for success in an enterprise culture should lead anyone to care about neighbourhood or nation, let alone (as in Burke's chain but not, I notice, in Hurd's) mankind.

The appropriate philosophical answer is supposedly contractarian: that ideally rational egoists are too long-sighted to cut off their separate noses to spite their collective faces. By idealising the agents, recent contractarians hope to improve on *Leviathan* – the seminal text for an enterprise culture – and Hobbes's contention that the benefits of trust and cooperation can be had only by instituting 'a common power to keep all in awe'. For Hobbes's breed of rational agent it may be true that 'covenants without the sword are but words'. But ideally rational agents appreciate that this kind of common power ensures only the minimum of voluntary input and requires a policing whose costs are a deadweight loss. So perhaps they can be rationally persuaded to adopt a moral point of view and thus comply in full without needing more than an assurance that others are as rational as they.

The moral point of view, for these purposes, is that of an impartial umpire applying universal rules which do the best for all consistent with the basic interests of each. Rawls's hunch in *A Theory of Justice*[4] was that rational egoists, set to draw up a constitution while knowing nothing of their own particular prospects, would hit on and agree to those very same rules: moral principles are equivalent to the shrewdest all-risks insurance policy for the unborn. That sets an awkward problem of why the better off will rationally comply, however, once they know that they are among the strong and fortunate. Hence the rational citizens of an enterprise culture may be more impressed by David Gauthier's *Morals by Agreement*,[5] where people who know their endowments still find that it pays to act morally, at least until they suffer for it. Gauthier's rational agents are not 'Straightforward Maximisers', who would defect whenever it

---

[4] Oxford: Oxford University Press, 1971. But cf. his *Political Liberalism*, New York: Columbia University Press, 1993, where mutual self-interest is not the source of obligation and he seems to deny that it ever was, even in *A Theory of Justice*.

[5] Oxford: Oxford University Press, 1986.

pays and thus be sunk by the free-rider problem, but 'Constrained Maximisers', who play fair with others whom they recognise to be Constrained Maximisers. Covenants between members of this charmed circle are more than words, since they are kept even on occasions when the sword could not provide an incentive.

But Gauthier's nakedly mutual-back-scratching approach gives the strong no reason to deal justly with the weak. The strong are not altruists and regard society as an association for mutual advantage, rather than as a community. Their idea of playing fair is to play Tit-for-Tat with those who have enough to offer, and enough power of reprisal, to make the policy profitable. They are not even much impressed by Hobbes's warning that 'the weakest has strength enough to kill the strongest, either by secret machination, or by confederacy with others' (*Leviathan*, chapter XIII). These days they can keep the weak under surveillance and divided, while giving them enough of a minimum to lock them into the market for fear of destitution. It is a market society where any concern for the interests of losers is merely instrumental. The root problem of an enterprise culture is unresolved.[6]

Furthermore, even the problem of compliance among the strong is unsolved, granted the line about cartels which I took in 'Honour among thieves' above. Defections which would be foolish on the part of a single individual can become profitable for sub-groups. An antique dealers' ring, for instance, which practises honour among thieves in order better to exploit outsiders, will be able to cover for each other and get away with free-riding on the norms whose observance by outsiders keeps the vehicle running. For a rather different example, consider the Mafia, whose activity is more open but whose power to lock outsiders into the game is correspondingly greater. The model here is 'Battle of the Sexes' (introduced more fully in 'Moves and motives' above), whose Nash-equilibria are local maxima.

In the abstract, there is no reason to expect the players to

---

[6] This paragraph is not meant to do Gauthier justice; but it hints at a line which I have taken elsewhere, in 'The Agriculture of the Mind', in D. Gauthier and R. Sudgen, eds., *Rationality, Justice and the Social Contract*, Hemel Hempstead: Harvester Wheatsheaf, 1993, pp. 40–52.

Player A

	a_1	a_2
b_1	2, 1	0, 0
b_2	0, 0	1, 2

Player B

Battle of the sexes

coordinate on one equilibrium rather than the other (or, indeed to coordinate at all). But if A can convince B that he will play a_1, then it is rational for B to play b_1. This solution tends to become established, even though the converse is equally true and (a_2, b_2) suits B better, because either equilibrium is better than none. But it also depends on which player can more easily absorb the loss of playing out of equilibrium to see if A will give in. In real-life battles of the sexes, it is rarely the women.

ROMANS

The last paragraphs are not meant to refute contractarianism out of hand. But I hope they cast serious doubt on whether mutual self-interest can supply the social cement of a civilised or even merely viable society. At any rate, they will serve to introduce the 'Romans' of my title. Gauthier's 'Constrained Maximisers' adopt a disposition to play fair with those who play fair with them, and are willing to presume that other people have this disposition, until proved wrong. To that extent they regard themselves as dealing with fellow members of their circle. But they do not regard themselves or others as entering the sort of relationship which, according to Rousseau, produces 'a remarkable change in man' (*The Social Contract*, Book I, chapter VIII). They remain 'Consumers' first and become citizens only for instrumental reasons. Granted, for the sake of argument, that the compliance problem is insoluble without a deeper change of heart, I shall next try reversing this priority.

By 'Romans' I mean members of political communities, whose identity is defined by where they belong. The plural is meant to signal a variety of groups more historically and contingently situated than Burke's 'mankind'. These communities need be political only in the Aristotelian sense that politics concerns '*ta koina*', the public life of civil society. The variety envisaged ranges from totalitarian states, where all activity is public in principle, to republics, which insist only that public duties are prior to private rights. The common factor is a *conscience collective*, a shared sense of morally binding incorporation in a collective undertaking, which makes Romans self-consciously Romans or Roumanians self-consciously Roumanians. Witness these examples, however, the abstract terms of incorporation are pretty indefinite, leaving it unclear quite who is to be deemed incorporated and quite what is the unifying bond.

In the abstract, the idea is to extend the boundaries of the self to include relations with other people, mediated by shared incorporation in the polity. The problem is to set a limit, so that the self is not swallowed up by an overweening state. By way of illustration, consider those orphans in Ceausescu's Roumania, who were nurtured with the sole aim of producing utterly loyal members of the *Securidade*. They grew up to become not individuals, not even, one might say, comrade-citizens, but comrade-soldiers and comrade-officers in a branch of the state which behaved as if it was the soul and will of the state. Something had gone radically wrong in applying an idea of political community, whose unperverted form might be hoped to yield social relationships in the republican tradition. But it is not easy to state the limit which a true idea of community must not overstep.

It might perhaps be done by attempting a liberal reading of Rousseau. In *The Social Contract* The People embodies a General Will, which expresses the desire of each citizen to bring about what is best for the community. While this sovereign body functions perfectly, it makes each citizen 'as free as before' even when forced 'to conform to wills not his own'. For, even when assigned a role as a subordinate, one is still not 'personally dependent' on the will of superiors but is playing one's part in the community and is protected by it from abuse. 'Freedom is obedience to laws which we prescribe to ourselves.'

This balancing trick depends on a positive notion of freedom as the ability to choose what is for the best. It depends also on the brief chapter 8 of Book I, where Rousseau contrasts the natural liberty of a state of nature, populated by narrow, stupid animals, with the civil and moral liberty of a society where, by becoming a citizen, one is transformed into 'a creature of intelligence and a man'. Such citizens retain a private will as individuals, but put their civic duties first. Even if they are tempted to regard citizenship as a burden, and so 'seek to enjoy the rights of a citizen without doing the duties of a subject', the temptation is resisted by truly free and rational persons and the free-rider problem is overcome, as Rousseau supposed it to have been in ancient Sparta or the early Roman republic.

Even if a liberal reading can be sustained, it is precarious. As practical advice, it carries an alarmingly high risk of tyranny. The state has but to become a little corrupt and the noble equation between the good of each and the good of all ceases to hold. Since the citizens have laid down all their defences when joining the social contract, they are at once in the chains from which Rousseau claimed to rescue them. Nor is it easy to know when corruption has set in. Formally, what emerges from the process of government is then no longer a General Will. Practically, since there is no independent way of identifying a General Will except as whatever emerges from a process satisfying the conditions which Rousseau specifies, departures from the ideal will be as undetectable as they are insidious. Disturbances have no inherent tendency to return to the ideal equilibrium, once the ballast of power has shifted.

Rousseau's readiness to let a community prescribe moral imperatives to itself without theoretical limit offends against the liberal conviction that autonomous citizens must be left a personal choice of ends. Yet this conviction cannot be sustained in any pure form which makes the principles of justice and social organisation purely procedural. (Although I cannot prove this point in short compass, it is instructive that Rawls's [1993] *Political Liberalism* more or less concedes it; and I shall assume it for purposes of argument.) Hence the liberal conviction needs to be that some morally justified limit has to be set to what The People can insist on in the name of a conception of the good. Thus laws which discriminate by race, gender or religion are ruled out not because they offend procedurally but because they are morally offensive. Pluralism is not morally neutral throughout. It relies on a positive, objective notion of autonomy which sets substantive limits to the collective options which a society may choose.

This raises the question of whether citizenship is an identity in some sense stronger than associate membership. Communitarian thinking tends to suggest that it is, witness those explicit versions where the community demanding its members' total loyalty is a nation or a church. Here, if sub-communities are tolerated, it is within limits hierarchically ordered, so that conflicts of loyalty are always settled in favour of the central body. Pluralist versions, however, are ambivalent. On the one hand they recognise and respect differences between, for instance, Muslims and Christians, men and women, blacks and whites, gays and straights. On the other they set limits to dissent, as when confronted with Muslim attitudes to Salman Rushdie or the education of women for subordinate roles. Where the limits lie is obscure. Is a plural community to allow conscientious objection, polygamous marriage and Lesbian parenting, for example? Such questions call for a definition of citizenship which specifies a moral core to the concept, even if as modest a core as it can. That sets a dilemma for those, like Douglas Hurd, who declare that men and women are *social* beings but remain staunchly individualist at heart. What is it that social beings have essentially in common, regardless of sex or gender, race or ethnicity? If it is merely that they have wants or needs which can be satisfied only by social intercourse, then the earlier destructive atomism resurfaces. If it is that they are ultimately their social selves, then it is unclear why the claims of nation or religion cannot be supreme.

FRIENDS

A 'plural community' thus threatens to be a contradiction in terms, with 'community' demanding that all members subscribe to a single, shared identity and 'plural' refusing this demand. This is a practical problem too, witness the havoc caused by efforts to state and apply the proper recipe for multicultural education, when faced with the claim that ethnicity or creed constitutes identity. Yet I do not despair of a notion of plural community as liberal republic, which can parry the threat of a contradiction in terms. Meanwhile, in search of an escape from the impasse, I turn to the 'Friends' of my title, meaning an attempt to think of 'social selves' in terms of small-scale, fragmented relationships. Burke's image was of links in a series proceeding from 'the little platoon' to 'country' and thence to 'mankind'. Let us try recasting it as one of concentric circles, with each individual as a notional blob in the centre of an inner ring of personal, intimate relations, like family and friends, then an intermediate ring of semi-personal role-relations, like neighbours and colleagues, an outer ring of fellow citizens and an outermost, universal ring for 'mankind'. Might the inner ring, typified by 'friends', hold the key to the rest?

If so, it is because the inner ring contains basic non-contractual relationships, which express the self rather than serve it. I assert this contrary to recent contractarian theory, which deals wholly in rational egoists, whose primary reasons for action are always instrumental. Certainly intimacy can be treated in this way, as when partners to a prospective marriage start by writing what they hope is a fully contingent contract specifying the division of household labour, child care, career options and, in the event of divorce, records and rugs. For, as Gary Becker strikingly remarks, 'a person decides to marry when the utility expected from marriage exceeds that expected from remaining single or from additional search for a more suitable mate'.[7] But this perversely imports the contractarian problem of trust among rational egoists into a relationship one of whose charms, when it flourishes, is that it by-passes the problem. Equally friendship can be reduced to commerce but, to be brief, the result is not friendship, for reasons to do with the master-slave dialectic. By 'Friends' I mean to gesture to small-scale, local and intimate

---

[7] G. Becker, *The Economic Approach to Human Behaviour*, Chicago: Chicago University Press, 1976, pp 3–14.

relationships which constitute who one is and where one belongs. They are contingent in that they are voluntary in their exercise, even if some of them are not chosen, and historical in that they are governed by social norms which vary through time and place. Without them we would not be social beings.

The image of concentric circles is one of sharp boundaries and so misleading. The self, once tempted out of the vanishing point in the centre, becomes a polypod. Family ties, for instance, can be more constraining than expressive; friendships, like marriages, come and go; some roles are crucial to the shape of a life, whereas others are means to unrelated ends. Concentric circles belie the fluid character of what matters. But they do convey the thought that they can rotate in conflicting directions. The usual idea behind attempts to identify a moral point of view is that the self should be guided by the demands of the outermost ring – the greatest good of the greatest number or the categorical imperative, for example. There is no obvious reason why these demands should be consistent with those of roles and commitments, which in turn need not be consistent with each other. The suggestion being made is that citizenship involves normative expectations of a locally variable sort and that, in cases of conflict, our loyalty should be to our own.

Yet, if this means that we should in general put personal ties before others, it cannot be right. Indeed it would be hard to find a neater definition of corruption in public life. Good citizenship is precisely not using one's offices for the benefit of one's friends. It will not do to replace 'Romans', who put duties to the state before all personal duties, with 'Friends' who simply reverse this priority. An active citizen needs to be so located that both pulls are at work, regarding fellow citizens as neighbours but impartial in contributing to the common good. Furthermore, if the retorts to egoism for each local community are not to sum to the original snag on an international scale, some notion of a citizen of the world will need to be included.

The Speaker's Commission thus had a daunting task in defining what it sought to activate in public life. Fortunately it could avoid having to draw up a blueprint for an ideal democracy. Recall the objection to Rousseau that there is no way of identifying the General Will independently of the fragile process of local discourse and decision. The best reply, it seems to me, is to grant the point but blunt it by contending that we can work out some ideal-speech conditions, in which discourse and decision will produce something as close to a General Will as is humanly possible. Similarly one can try to work out what sort of active engagement may be trusted to sum to a flourishing public life, without having to delineate the result in advance.

There is nothing amiss with the broad aim to animate 'the citizen acting in a voluntary capacity'. My objection is only to regarding this as a novel 'fourth dimension', with 'voluntary' construed to mean independent of government. As remarked earlier, the scheme of 'entitlements and duties within a framework of law' is doomed without voluntary activities by people whose citizenship, incidentally, is of right rather than 'bestowed' on them. That is why I rejoice in local government. It is the obvious forum where the process of public decision can harness the virtues of neighbourliness and hold the decision-makers accountable by making them live with the outcome. By the same token it offers a practical response to doubts about what is for the best, when abstract theory gives no clear guidance. Local government, with its pragmatic sense that the best is the enemy of the good, settles for defensible choices which the defenders must then live with in person.

CITIZENS IN MIDSTREAM

That is not a final answer to the question 'Who is my neighbour?'. Here I am not sure what to conclude about the blending of personal aims and public good. So, to focus discussion, I offer a small allegory about an environmental group campaigning for a clean-up in the area around the Chesapeake Bay in the coastal strip of Virginia and Maryland. It used to be a verdant landscape, where every prospect pleases; but, as usual, man is vile and the campaign is almost too late. Homes have been springing up in the trees, each pleasantly sited when it was built but each new one whittling away a little more of what Nature provided. Gradually there is more waste to dispose of in the shrinking woods or in the darkening rivers, where it joins the profitable fertilisers sluiced off smiling farmlands. Fish are poisoned as the water carries the silt away and down to the dying Bay. This is a familiar story of the search for positional goods, but the campaign slogan is unusually instructive: 'We all live downstream.'

This message is both uplifting and absurd. How uplifting to hear that we are all part one of another, all exposed to one another's evacuations and all with the same interest in cleaning up! How absurd to fancy that those upstream will give it the slightest credence! Yet it is not mere foolishness. Consider those who live in midstream with upstreamers above them and downstreamers below. At present, perhaps, they greet the pollution arriving from higher up with righteous anger, but save themselves trouble and expense by adding to the pollution lower down. Since they live halfway down, they might be rationally willing to subscribe to a clean-up. But, since they live halfway up, they have a free-rider's resistance to a categorical maxim that no one shall foul the water. So the campaign organisers have thrown in an incentive designed to appeal even to those living squarely upstream. Everyone already ensconced is vulnerable to a threat of further newcomers. To repel these potential boarders there will have to be planning controls. But that requires the votes of those who currently live downstream and the price of their votes is a genuine clean-up after all. Thus, you see, we do all live downstream.

In this allegory what persuades the advantaged not to enjoy the rights of a citizen without doing the duties of a subject is a common interest in keeping outsiders out. The categorical imperative gets a hypothetical grounding. But there will be trouble presently. Since upstreamers do not truly live downstream, they constitute a potential faction, which will become active once planning controls are in place. The wider alliance, which works while the strong need the votes of the weak, will shrink when the power of the weak can be safely eroded. This is a fair portent for an enterprise culture, which bids each of us move as far upstream as we can get and then reflect that those left downstream have failed through lack of enterprise. If the

message is seriously meant to be that we do indeed all live
downstream, then it implies the kind of voluntary activity which
brings about a remarkable change in man by turning acquaintances into friends and strangers into neighbours.

Citizenship, then, requires an animating sense of the common
good which Consumers lack. But it cannot embrace the idea
that we all live downstream in a global village. Citizens form a
sovereign body, whose leaders are accountable to its members
and whose members have special duties to one another. This
depends on setting a boundary between neighbours within and
strangers without. Burke's series, starting with little platoons
and progressing to love of country, does not extend to the global
love of mankind. Rich nations need not go out of their way to
injure poor ones but rich governments rarely accept much duty
to help, even when their way has had this effect. Sovereignty
and accountability belong in midstream.

Viewed globally from downstream, sovereignty matters less
than it used to. Interdependence is growing, both because
commerce laughs at boundaries and, more ambiguously, because
we all inhabit the same greenhouse. Sovereignty allows of
degrees. Local government can flourish without full control over
its activities and supported by budgets dependent on national
grants and taxes. So too nations can group into confederations,
then into federations and finally into unions. Although it would
be rash to suppose that consolidation into blocs tends towards a
single world government or perpetual peace, autonomy does not
demand complete separation.

Accountability is more fragile. Citizenship changes character
in the process of turning strangers into neighbours. As it
becomes more distant and formal, less personal and friendly,
public life takes on a different complexion. Local government is
again instructive. The 1980s in Britain set about turning it into
an agency of national government, by eroding its powers in
education, housing and most other areas. The power to levy
local taxes and rates was severely capped and made nationally
much more uniform, thus snapping reciprocal links with local
electors and local businesses. Local councillors, accountable to
their local electors, were increasingly replaced by decision-makers

in London and by Quasi-Autonomous Non-Governmental Agencies, who are emphatically not. By 1994 QUANGOs were spending four times as much public money as all local Councils put together. One could argue that this was in part the inevitable result of a homogenised Britain becoming more interdependent in a growingly interdependent Europe. But it was also a conscious denial of political pluralism and degrees of decentralised authority.

There is a delicate balance here, which, abstracted from current British politics, poses a final dilemma for believers in liberal democracy. On the one hand liberal persons are no doubt delighted when the European Court of Justice settles issues of individual rights by overriding illiberal national directives. Such a higher authority is an attractive way to shed reforming light not only on the practices of governments but also on forces like anti-Semitism which flourish in the dark shadow of nationalism. On the other hand accountability flourishes only in the shade of a local autonomy which, however constrained from above, still lets boroughs, provinces or nations go their own way. The claims of citizenship are not simply those of universal rights.

I urge the virtues of local government not because they are unsullied but because they protect the shade for neighbourliness among citizens. If more global authorities have scope for spreading greater wisdom, they also have scope for greater corruption. So I settle for some midstream mixture of Friends and Romans as an account of citizenship in a Europe which has buried its Caesars. I had hoped to end with a final word from Shakespeare on how best to blend these elements. But Mark Antony is of no further help. When he had finished turning Romans into friends with a promise of seventy-five drachmas per head from Caesar's legacy, he remarked simply

> Mischief, thou art afoot,
> Take thou what course thou wilt

and added, most implausibly for today's world,

> Fortune is merry
> And in this mood will give us anything.

CHAPTER 11

A death of one's own

*The wish to have a death of one's own is growing ever rarer. Only a
while yet and it will be just as rare to have a death of one's own as it
is already to have a life of one's own.*

Rainer Maria Rilke

Rilke's remark conjures up an officious array of well-meaning
persons bent on completing our orderly passage from cradle to
grave. They tidy our files cosily about us, inject us with extreme
unction and slide us into the warm embrace of the undertaker.
At the forefront of the array stands the doctor, part mechanic
and part priest. His official task in life is to repair the living with
resources whose effective and impartial allocation is a chief topic
of medical ethics, and in death to certify that they have been
duly expended. But at heart his role is not that of an impartial
allocator: his patients want his partisan support. This builds a
moral tension into a role played out where system meets patient,
and one made instructively plain in the care of the dying. The
system no doubt prefers death to be measured and orderly; but
this thought may not move someone like Rilke wanting a death
of his own. The doctor is then caught between his general duty
to patients at large and his particular duty to the patient in front
of him, a tension tautened for a Hippocratic promoter of health
and life by a patient in search of an exit.

To put flesh on the theme, let us start with an awkward case

This essay first appeared in M. Bell and S. Mendus, eds., *Philosophy and Medical Welfare*,
Cambridge: Cambridge University Press, 1988, pp. 1–15. I would like to thank Dr Brian
Cole warmly both for its starting point and for help in seeing what might be done with
George's case philosophically. I am also grateful to Albert Weale for comments on an
earlier draft.

for the doctor. George is an old man, a widower, in hospital after a stroke. Although fairly well recovered, he still is fragile and has poor balance. But he is clear-headed, especially about his wish to go home. He says firmly that he could manage on his own; and so he probably could, if he had enough support. Otherwise there is a real danger of his falling, fracturing a leg and being unable to summon help. There is a risk of hypothermia. He may easily become dirty, unkempt, emaciated and dehydrated, since it is not plain that he can dress, toilet and feed himself for long. He may not manage to comply with his medication. He might perhaps become a risk to others by leaving his fire unattended or causing a gas leak. None of this would be worrying, if there was a supporting cast. But his house is not suited to his condition. His only relative is a daughter, living elsewhere, with her own job and family and not willing to take George on. His neighbours are unfriendly. Social Services can offer something – perhaps a home help, meals on wheels, a laundry service, day care, an alarm service. But this does not truly cover nights and weekends and, anyway, George is liable not to eat the meals and not to accept the day care. Meanwhile the advice from Social Services is that he should stay in hospital. It is good advice for the further reason that there will be no second chance. Often one can allow a patient a try at looking after himself, knowing that he can be scooped up and returned to hospital, if necessary. But George is too fragile and too alone for this to be a promising option. Yet he is in no doubt that he wants to go home and denies that he needs any of the missing support.

This situation was described to me by Dr Brian Cole, an experienced GP, as one commonly encountered and ethically difficult. He added two questions. How much self-determination should George be allowed, given that his insight is poor? How much responsibility does the doctor shoulder, if he colludes with George's wishes? Both questions sound easy, if one begins by disputing their assumption that they can be posed primarily from the doctor's point of view. Or so I supposed, until I tried the familiar philosophical tactic of challenging the assumptions and found that the still waters run awkwardly deep. In what follows, I shall open with George's point of view and try to extract a line which gives the doctor clear guidance. Having failed, as the GP predicted, I shall then address the tension between system and patient as claimants on the doctor's integrity, before finally reverting to George's own wishes for his life or death.

The first question was how much self-determination George should be allowed, given that his insight is poor. As a preliminary, the story, as told, does not guarantee that George's insight is poor at all. It could be that he has a pretty shrewd idea that he will not last long on his own but simply wants to go home to die. Being also shrewd enough to know that he cannot expect the doctor's cooperation on those terms, he takes on the conventional patient's role in a well-tried dramatic dialogue between confident patient and concerned doctor. It is both polite and politic to offer the doctor clean hands by persuading him that the patient has the determination to cope. It is both polite and politic for the doctor to collude in what is, after all, not exactly the doctor's business, once he has been offered enough to satisfy any later enquiry into negligence. Under the surface of the conventional dialogue another has been conducted. George's unasked questions about his true condition have been answered amid the professional advice given. George has rejected the advice, absolving the doctor of private and public responsibility. Honour has been satisfied on both sides.

I raise this possibility as a way of ushering in what one might call a decent liberalism. Traditionally the doctor's role is attended with more paternalism than a liberal doctor may relish. The liberal reminds us that today's doctor is no longer God and should not play God. He is the patient's servant, not his master. If George really did want to live out a full, self-sufficient life and was suffering from illusions, brought on perhaps by resentment at the humiliations of hospital routine, then the doctor might have a duty to be obstructive. But a good servant accepts his master's wishes and, in so far as George is weary of the world, the doctor is not his judge. Doubts about George's autonomy, a liberal would say, should be resolved in George's favour and a discreet way found of avoiding scandal. George's insight is not outrageously poor and there is a fair chance that it is not poor at all.

The crux for this liberal line does not depend on whether the doctor has a formal power to keep George in hospital or is merely giving authoritative advice which he can make prevail. Whichever kind of authority it is, he should use it to uphold George's genuine wishes. This directive applies broadly, even where George is under some illusion about his likely power to cope but is not exactly brimming with the will to live. The doctor's moral responsibility is to be supportive when he can, and *in loco parentis* only when he must.

We can distinguish two routes to this result. One starts by thinking of patients as bodies and of doctors as mechanics. George has, so to speak, brought his rickety old Ford to the garage with a big end gone and been told, that, although pretty clapped out, it would do a few thousand more miles, if left in for further repairs. Some garages are gleaming hi-tech affairs, which strip the car down in a flash and will not give it back until the bemused owner has signed an open cheque for whatever the garage sees fit to do. The medical equivalent of these motoring pits are hospital wards ruled by lordly consultants with acolytes, who strip away the patient's identity and turn him into an object before pretending to consult him on the technology of his health. But there are liberal garages too. There the owner is given an assessment before the dismantling starts and, even if nudged with a spot of advice, is left to make the decision. What makes this traditionally liberal is partly its general view that, as J. S. Mill put it, there is a circle round every individual human being, which no government ought to be permitted to overstep, and partly its cerebral presumption (also to be found in Mill) that a person is a mind in charge of a physical machine whose disposal is up to the driver.

The liberal line becomes trickier, if, as has become fashionable of late, one reverts to the ancient view that patients are not bodies but persons, and adds that a person is not a mind lodged in a body like a pilot in a vessel or motorist in a car. This subverts the idea that the doctor is just a mechanic and hence subverts one neat way of denying that the doctor is God. The other liberal route to granting the patient's autonomy thus starts from an idea of respect for persons. For all its greater current plausibility, it is stonier, however, and I am not sure that it gets there. Here are some of the complications.

George's chances of coping on his own seemed at first to depend merely on the support available for his rickety physical machine. But, if he is thought of as a person, we shall have to notice that psychological and social factors matter too. To discuss the social factors would take us too far afield. So let me just say that George's chances of recovering manageably from a stroke may well vary with his class, gender, income and previous occupation, and that strokes may belong in a mysterious category, along with, for example, cot deaths and schizophrenia, where it looks as if social factors may even be causal. Meanwhile there is the obvious social point that he would get on better if he had friendly neighbours. In brief, the likely health of persons cannot be assessed in social isolation.

More directly relevant are the psychological factors. George's chances depend on his state of mind – his desires, beliefs and strength of will – which the doctor who treats him as a person must take into account. An instant complication is that the doctor's diagnosis or prognosis can affect George's chances. In cultures imbued with belief in witchcraft, people have been known to curl up and die on learning that they have been cursed. In George's case there is an obvious risk that, in probing his chances of survival, the doctor will upset his fragile balance and thus improve his insight at the expense of his health. In general the liberal view is that knowledge is always a Good Thing and, in general, I shall not doubt it. But even a liberal admits some exceptions, where true beliefs are a handicap. For instance the skater may be better off unaware that the ice is thin, the tightrope walker unaware of crossing a snake pit, the soldier unaware that the ground is mined. George may need his self-confidence and a doctor who believes in improving people's insight may be something of a health risk.

The point is less quirky in relation to desires, as opposed to beliefs. Having it borne in on him just how lonely, friendless and helpless he is can seriously damage George's will to live. The doctor cannot assess the situation by, so to speak, hidden camera and one-way mirror alone. He must interact with George, must probe his determination or apathy and, in short, must prod the roots of the plant to see how well they withstand prodding. That is also a comment on the earlier thought that George may be wholly clear about consequences but too diplomatic to say so: the doctor cannot act on the mere possibility that it is so. If George started with an unresolved mixture of hope for an independent life and weariness of a lonely one, he may well finish with a newly defined wish to go home to die. To put it too starkly, no doubt, respect for persons threatens sometimes to mean killing them off.

It is rapidly becoming unclear whether we are concerned with George's wants or George's interests. Which is indicated by the maxim that patients should be treated as persons? The easier answer is the economist's: let there be consumer sovereignty for George's wants; if he still wants to go home after becoming clear about the risks, then the doctor has no business to obstruct him further. A merit of this answer is that it avoids having to tangle with the awkward concept of interests. Who can say that it is in George's interest to drift on into an institutionalised decline rather than to shorten his loneliness by returning home? The doctor is, at most, to probe the difference between considered and unconsidered wants. Having established what George truly wants, he need not worry about whether the preferred outcome is in George's interests. Autonomy, in other words, goes with considered wants, not with real interests. This is the liberal attitude which I had in mind for the initial question of how much self-determination George should be allowed. The doctor is not to set up as an authority on the riddle of existence: on that each patient is sovereign.

The suggestion, generalised, is that the doctor's role should be patient-centred, with patients sovereign and doctors their servants. A death of one's own is the ultimate in consumer choice. When generalised thus, however, this version of liberalism runs into difficulty. I shall try to show first that patient-centredness is not a clear guide to action and then that, even when it is, it may not be a good guide.

A Scottish doctor recently landed himself in trouble by adopting a novel approach to the problem of when to stop

treating senile patients who catch something lethal like pneu-
monia. He began taking instructions from his patients at an
earlier stage, when they were old and thinking about getting
older. He asked them what they would wish done, if they
became senile and the problem arose. Many replied firmly that
they would wish to be allowed to die in those circumstances, and
wrote it down as a, so to speak, penultimate will and testament.
The doctor reasoned that, since one cannot consult patients with
senile dementia, the next best thing is to consult their former
selves. But the British Medical Association would have none of
this. The responsibility for a senile patient, it said, is and must
remain the doctor's. He should consult relatives, but the
presumption must remain that patients wish to live and that
doctors are there for the purpose. The patient's younger self
cannot be an authoritative voice.

The BMA was, I think, careful not to say too much. There are
some discreet conventions about the withholding of treatment
for patients where prospect of a fair quality of life is gone beyond
recall; and the BMA said nothing on this score. Its objection was
to involving the patient's former self. It has to be an objection on
behalf not of patients' wants but of their interests. It is no good
arguing that the senile patient would *want* to live on, if able to
consider the matter rationally, since the problem arises only
when the patient cannot consider the matter rationally. The
objection has to be that the patient's earlier utterance misstates
the patient's later *interests*. The Scottish doctor might seem to
have the stronger ground, if one believes that a patient-centred
approach is to be one governed by the patient's *wants*, since he at
least has an earlier statement of a *want* to go by. But one suspects
that he too is not acting on the mere fact of a want expressed but
on his own belief that death has become in the patient's interests.

Thus prompted, we should notice that the classic liberal
spokesman on the sovereignty of the individual words the case in
terms of interests. The argument of Mill's *On Liberty* is that it is in
our *interests* to be left to pursue our own good in our own way (so
long as we do not interfere with the liberty of others). In *The
Principles of Political Economy* he maintains that individuals are
the best judges of their own *interests*. This at once raises a

question about whether individuals' *wants* are sovereign, when they conflict with their interests. Mill gives a clear answer – No. In *On Liberty* he insists that the only liberty worth the name is that of pursuing our own good in our own way and argues that neither legal nor physical force may be used to compel or obstruct this pursuit. But he has no scruples about applying social pressure to ensure that we use the liberty to achieve the individuality and autonomy, which he holds to be in our interests, whatever our foolish wishes to the contrary. In the *Principles* (Book V chapter 11) he considers seven exceptions to the general maxim that individuals are the best judges of their own interests and bids government take action in each of them to make sure that what is done is truly in individuals' interests. Among them are cases where the individuals concerned are not mature and sane adults in full possession of their faculties, and where an individual attempts 'to decide irrevocably now what will be in his interest at some future time'. The Scottish doctor can still invoke Mill against the BMA, but only by arguing that the senile patient's younger self remains a reliable guide to the *interests* of someone who has ceased to be a sane adult in possession of his faculties and whose 'own good' is to die.

Death is, in general, an awkward case for a liberal debate about what is in someone's interests. If death is the end of a person, then it closes our profit and loss account, making it hard to maintain that we shall be better off, if we no longer exist. Even the thought that George's life would be in the red, were he around to live it, becomes awkward with senile dementia. On the other hand, if death is not the end, then who knows how to adjust the profit and loss account for another world? Yet a fully patient-centred approach would need a view on these enigmas. Perhaps that is why the Exit Society, which advocates euthanasia and helps people in search of a death of their own, cannot persuade the medical profession that doctors should be as obliging about death as about life. It is worth noting, however, that societies vary. In Holland, for instance, exits seem to be very much easier to come by – a fact worth noting not only because more old people are living on to a stage where life is a burden but also because AIDS will soon be reaping the young in numbers too large to be furtive about.

At any rate, a patient-centred approach cannot avoid tangling with questions of *interests* as soon as patients start wanting what is bad for their health. This is not to say that good health is always an overriding interest, since doctors are sometimes asked to support people doing dangerous or exhausting tasks which shorten their lives. But no doctor is required to help masochists suffer more pain in the name of consumer sovereignty. The most libertarian version of a liberal-inspired patient-centredness on offer is one which gives patients the benefit of the doubt, when it is not clear that their wants are in their interests.

Patient-centredness is thus not the enemy of paternalism that one might suppose. It invites us to decide in the patient's interests but leaves the doctor often the better judge of them. All the same, I imagine that sympathies still lie with George, old, lonely, uncared for and wanting release. The first question was how much self-determination he should be allowed, given that his insight is poor. Treating George as a person will, I imagine, be held to imply only that the doctor should make sure that his insight is not so poor as to frustrate his clear interests. So far, presumably, George goes home.

But I have almost commanded this answer by asking about a single patient and exploiting the obvious attractions of patient-centredness as a guide to medicine. The other question was how much responsibility the doctor shoulders, if he colludes with George's wishes. A natural thought is that, if the answer to the first question is to give George the decision, then the doctor must be morally in the clear for the purposes of the second. But, on reflection, it is not so simple. Even a patient-centred approach saddles the doctor with moral responsibilities which are not exhausted by serving George's interests. I open my case by asking which patient is to be at the centre of a patient-centred approach.

It is time that the doctor had a name too. Resisting a revealing temptation to call him Dr Smith, I shall christen him Henry. (In what follows Henry is the hospital doctor overseeing George's treatment and discharge. But, since the moral relationship which I want to discuss is a professional yet personal one better typified by a GP, he can be thought of as George's GP also. This elasticity, I trust, will not spoil the argument.) It is a trick of the example to suggest that Henry is involved only as George's medical adviser and that only Henry is involved in the decision. Henry has other patients beside George and belongs to a medical profession most of whose patients are not Henry's. Equally I blanked out other people concerned with George, notably the Social Services department, but they are still in the wings and they too have other clients and commitments. None of this matters to George, seeking the patient-centred solution which fits in with his wishes, but it is bound to weigh with Henry. Morally speaking, collusion will not be an isolated act.

George is occupying a hospital bed. There are other people waiting for beds and George does not really need one. At first sight this is not Henry's problem, partly because it is not his fault that there is a lack of outside support to keep George going and more generally because ordinary hospital doctors and GPs are not responsible for the overall allocation of resources. But that is too a formal a way of looking at a doctor's responsibilities. If Henry is an experienced and respected GP, he has a *de facto* power to call up social service support or to secure hospital beds, while his credit remains good. His credit is staked on every case and depends on his not staking it too casually. He can mortgage it for any one patient, but, if his fellow professionals do not agree that the case merited the resources by comparison with other cases, it will be that much harder for Henry to secure help for his next patient. Hence Henry's considered pronouncement on George may have costs and benefits to Henry's other patients. To serve *all* his patients, he needs a good reputation among those who allocate scarce resources which cannot meet all claims by all doctors. George, let us assume, simply wants the best result for himself. Henry aims more widely at the best for all his patients. These aims can conflict.

Moreover Henry is not the champion solely of his own patients. He has a doctor's concern for all the sick, shared with fellow doctors and with others in the work of promoting health. That opens up an interesting ambiguity in the notion of patient-centred care. Should each doctor care for his own patients (and, to generalise, each professional for his own parish)? Or should each behave as a member of a group whose aim is the good of all patients? These alternatives do not yield the same result. Just as Henry's 100 per cent effort on George's behalf may do what is best for George at the expense of Henry's other patients, so Henry's 100 per cent commitment to his own patients may be at the expense of other doctors' patients. Similarly a powerful consultant, administrator or health team can get more than proportional resources for their own parish, if their own parish is what counts. Patient-centredness is ambiguous on the point. Offhand one is inclined to say that the care patients receive should depend not on who they are, where they live or who their doctor is, but on what they need. That suggests a sort of Kantian universality, bidding us look on all cases evenly from some central vantage point. On the other hand, the obvious universal Kantian imperative to each doctor or carer is 'Do your best for *your* patients' and this comes with the tempting utilitarian thought that, since each doctor has a personal bond with his own patients (and each professional with his own patch), the total amount of good care resulting will be greater.

If Henry is an experienced, effective doctor who knows how to work the system better than most, and if the general principle is equal care for equal need, then Henry, it seems to follow, should *not* do his best for his patients. To block this odd conclusion, we might try envisaging the care network as a system of checks and balances. Henry is to do his best for his own patients but other professionals, with their rather different concerns, do their best to stop him getting away with unfair allocations. That offers a promising rationale for the division of caring labour, given an ideal allocation of resources (including professional skills). If the doctor can count on social work support but only when his request for it is reasonable in relation to other requests, then we perhaps have something like a game where each player can go flat out in the knowledge that enforced rules of fair play will stop him and others gaining unjust advantages. The best efforts of each in his own parish can then sum to the best which the system can deliver as a whole.

But this is to take a very idealised view of the social world about us. In George's case, it supposes that the Social Services department has proper resources, so that it can support George at no cost to its other more desperate clients, if the request for support is reasonable. In practice Social Services departments are sure to be stretched thinner than this. Being under-resourced and, most unfairly, the target of political suspicion or hostility, they can treat each case in a way which will withstand public scrutiny, when things go wrong, only if they take on fewer cases than ideally would be for the best. As I presented George's story, Social Services were offering some support but probably not enough to keep him going in earnest. Although this may have reflected their view that, given the lack of family and friends, he should stay in hospital, it may also have been because they could not spare the resources for major support, given the other claims on them. At any rate let us suppose it so and ask how that affects Henry's ethical responsibilities.

The general puzzle is one of professional duty in an imperfect world. It is not one of legal obligation, since Henry can see to it that his back is covered, whatever he does. He can steer George either back home or back into his hospital bed and cover himself by the wording of his professional judgement. Ethically, however, we still want to know how much responsibility is his, if he steers George home, knowing that the social work support really available is not really enough. It is not his responsibility to provide enough support to free George's hospital bed with a clear conscience. But he has a moral decision to make and he is answerable for it in a way which George is not and which is not trumped by George's wish to go home. He might consider, for instance, encouraging George to go home partly because that is one way of putting pressure on those who allocate the budget to Social Services. This would be for the future benefit of others in need, but hardly for the present benefit of George. This sort of consideration is endemic in the ethics of professional roles, when played out among roles which mesh imperfectly, and it is one on which patient-centredness gives no guidance.

A final ambiguity about 'patient-centred' is found by asking whether it means 'answerable to the patient'. The initial reaction is probably that it does. The doctor-patient relationship is usually deemed one-to-one, in that it is a confidential relation of trust between a doctor and a patient with a right to an undivided commitment. But a couple of examples will show that there is more to it. In the days before syphilis was curable and Wasserman tests required before marriage, a New York doctor diagnosed syphilis in a patient and advised telling his fiancée. The patient refused. Recently (although it may be just a new urban legend) a London doctor diagnosed AIDS in a patient, who demanded utter confidentiality, and was presented a few months later with the man's unsuspecting wife, radiantly pregnant. Both women happened also to be patients of the respective doctors but this point only focuses the ambiguity about which patient to centre upon. The broader question is whether a patient-centred practice is answerable to a wider tribunal. The doctor is not like a priest upholding the secrecy of the confessional in the face of enquiries by the temporal authorities. He is an agent licenced by that state, akin less to a priest than to a social worker who is explicitly the state's appointee, wielding its authority even in seemingly personal relations with clients. The doctor is answerable to the community at large and, although it is relevant whether or not syphilis and AIDS are legally notifiable diseases, his professional conscience is not fully absolved by this test. How much responsibility does Henry shoulder if he colludes with George's wishes? The question is incomplete: how much responsibility *to whom*?

It has emerged by now, I hope, that, if we try for something patient-centred, to the effect that the doctor's duty is to his patient, the idea is thoroughly ambiguous. Even concentrating on the particular patient in the immediate case, we find that the duty is to serve the patient's interests as a person rather than his declared wants for his physical machine. Liberal notions of autonomy leave the patient's wishes the benefit of the doubt as a guide to his interests, but override them when his insight is clearly lacking. Meanwhile patient-centredness cannot be construed thus one-to-one. Henry is answerable for more people than George and to more people than George. He is responsible at least for his other patients; perhaps, as a member of the caring professions, for the overall welfare of those in need of care.

Equally, he is responsible not only to George and other patients but also to fellow professionals and ultimately the community at large. As soon as resources are short or roles mesh imperfectly, Henry's best efforts for George have a price paid elsewhere. 'Patient-centred' starts with George but cannot mean simply 'George-centred' and gives no guidance on where to stop.

Yet George is still inescapably Henry's patient. So far I have turned a simple plea by an old and lonely widower for a death of his own into an intricate set of questions about Henry's duties. That is rough on George but, all the same, I propose to say a bit more about professional integrity as a factor in medical ethics before returning to death as a proper exercise of consumer sovereignty.

The difficult notion of integrity comes with some philosophical baggage which may need to be unloaded. Integrity, as a general moral concept, is commonly invoked as an objection to consequentialist ethics: even if it would save the Health Service a pile of money to let George die off quietly, Henry should refuse to be party to such base calculation. This admonition may be made from either of two points of view. One belongs to the kind of deontological or duty-based ethics which opposes principle to consequence and bids us do right and damn the consequences. From this point of view the Hippocratic oath is a sort of categorical medical imperative, which forbids doctors all compromise with lack of resources or any other obstacle to the patient's good health. Integrity demands acting on pure principle with the moral consistency of a tank. My short comment is that principle and consequence cannot be so starkly opposed. On the one hand utilitarians are applying a principle when they adopt whatever solution makes for the greater welfare of the greater number. On the other there are always questions of whether a principle is appropriate to a situation and of how it is to be applied – questions which demand care for results. Hence integrity does not provide independent leverage on what it is right or best to do. It demands only that, having identified the right or best thing to do, the agent goes ahead and does it.

The other common use of integrity is to appeal against all systematic ethics, whether of principle or of consequence. The *locus classicus* is the existentialist idea of authenticity which forbids the agent to accept *any* general guidance in advance of a situation, on pain of 'bad faith'. My equally short comment is that we can agree in refusing to let the doctor hide behind an unexamined conscience but cannot possibly construe professional integrity as *carte blanche* for professionals to do whatever they find most 'authentic' at the moment of choice.

That leaves two unmistakable tensions involved in the notion of professional integrity, both concerned with the relation of self to role. One has to do with conflicts between doctors' personal beliefs and the demands of their office. The other has to do with the degree for which they are personally responsible, when the duties of their role are overridden by other pressures.

Cases where personal belief can conflict with official duty are easy to find. The Catholic doctor's patients may include a woman in search of an abortion. If he personally regards abortion as murder and the abetting of abortion as the abetting of murder, how helpful does his role order him to be and how helpful should he therefore be? There are terminal patients in great pain who want only to die. Is a doctor who, personally, believes in euthanasia professionally bound to resist their death? There are ways of muting such conflicts. If he will not deal in abortions, no doubt he can refer the patient to a doctor who will. With a terminal patient he need not strive officiously to keep alive. But, even when muted, conflicts remain. In some authorities most doctors are anti-abortion. Does that imply a duty on each of them to pocket their consciences? Letting patients die is not always distinct from killing them. If one supposes that justice calls for similar treatment in any part of the country and from any doctor, can we countenance any luck of the draw in death?

The dilemmas of professional integrity are distinct both from personal dilemmas (shall I betray my country or my friend?) and from professional dilemmas (shall Henry improve George's insight at the expense of his health?). They cross the line between personal and professional. Presumably no one thinks that the doctor should hang up his conscience along with his hat and obey all possible orders by the authority which hands out his stethoscope. In that case he might as well take the job of medical assistant to a team of torturers. But integrity can seem so much a personal notion that the opposite view is tempting. Should he ever compromise his private conscience and, if so, when and why?

The easy part of the answer is that private conscience is not infallible and, where it is just another term for personal convictions, not safe from bigotry. A doctor may not eject patients from his surgery as he might visitors from his living room. He cannot refuse them on grounds of their race, sex, religion or politics. But, on the other hand, total moral neutrality is not what we ask of doctors. We expect them to uphold a professional code, whose rationale is their special situation in relation to a broader ethic of concern for others. The broader ethic cannot be wholly bland, and its special application to medicine is bound to conflict from time to time with what a doctor personally thinks right. Mismatch can occur in both directions. For example, official guidance for doctors on abortion, on severely handicapped infants, on patients long comatose and on the incurably senile can strike some as too strict and others as too lax. Then there will be tension because we need the doctor's personal moral commitment but not too much of it.

The same goes for the other kind of tension, when scarcity of resources interferes with the doctor's duty. The National Health Service had hoped originally to avoid this difficulty by giving doctors a free hand in prescribing what they thought best. But it is clear by now that the medical task is expanding, not shrinking, and cannot possibly be fully resourced. Two typical ways of applying the cork are to limit the doctors' efforts (for instance by restricting the list of prescribable drugs or by letting queues form) and to put decisions about allocation in non-medical hands (as with the rationing of kidney machines by committees of citizens). However it is done, doctors are then asked to acquiesce in what they may think a betrayal of their calling. They may doubt whether they are absolved from guilt, when their patients die of treatable renal failure, by the undoubted fact that they did not decide the allocation between health and roadbuilding.

What makes such tensions morally distinctive, in my view, is that the ethics of role are a *tertium quid* in the dispute between agent-neutral ethics and agent-relative ethics. An agent-neutral ethics is one of the golden-rule, Kantian or utilitarian kind, which holds that an action is right for me if and only if it would be right for *anyone* so placed. An agent-relative ethics maintains that each of us is morally peculiar, for instance because we are each morally constituted by some personal project which informs our lives, and hence that different people should behave differently in the same situation. It is not an easy dispute to umpire because both sides nuance their positions. Just as the golden rule on car parking need not be 'No parking' but 'No parking on yellow lines' or 'on Saturdays' or 'by lorries', so there can presumably be imperatives addressed to doctors. Conversely agent-relative theories tend to be surprisingly systematic about the claims of those near and dear to us, like family, friends, neighbours and compatriots. That makes it correspondingly unclear that the dilemmas of self and role are truly a *tertium quid*. All the same a doctor's dilemma seems to me resistant to both pulls. In the universalising direction, there is no problem where doctors merely have a special *duty* to do what people at large are *permitted* to do. But what if they sometimes have a duty to kill patients when the universal rule is 'thou shalt not kill'? In the particularising direction, there would be no problem if doctors could express themselves in their practice in whatever way suited their own project in life. But this is absolutely not what we intend by a licence to practise medicine. To become a doctor is to accept a code which may be doctor-relative but is certainly not relative to the individual doctor. There is a *tertium quid* as soon as we think of role in general terms and self in particular terms, thus creating a threat of incommensurability.

The shoe pinches harder for some professions than others. For example, social workers are professionally expected to make personal friends with their clients so as to wield their statutory authority in a fully informed way. This injects an ambiguity, bordering on a duplicity, into a role which would not work as well without it. In their assessment of whether a child is at risk of abuse and needs removing to a place of safety, they have to mortgage their personal judgement, in the knowledge that it is not possible to remove in total all the children for whom there is a genuine risk.[1] Yet the system would not work, and more children would be abused and killed, if social workers refused to live with this constant threat to their integrity. Doctors are less exposed, because protected by the white coat of clinical judgement. But it is not a coat of infallibility and what it covers is often not solely a scientific assessment. Here too the role involves special duties and hence moral decisions in a professional capacity, whose ethical basis is obscure.

But if I shuffle the paper much longer, George will simply die of old age. So let us draw the threads together, answer the question about Henry's responsibility, if he colludes with George, and let the poor fellow go home at last.

I have been offering an oblique comment on a natural approach to medical ethics, which goes, so to speak, top down. We start with a broad aim for the system, like maximising welfare subject to constraints of justice, and try to translate it into policies for allocating resources and applying them to individual patients. I do not think this a false approach and I have not tried to belittle the problems it identifies, which are typically to do with scarcity of resources and the need to weigh the claims of medicine against other priorities. My comment is that, however well one works things out top down, there is an ineliminable moral friction where top down meets bottom up. Where policy meets patient, the doctor has moral choices to make which no code of medical ethics can reduce to routine. Since a system of care is to be judged finally at its point of delivery, it is crucial to think about it from bottom up as well as from top down.

Considerations of justice and welfare are, in the main, impersonal, impartial and universal. Patients, in the main, expect their doctors to take a particular, personal and partial interest in them. Caught with Kant and Bentham on his bookshelf, Hippocrates in his waiting room and the ombudsman on the telephone, the doctor finds his role underscripted, his ethics ambiguous and his integrity prone to disintegrate. The

[1] This theme is explored in M. Hollis and D. Howe, 'Moral Risks in the Social Work Role', *Journal of Applied Philosophy*, 1987.

doctor-patient relationship is more than a *bricolage* of morally untidy choices but less than a systematic application of moral philosophy. It can be guided by an ethics of resource allocation but there is an endemic friction where system meets patient. Medicine has more to it than applying decision theory to diseases.

How much responsibility does the doctor shoulder, if he colludes with George's wishes? What he should do no doubt varies with George's insight, but the doctor's responsibility is constant. To collude with *very* poor insight is to act on the proposition that George is better off dead. To collude with *very* good insight is to endorse George's choice to die. To collude with hazy insight is to stand aside by letting doubt demand the benefit of doubt. Whichever it is, Henry has made a choice and staked his integrity on it. I imagine that most doctors will think it best to let George go, and will find this responsibility easiest to shoulder. Indeed, I think that they must, as more people live longer into a fragile and confused old age. But responsibility is not here lessened on the ground that letting die is not killing. Having learnt to postpone death, we have set ourselves problems of when to cut short the losses of an extended life. We have a collective responsibility for what Henry decides but Henry is responsible for his decision. Although he can cover his back by recording a clinical judgement that George's insight and prospects were adequate, he knows that there is more to the moral question than clinical judgement.

At any rate, George goes home. He remains on his doctor's conscience as he is carried out a month later to a forgotten grave. But so he would have done also, languishing on in a hospital bed. Without hoping to make it easier to see in the twilight, let me end with a patient-centred prayer, also from Rilke:

> O Herr, gib jedem seinen eignen Tod,
> Das Sterben, das aus jedem Leben geht,
> Darin er Liebe hatte, Sinn und Not.

Even when a death of one's own is a poor consumer choice, it is a proper exercise of human dignity.

III

Other cultures, other minds

CHAPTER 12

The limits of irrationality

The anthropologist starts with an empty notebook and it seems that everything he writes in it is discovered empirically. But is it? I shall argue here that the fact that the natives are 'rational' in some universal sense is not discovered empirically. To understand native utterances the anthropologist must relate them to one another and to the world. To translate them into, let us say, English, he needs to relate some of them to the world, since, in relating an utterance to others he does not learn what it means, unless he already knows what the others mean. Ultimately, then, he needs a class of utterances whose situations of use he can specify. These situations can apparently be specified either as he himself perceives them or as the natives perceive them; and it seems that the two specifications might be different. But, if he has to allow for this possibility, he cannot begin at all. For his only access to native perceptions and specifications is by translating what they say about what they perceive. He would therefore have to translate before discovering what they perceive, and to know what they perceive before translating. There would be no way into the circle. The class of utterances which form the bridgehead for his advance must be one for which his specification and his informants' coincide.

His line of attack, then, is that a native sentence can be

Originally published in *Archives Européenes de Sociologie*, 7, 1967, pp. 265–71, as a companion piece to Steven Lukes's paper 'Some Problems about Rationality' in the same issue, both reprinted in B. Wilson, ed., *Rationality*, Oxford: Blackwell, 1971. I owe much to his paper and to many discussions of the topic with him over the years. The references for Evans-Pritchard on the Azande and the Nuer are given in the next essay, 'Reason and ritual', which expands the theme trailed in the present one.

191

correctly translated by any English sentence which can be used in the same way in the same situations. Although sentences related like this need not be semantically equivalent, there is no more direct attack on meaning available. In taking this line he makes two crucial assumptions, firstly that the natives perceive more or less what he perceives and secondly that they say about it more or less what he would say. I shall defend my claim that these are assumptions and not hypotheses; and then draw some implications for the problem of rationality.

Suppose he gets his bridgehead by pinning down the native counterparts of English sentences like 'Yes, this is a brown cow.' There are no native counterparts to pin down unless the natives perceive brown cows and assert that they do. For, since these are conditions for the English sentence meaning what it does, they are also conditions for any native sentence meaning the same. This is banal enough. But is it not a hypothesis that anthropologist and natives share certain percepts and concepts, a hypothesis, moreover, which later successes in translating abundantly confirm?

I suggest not. A hypothesis must be refutable. This one is not. The force of calling a set of utterances a bridgehead is that it serves to define standard meanings for native terms and so makes it possible to understand utterances used in more ambiguous situations. In order to question the perceptual and conceptual basis of the bridgehead, the anthropologist would have to ask the natives what they perceived when confronted with a brown cow and whether their utterances were to be construed as assertions. Also he would have to understand their answers. He can neither ask nor understand, unless he already has a bridgehead. Consequently he cannot refute the 'hypothesis' by establishing a rival one. At most he can merely draw a blank and fail to produce any translations at all. But even this failure would not show that the natives perceived the world after some idiosyncratic fashion or had a language with idiosyncratic functions. It would serve to suggest only that they had no language at all. No successful translation can destroy his bridgehead, since all later translations depend on its being secure.

Nor is the 'hypothesis' confirmed by success. He has indeed discovered what native sentence to pair with 'Yes, this is a brown cow', but he has not discovered that the natives perceive a brown cow when they utter the native sentence. For, if that were in doubt, so also would the pairing be. And, as has been argued already, if both are in doubt, there is no way in to the circle. Similarly, although it is an empirical matter to discover how the natives signal the difference between assertion and denial, 'yes' and 'no', 'true' and 'false', it is not a hypothesis that they have such distinctions. For, to check such a 'hypothesis', the anthropologist would have to establish the meanings of utterances in the bridgehead independently of whether they were used to assert what was taken to be true. But this cannot be done, as their translation depends on what linguistic function they are taken to perform. Consequently the only alternative to finding an overlap in concepts and percepts is to find nothing at all.

If this is right, then the assertions comprising the bridgehead will have to be coherent and, indeed, true. Again it looks as if native notions of coherence and truth need not coincide with the anthropologist's own. But again, if this is taken as a hypothesis, it generates a vicious circle. For the only way to find native terms for relations among utterances is to translate the utterances and then to interpret the linking terms so that the utterances are linked coherently. Equally the only way to find the native sign of assent is to translate the utterances and then to interpret whatever sign accompanies most of the true ones as assertion. But this makes it impossible for alternative concepts of coherence and truth to show up. If these concepts were in doubt, the anthropologist would have to know what they were, before he could translate the utterances which they linked, and would have to translate the utterances in order to find how they were linked. Again there would be no way in to the circle.

So some overlap in concepts and percepts is a necessary condition of successful translation. The *sine qua non* is a bridgehead of true assertions about a shared reality. But plainly societies differ about what is real and rational and the philosopher's problem is to see where the necessary limits on these divergences lie.

This problem is raised, for example, by belief in agencies and forces which we class as 'supernatural'. It seems that none of the tests for the identification of beliefs in the bridgehead apply the

Nuer's *Kwoth* or the Dinka's *Deng*. Utterances expressing the belief that 'twins are birds', for instance, apparently do not have to be translated so as to make the belief true or coherent or even plausible. On the one hand, there must be some test of success in identifying 'supernatural' beliefs, otherwise any account would be as good as any other. On the other hand, any test proposed looks parochial, in that it forces other cultures to subscribe to a Western and twentieth-century view of what is true, coherent or plausible. So can we hit on a test which is innocent of parochialism?

There seems little point in testing beliefs about *Kwoth* for correspondence with reality. For, unless the anthropologist happens to believe in *Kwoth*, he can report only that they do not correspond with reality. Nor is it yet any help to remark that the natives take beliefs about *Kwoth* to be empirically true, since we do not yet know what the beliefs are. Equally, we cannot invoke the notion of a wider reality to give the beliefs something to correspond to, since we can get at the wider reality only through the beliefs.

There is more point in testing the beliefs for coherence. But this cannot be the whole story, since more than one set of beliefs about *Kwoth* may be coherent and since a belief-system may in any case contain incoherences. Incoherence is a *prima facie* reason for rejecting alleged identifications of native beliefs, but it can always be removed by showing why the natives do not perceive it. Thus Evans-Pritchard's twenty-two reasons why the Azande fail to perceive the futility of their magic serve to justify his account against a charge of incoherence. The charge would stick only if it were more likely that the natives would notice the contradiction than that it existed. Even if this test eliminates some interpretations, it is still likely to leave more than one. Coherence is at best a necessary condition of success.

A more promising requirement is that the everyday meanings of native words used in utterances expressing 'supernatural' beliefs should have been firmly established. Thus, it might be said, we know that some Australian aborigines believe that the sun is a white cockatoo because we have definitive uses in everyday contexts for terms meaning 'sun', 'is', 'white' and 'cockatoo'. But this is at best inconclusive, since words can bear more than one sense. The anthropologist can invoke the notions of ambiguity or metaphor, when he does not wish to be bound by the everyday meanings of native terms. Since one way of putting the question at issue is to ask when an utterance may be given a special or metaphorical interpretation, we cannot rest content with assuming that words always carry the sense they were allotted at the bridgehead.

We must therefore find internal relations among the beliefs which make their identification plausible. Neither deductive nor inductive relations will do. Deductive inference from true premises is bound to give true conclusions; and so all beliefs deducible from those in the bridgehead would be true. Besides there is no contradiction in asserting everything the Nuer believe about the everyday world and denying everything they believe about *Kwoth*. Inductive inference proceeds from known cases to unknown cases of the same sort. So it seems that everyday beliefs give the natives inductive grounds for holding 'supernatural' beliefs, in as much as there is no discontinuity in the native thought between natural and supernatural. (If, for instance, lightning and arrows are phenomena of the same sort, then agency in the one gives inductive ground for supposing agency in the other.) But this is of no help in identifying 'supernatural' beliefs, unless the notion of 'the same sort' can be made clearer than I can make it. If we take a scientific criterion of resemblance, we set up an impassable discontinuity between natural and supernatural. But if we accept a loose criterion, then, since everything resembles everything from some point of view, we are left without limits on the supernatural beliefs which might be grounded on the everyday beliefs.

This drives us to testing alleged native beliefs for rational interconnection. Each new identification of a native belief has to be plausible, given what is already established. In other words, to justify an identification, we must show that natives who believed what we already know they believe would have good reason to believe what we now claim they believe. Here we seem to have met an impasse, since what counts as a good reason appears to be a social matter and so has to be discovered in each case by empirical investigation. This would generate another vicious circle, since we should have to know what the natives believed, in order to find out what was a good reason for what; and we should have to know the native criteria for rational belief, before we could find out what they believed. We can avoid the circle, however, if we distinguish the definition of a concept from the examples which are held to satisfy it. It would be fatal to allow that anthropologist and natives might differ over what it means to say that one belief gives good reason for holding another. But, if we add to the list of necessary conditions for the possibility of anthropology a shared concept of rational belief, then we can allow that some societies find beliefs rational which others find irrational.

I contend, therefore, that there are criteria of rationality which are necessary, and hence universal, even if there are others which are a contingent feature of local conceptual schemes. (Such local criteria would also be universal, if all societies happened to hit on them, perhaps for some practical reason, but they would still be contingent even so, in the absence of any quasi-transcendental reason for holding that they are preconditions of the possibility of making sense.) If anthropology is to be possible the natives must share our concepts of truth, coherence and rational interdependence of beliefs. Otherwise our theories will be caught in vicious circles. Western rational thought is not just one species of rational thought nor rational thought just one species of thought. If we supposed it was, and so had to discover empirically which societies espoused which brand of rationality, we would destroy our only test for the identification of native beliefs. In this sense some criteria of rationality are necessary. But anthropologists often come across beliefs that seem false, incoherent and unconnected. These beliefs are rendered harmonious by appealing to theoretical options, like ambiguity, metaphor and local variations in what is regarded as rational. They are options, in the sense that the interpretation to be placed upon native utterances is partly a function of the anthropologist's own view of the possible uses of language and the possible connections among beliefs. If my argument has been sound, the only way to produce justifiable accounts of other cultures is to make the natives as rational as possible.

The argument has been wholly general and applies equally within a single culture, for instance to the study by an Anglican of what other Anglicans believe. If it applies here, where each enquirer is his own bilingual, then it cannot be objected that an anthropologist who works with a native informant by-passes the problems discussed. Equally the behaviourist's contention that we should study causal relations in social behaviour rather than the structure of beliefs is weakened, if theology is from this point of view sacred anthropology. On the other hand the existence of (philosophical) Idealists, with their own concept of Reality, and of Pragmatists, with their own concept of Truth, seems to be an embarrassment. If we can understand their doctrines, does that not show that the arguments here are wrong?

I shall not consider here whether these philosophies are true. For the difficulty arises even if they are false. It is that they seem to have their own ultimate criteria of rationality, and that, since other philosophers find them intelligible, there can be no necessarily universal criteria. Yet Idealists do not deny that everyone perceives the same sort of reality. They do not maintain, for example, that some people perceive cows and others sense-data. Nor do Pragmatists maintain that some empirical truths correspond with reality, while others are merely useful to believe. Each, rather, offer their own account of the world we all share. So there is as yet no threat to the thesis that overlap in percepts and concepts is a necessary condition of communication. The difference comes not in concepts but in concepts of concepts. But here, as can be seen by comparing different commentaries on the same thinker, the problem of this essay arises all over again. Like rival anthropologists, rival commentators have to decide what standard of plausibility to set for the identification of their subject's beliefs. Their decision affects their interpretations; and this applies even to the limiting case of thinkers expounding their own thought. So my argument is not, I hope, refuted by this objection alone.

The anthropologist emerges as part chronicler, part philosopher and part social theorist. As chronicler, he collects observed facts of native behaviour. As philosopher, he sets *a priori* limits to possible interpretation of facts. As social theorist, he decides which of the interpretations consistent with the facts is empirically correct. It has been argued here that relativism, far from being a due recognition of the scope of empirical science, makes anthropology theoretically impossible. We cannot understand the irrational and to suppose that we can is to run into vicious circles; but we can understand the rational in more than one way.

CHAPTER 13

Reason and ritual

Certain primitive Yoruba carry about with them boxes covered with cowrie shells, which they treat with special regard. When asked what they are doing, they apparently reply that the boxes are their heads or souls and that they are protecting them against witchcraft. Is that an interesting fact or a bad translation? The question is, I believe, partly philosophical. In what follows, I shall propound and try to solve the philosopher's question, arguing that it has large theoretical implications for social anthropology.

Anthropologists set themselves to understand a culture which is not their own. They have succeeded when they understand everything the natives say, do and believe. But do they always know that they have understood? What, for instance, would give them the right to be sure that the Yoruba believe boxes covered with cowrie shells to be their heads or souls? It is a curious belief to find among people who are often as rational as we. Yet we claim to know that rational people do sometimes hold curious metaphysical beliefs; so presumably we have some way of identifying such beliefs. On the other hand we sometimes reject proffered accounts of beliefs on the ground that the beliefs are unintelligible. How, then, do we decide when it is more plausible to reject a translation than to accept that a society believes what the translator claims they believe? I shall call those metaphysical beliefs which inform ritual actions 'ritual beliefs'.

Originally published in *Philosophy*, 43, 1967, 165, pp. 231–47. I am grateful to Frank Willett of Northwestern University for the Yoruba example and the possible explanation of it given later; and to Steven Lukes, Peter Hacker and Anthony Kenny for many helpful discussions of the matters raised.

The problem is how we know when we have identified a ritual belief.

This looks like an empirical question. For, it might be said, the problem is that of knowing when a language has been correctly translated and it is surely an empirical matter what native utterances mean. The anthropologist can learn Yoruba and ask the natives what they believe. Provided that his attempts to speak Yoruba have met with success in everyday contexts, and he has no reason to suppose that the Yoruba are lying about their ritual beliefs, then there is no reason to doubt the resulting translations. Besides, he can always recruit an intelligent bilingual to settle any doubtful points. Admittedly, ritual beliefs, like Yoruba boxes, may seem unintelligible in isolation. But that means only that they should not be taken in isolation. They belong in a ritual context and will be found to make sense when the whole context is grasped. Moreover, ritual is of its essence expressive rather than informative and mystical rather than rational. Consequently, a literal translation need not produce a statement which the natives believe literally. Metaphor is to the temple what literal sense is to the market place. There are, in short, no *a priori* limits on what a society may believe and it is thus an empirical matter whether an anthropologist's account is correct.

If this line of thought is right, there is nothing for a philosopher to discuss. But, I shall argue, far from making anthropology an empirical matter, it makes it, instead, impossible. If a ritual belief is to be identified after the manner of an everyday belief, then it cannot be identified at all.

The identification of everyday beliefs is indeed (within limits to be discussed later) an empirical matter. The anthropologist learns the native language by discovering the native signs for assent and dissent and the native names for common objects. He then composes statements about objects and elicits assent or dissent from the natives. He thus frames hypotheses by assuming that the natives assent to true statements and dissent from false ones. The exact history of his progress does not concern us, but the last assumption is important. For, unless the native utterances make sense in simple everyday situations, the anthropologist will not even begin. If the natives made no statements about the cat on the mat and the cow in the corn which can be translated to yield truths, then the anthropologist has no way into the maze. In general, identifying an everyday belief involves knowing the truth conditions of the statements which express it. This does not imply that every native belief must, when translated, yield a true statement, but it does imply that most of them must. Equally any claim that the natives say something false must be backed by an explanation of why they fail to see that the belief is false. Otherwise the falsity of the belief, as translated, will be a sufficient reason for rejecting the translation. Caesar tells us that some German tribes believe that the elk has no joints in its knees and therefore sleeps leaning against a tree, since, if it lies down, it cannot get up again. Without some explanation of how they manage to believe this taradiddle, we shall have sufficient reason to suppose either that the Germans did not believe it (Caesar's informant was perhaps pulling his leg) or that there had been a mistranslation. In neither case will Caesar have identified a belief which the Germans held. The point is that everyday beliefs have objectively specifiable truth conditions. That the truth conditions are objective both gives the anthropologist a lead in and, in the absence of a special explanation, provides the tests of his hypotheses.

Ritual beliefs, by contrast, do not have objectively specifiable truth conditions. To be sure, a Yoruba, who believed a box covered with cowrie shells to be his head or soul, might take that belief to be true. But this is not to say that any fact referred to is objectively specifiable. Consequently the anthropologist cannot use the facts to get at the beliefs: he can, at best, use the beliefs to get at the facts. Here, then, is a first difference between ritual and everyday beliefs.

But this does not dispose of the claim that we are dealing with a wholly empirical question. Is it not an empirical matter what words mean, even in a ritual context? May we not translate ritual literally, marking the fact that we are translating ritual utterances by noting that the statements may be taken metaphorically? For instance, we know that some Australian aborigines believe the sun is a white cockatoo, because we have firm everyday translations for 'sun', 'is', 'white' and 'cockatoo' and aboriginal assent to the resulting utterance. Of course the claim would be absurd, if the aborigines were expected to take the belief literally; but it is a ritual belief and they take it metaphorically.

As it stands, this move is useless, since it relies on using the notion of metaphor, without giving it any independent leverage. The notion of metaphor, like that of ritual, must do more than signal a failure to produce sense. If we take a ritual utterance, translate it literally and dub the result 'metaphorical', how do we know that what we now have is equivalent to the original? To put it another way, how do we know what the metaphorical sense of an utterance is, seeing that any utterance might have many metaphorical senses? To put it yet another way, how do we know that words are not used equivocally in ritual contexts? If any piece of literal nonsense can be taken metaphorically, then anthropology rapidly becomes impossible. For there is no way of telling which of rival accounts of ritual beliefs is the right one. The literal nonsense which one anthropologist interprets in one way can always be given a different metaphorical sense by another anthropologist. We need, then, a better test of success than the accuracy of a literal translation.

Let us try next to give the notion of ritual some independent leverage. What is the force of calling something a ritual belief? We have said that ritual beliefs are metaphysical and inform ritual actions (in the sense that ritual actions are identified as the actions which express ritual beliefs). But, so far, this serves merely to sweep them under the rug as beliefs which we have failed to identify by making literal sense of the utterances used to express them. What then is the category of ritual more than a waste bin for unidentified beliefs?

This question has been given an interesting answer by Suzanne Langer in her *Philosophy in a New Key*.[1] Man, she says, is a symbolising animal, whose symbolising takes two main forms. First, there is practical symbolism of the kind used in everyday discourse and in science. Practical symbolism is experience

[1] S. Langer, *Philosophy in a New Key*, 3rd edition, Cambridge, Mass.: Harvard University Press, 1963.

transformed into a form in which it can be talked about, as a means to some practical end. Practical symbolism in effect comprises all and only those utterances which a Logical Positivist would allow to be literally meaningful. Secondly, there is expressive or presentational symbolism of the kind found in music or religion. Expressive symbolism is an end in itself and any example of it (like a piece of music) forms a whole, in the sense that its meaning is not a compound of the discrete units which constitute it. Language is the best example of practical symbolism, because it is analysable and instrumental; whereas music is the best example of expressive symbolism, because its meaning is total and it is an end in itself. Langer puts the distinction thus:

It appears then that although the different media of non-verbal representation are often referred to as distinct 'languages' [*e.g.* the 'language' of painting], this is really a loose terminology. Language in the strict sense is essentially discursive; it has permanent units of meaning which are combinable into larger units; it has fixed equivalences which make definition and translation possible; its connotations are general so that it requires non-verbal acts like pointing, looking or emphatic voice inflections to assign specific denotations to its terms. In all these salient characters it differs from wordless symbolism, which is non-discursive and untranslatable, does not allow of definitions within its own system, and cannot directly convey generalisations.[2]

Ritual beliefs, then, if we follow Langer, are the significance of acts of expressive or presentational symbolism. Thus the behaviour of Yoruba towards their boxes covered with cowrie shells may perhaps express a total view of the nature of man, rather as Beethoven's music is sometimes alleged to express a total view about the order of the universe. The reason that Yoruba statements do not make literal sense is that they are, if used to express ritual beliefs, not statements at all, and, if used to describe ritual beliefs, not so much statements as clues. Equally, if Beethoven was expressing any total belief in his music, then that belief cannot be more than hinted at in words. For, according to Langer, the vehicle of expression is not a means to an end but an unanalysable end in itself. If so, then the reason

[2] *Ibid.*, pp. 96–7.

that ritual statements cannot be taken out of context is that they do not mean anything out of context. Ritual beliefs are the beliefs they are because of their place in a whole. Identification of each depends on the identification of all.

In distinguishing practical and expressive symbolism as she does, Langer is following Carnap, from whom she quotes these remarks:

> Metaphysical propositions – like lyrical verses – have only an expressive function, but no representative function. Metaphysical propositions are neither true nor false, because they assert nothing...But they are, like laughing, lyrics and music, expressive. They express not so much temporary feelings as permanent emotional and volitional dispositions.[3]

When Langer's view of symbolism is added to Carnap's view of metaphysical propositions, the result is a close analogy between ritual and music. This may seem a promising start at characterising ritual beliefs. But it would be defeat to accept it, as it makes it impossible to identify the ritual beliefs we are characterising. A ritual belief, on this view, not only lacks a truth-value but also is unanalysable and untranslatable. If this is right, then all we can ever say about two rival anthropologists' accounts of a ritual belief is that they are both wrong. An anthropologist's account of ritual would be limited to what his camera (equipped for sound) could record: as soon as he told us that the Yoruba believed that their boxes were their souls, he would have tried to translate the untranslatable. His and any rival account, then, would be bound to break down, as soon as they tried to put the significance of the ritual into words.

So far, then, we do not see how to exploit either the fact that natives take their ritual beliefs to be true, or the fact that ritual beliefs can be expressed in words or the fact that ritual has affinities with art, in order to identify these elusive beliefs. But before offering a *dénouement*, I would like to glance at a way of trying to by-pass the problem. We have been assuming that the significance of ritual must lie in the beliefs which it expresses, and this has left us trying to grapple with seemingly untranslatable

[3] R. Carnap, *Philosophy and Logical Syntax*, London: K. Paul, Trench, Trubner and Co., 1935, p. 28; quoted by Langer in *Philosophy in a New Key*, chapter IV, p. 84.

alien metaphysics. Perhaps, then, the significance of ritual is to be sought strictly in its social effects. Evans-Pritchard found in his studies of the Azande that Zande beliefs in witchcraft, oracles and magic served, *inter alia*, to maintain the power structure of Zande society.[4] It is tempting to argue from this that Zande ritual statements simply are statements 'about' social relations among the Azande. The attraction of such a move is that it gives us something objective for ritual statements to be 'about' and so allows us objective truth conditions to back our identifications.

But, in referring ritual beliefs to the social structure, would we be identifying them or would we be, at most, explaining how they come to be held? The latter, I suggest. A Zande, who believes he has been bewitched, surely does not believe that he has offended some social authority or other. If he did, he could perfectly well say so. He surely believes, rather, that he is the victim of supernatural interference. If so, facts about the Zande social structure serve at most to explain why, scientifically speaking, he believes this and perhaps why such a belief is common among the Azande or takes the form it does. But they will not serve to identify the belief as they do not constitute it. Equally, Catholic beliefs evidenced in the Eucharist might be found to be causally connected with some facts of human social history. But no convinced Catholic would agree that the beliefs were about social facts, if this meant denying them the status of metaphysical truths. Admittedly, it might be possible to argue in reply that Azande and Catholics simply did not know what their beliefs were about or even that their beliefs did not exist, being fictions inferred from social behaviour.[5] But this takes us too far afield. I shall continue to assume that there are ritual beliefs and that our problem is to show how they can be identified. If this is the problem, then social explanations are not identifications.

So our problem is not to be solved by looking for empirical

---

[4] E. Evans-Pritchard, *Witchcraft, Oracles and Magic Among the Azande*, Oxford: Oxford University Press, 1937. I am not implying that Evans-Pritchard takes a functionalist line himself.

[5] Cf. E. R. Leach, *Political Systems of Highland Burma*, London: Bell and Sons, 1954, p. 14: 'In sum then, my view here is that ritual action and belief are alike to be understood as forms of symbolic statements about the social order.'

truth conditions nor by sanctifying a literal translation with the name of metaphor. Nor is it removed by saying metaphorical propositions are non-assertive and untranslatable. Nor is it by-passed by concentrating on social facts. So how is it possible to identify a ritual belief? The answer is, I believe, to appeal to our own criteria of rationality.

Langer claims that her account of presentational or expressive symbolism has the merit of making it rational. She writes:

The recognition of presentational symbolism as a normal and prevalent vehicle of meaning widens our conception of rationality far beyond the traditional boundaries, yet never breaks faith with logic in the strict sense.[6]

Rationality is the essence of mind and symbolic transformation its elementary process. It is a fundamental error, therefore, to recognise it only in the phenomenon of systematic explicit reasoning. That is a mature and precarious product.[7]

This will hardly do as it stands. Presentational symbolism, she has just finished saying, 'is non-discursive, untranslatable, does not allow of definitions within its own system and cannot directly convey generalisations'. Its best example is music. Very well then – how can it possibly fail to 'break faith with logic in the strict sense'? Logic in the 'strict sense' (whatever quite that may be) requires the notions of well-formed formula, truth and falsehood, contradiction and so forth which are notably absent in music. Above all, it has criteria of identity for formulae and decision procedures for checking inferences. These notions are, I agree with Langer, what we are looking for. They are not to be found in her presentational symbolism.

It is my thesis that we can identify a ritual belief only if it is rational by our standards of rationality. This will seem parochial: why should the natives share our standards of rationality? In answer I shall try to show that some assumption about rationality has to be made *a priori*, if anthropology is to be possible; and that we have no choice about what assumption to make. I begin by arguing that the anthropologist works

[6] Langer, *Philosophy in a New Key*, p. 97.
[7] *Ibid.*, p. 99.

with a number of *a priori* assumptions, of which rationality is only one.[8]

Let us start with those simple everyday beliefs which the anthropologist shares with the natives. The natives believe that the cat is on the mat and the cow is in the corn. That they hold these particular beliefs is a matter of empirical discovery, but the discovery can only be made if some *a priori* assumptions work. The anthropologist begins in earnest by eliciting from a native a true utterance about a common perceived object, or perhaps by eliciting assent to such an utterance. The assumptions here are that the object has properties which they both perceive it to have, that the utterance refers to the object and that the native believes the utterance to be true. Only if these assumptions are correct, may the native be taken to have said in his language what the anthropologist would have said in his own. I want to insist firstly that they are assumptions and secondly that the anthropologist has no option about making them.

Since the anthropologist knew nothing about the natives when he started, it may seem that he discovers everything he knows in the end. Very well; how does he discover that the natives sometimes perceive what he perceives? Possible answers are that he observes their behaviour and that he translates their utterances. But if there is anything to be in doubt about, then observing their behaviour will not help. For, he needs to discover that the natives discriminate among phenomena as he does, and this is not guaranteed by outward similarity of reactions to the phenomena. Until he knows how the natives discriminate, he is imposing his own classification of reactions on their behaviour; and this implies that he is also identifying the phenomena according to his own perceptions, or else simply assuming that the phenomena are common to both parties, which is what he is purporting to discover. To show that he had discovered how they perceived the world, and not merely

---

[8] I am much indebted to W. v. O. Quine, especially to the second chapter of *Word and Object*, Boston: MIT Press, 1960, for several ideas in this paper. But his doctrine that all beliefs are revisable groups him with empiricists, even if his pragmatism is at odds with empiricism in other matters, and I hope to show that no empiricist can sail so close to the rationalist wind.

credited them with his own perceptions, he would have to translate their judgements of perception.

He cannot translate these judgements, however, until he has made some assumption about what the natives perceive. In translating a native word as 'cat', for instance, he is bound to be guided by the fact that it applies only to cats. But now it is too late to discover that they do not perceive what he does when he perceives a cat. He can, of course, be so open-minded that he fails to translate any native word at all. But he cannot first translate the word 'cat' and then discover that the natives perceive cats. That 'discovery' must come first, and the later translation does not confirm it, since the translation depends on it.

The *a priori* element in the process is obscured by some seductive empirical facts. It is an empirical fact that the natives have a word for 'cat', and, indeed, that they have a word for anything. It is also an empirical fact that they react to phenomena and that they make perceptual judgements. All these facts might not have been so; and the anthropologist has *discovered* that they are so. He has not discovered, however, that they perceive phenomena one way and not another way, that they make judgements about phenomena instead of making them only about something else, that they take blue objects to be blue and not pink. Equally, to advance a little further, he has not discovered that when they assent they mean 'yes', nor that when they sincerely assent to something they believe it to be true. He needed this information in order to translate any utterances at all, and it is then too late to discover it false.

This contention floats uneasily between the Scylla of the Whorf hypothesis and the Charybdis of the doctrine of analyticity. I shall next try to avoid both dangers.

The idea common to the many variants of the Whorf hypothesis is that what people perceive is a function of their language, in the sense that 'we dissect nature along lines laid down by our native languages'.[9] So long as this is a thesis about limited differences in perception embedded in a general agreement in perception, it is an empirical hypothesis, which a philosopher

---

[9] Benjamin Lee Whorf, *Language, Thought and Reality*, Boston: MIT Press, 1956, p. 213.

has no business to dispute. But it ceases to be an empirical hypothesis, if it is suggested that two people or societies might have no perceptions in common at all. Such a claim could not be shown empirically false, since there will always be cases uninvestigated. Nor, and this is what counts, can it be shown empirically true. For this would require that the totally different perceptions be the product of a translatable language and translation depends on some apparent agreement of perceptions.

I say 'apparent agreement' advisedly. Let us in a flight of philosophic fancy suppose that a tribe with only the sense of sight meets a tribe with only the sense of touch. Each tribe has a language for describing the world, one without tactual terms, the other without visual. Communication seems impossible, since, without any overlap in perceptions, neither tribe can establish any bridgehead. But now suppose that the tribes inhabit a world where every visual property of objects is, in fact, correlated with just one tactual property, where, for instance, all and only red objects feel square, or, more disingenuously, all and only objects which look square feel square. In these special conditions each tribe could successfully assume that there was overlap in perceptions. While restricted to its peculiar sense, neither could detect or correct the mistake. And so each could chart the other's language to its own satisfaction, provided the languages had the same structure. Now, if this flight of fancy is coherent, it is logically possible for one person to be totally, though systematically, mistaken about the content of another's experience. If the flight of fancy is incoherent, then it is so on *a priori* grounds. In neither case is it an empirical hypothesis that perception is a function of language. Apparent success in translation guarantees identity of the conceptual structure given to experience but not of the experience itself. Identity of content remains, however, a necessary condition of correct translation.

So is it not then analytic that languages are genuinely intertranslatable, only if speakers share experiences and conceptualise them in broadly the same way? That depends, I think, on the sense given to 'analytic'. If 'analytic' is defined broadly and neutrally as '*a priori*', there is no Charybdis of analyticity to avoid. Indeed, I shall argue later that what is here true of two languages applies equally to one and that we are seeking *a priori* conditions of the possibility of language in general. But 'analytic' is usually given a narrower and more loaded definition, suggesting that analytic truths rest on conventions which are a matter of choice. If it turns out that the anthropologist's assumptions are *a priori* without being optional, then I suggest that we are committed to some rationalist doctrine about the place of necessary truths in knowledge. With this in mind, I shall first extend the list of assumptions and then continue to argue that we have no option about what to assume.

The assumptions required for identifying everyday empirical beliefs are common perceptions, common ways of referring to things perceived and a common notion of empirical truth. Unless these assumptions work, the anthropologist cannot get a bridgehead – a set of utterances definitive of the meanings of everyday words. Thus to identify the native signs of assent and dissent, he must assume that the natives in the main assent to what is true and dissent from what is false. If his translation has them doing the opposite, that is sufficient reason for rejecting it. If it has them doing something quite different, for example expressing aesthetic reactions to the sound-pattern of the words, then he cannot claim to know what the words mean. Translation is possible only if the natives speak sooth about everyday objects as the anthropologist does; and no translation can either verify or falsify this assumption.

The notions of truth and falsehood cannot be separated from the notion of logical reasoning. They form a pair whose identity depends on the law of non-contradiction. An anthropologist does not know what he can say in the native language, unless he also knows what he cannot say. (This is why it is much easier to work with a native informant who can say no to a question, than with a set of texts, which cannot.) A language has a word for negation only if its speakers take the truth of a proposition to entail the falsity of a denial of that proposition. A language without a word for negation is translatable only if it is embedded in one which distinguishes what can and cannot be said. The anthropologist must find the word for 'no', and, to do so, must assume that the natives share (at least partly) his concepts of identity, contradiction and inference.

The case for this needs to be made out with care. The idea of an alternative logic to our own is not obviously absurd and, indeed, it has been claimed that pre-logical peoples actually exist.[10] The right of the law of the Excluded Middle to feature in the corpus of indubitable axioms can certainly be disputed. What, then, is special about the laws of Identity, Non-Contradiction and Inference?

The answer is, I believe, that these notions set the conditions for the existence not only of a particular kind of logical reasoning but also of any kind whatever. Try contemplating a culture whose members reason logically but not according to the schema 'If *P*, and if *P* implies *Q*, then *Q*'. They must reason somehow, however, so let us suppose them to infer something like this:

$$P * Q$$
$$P$$
$$\overline{}$$
$$! \, Q$$

How might we translate this? Well not by 'If *P*, and if *P* implies *Q*, then *Q*' as that would not yield an alternative to *modus ponens*. Nor by 'If *P*, and *P* implies *Q*, then *not Q*' as that would involve a self-refuting claim that '*P*', '*Q*', '*', '!' and '—' have the meanings or functions in the native language which '*P*' '*Q*' 'if...then' and 'implies' have in English. In general we cannot first identify a native constant as 'if...then' and then go on to show that *modus ponens* does not hold, since, if *modus ponens* does not hold, then the constant has been wrongly identified. Nor can we identify a native logical constant without saying what constant it is, since we need this as grounds for believing it is a constant. Native logic must either turn out to be a version of our own or remain untranslatable.

If this is right, '*P* →*P*', '~ (*P* & ~*P*)' and '(*P* & (*P* → *Q*))→*Q*' express more than axioms in a particular system or

[10] e.g. L. L. Levy-Bruhl, *La Mentalité Primitive*, Herbert Spencer Memorial Lecture, Oxford, 1931, p. 21. But see also his *Les Carnets*, Paris: Presses Universitaires, 1949, p. 130.

rules in a particular game. They express, rather, requirements for something's being a system of logical reasoning at all. To look for alternatives is like looking for a novel means of transport which is novel not only in that it has no engine but also in that it does not convey bodies from one place to another. Anything which satisfies the latter condition simply could not be a means of transport. If the natives reason logically at all, then they reason as we do.

I suggest, then, that what sentences mean depends on how the beliefs which they express are connected, and that, to justify a claim to have identified a belief, one must show how the belief is connected to others. Logical connection is not the only kind and to identify ritual beliefs, we need to introduce the notion of rational connection. I shall try to show that a ritual belief P can be identified only if there is a belief Q which supplies the holder of P and Q with a reason for believing P.

Return for a moment to the Yoruba and their boxes. One possible explanation which has been put forward is that these Yoruba believe each person to have a spiritual counterpart in heaven, who is susceptible to witchcraft. Witchcraft can be fended off by ritual treatment of the box, which represents the spiritual counterpart of its owner. Thus, when the Yoruba say the boxes are their heads or souls, they are using an 'are' of symbolisation and not of identity. In this explanation a pattern of behaviour is referred to a set of ritual beliefs and some of the beliefs are used to determine the translation of sentences expressing others. In seeing why the explanation has any force, we may perhaps answer our original question about the identification of ritual beliefs.

Are we to test Yoruba beliefs for rationality at all and, if so, are we to pronounce them rational or irrational? As ritual beliefs rarely entail each other and are sometimes, as with the doctrine of the Trinity, nigh-on contradictory, and as they do not correspond to objective facts, they will be unidentifiable, unless connected according to some notion of rationality. Besides we must surely allow for the fact that the Yoruba think their beliefs (whatever they are) true; and whatever the Yoruba take to make them true will make them *pro tanto* rational from a Yoruba point of view. But this is not yet to say that we and they must have *our* concept of rationality, and we may be reluctant to do so, as that might convict us of being ethnocentric or oblige us to believe in witchcraft too. So I shall consider next whether Yoruba beliefs may be rational by their standards but irrational by ours.

It may seem irrational to hold as true a belief which corresponds to no empirical reality. Ritual beliefs, as defined in this chapter, are certainly of this sort. Equally, ritual beliefs can be incoherent, and this might also seem to make them irrational. But this is not to say that we can accept identifications which make the empirical falsity and logical incoherence explicit, general and recognised. For that would give sufficient reason to reject the identification on the grounds that, given this degree of laxity, we no longer have a way of deciding between rival translations. People may believe a contradiction but, if they were also to believe that it was a contradiction, that would cancel their claim to know what the belief was. Since beliefs in an incoherent system imply their own negation, the existence of identifiable beliefs in an incoherent system depends on the holders not being aware of their incoherence. Otherwise they might believe anything and neither we nor they could identify what they did believe. The only relevant fact about someone's ritual beliefs cannot be that we find them irrational.

Perhaps, however, the natives find rational what we find irrational, in the sense that they have a different notion of 'being a reason for'. We could discover this only if we could first identify the beliefs and then see how they were connected. In other words, we must be able to reach a partial translation of the form 'I believe $P * $ I believe Q' without translating '$*$' and then go on to translate '$*$' without making it our own (rational) 'because'. But now we are stuck. We could take '$*$' as 'although'; but this would still leave us with our concept of rational connection. There is no English word, however, for an alternative to our (rational) 'because'; and, if there were, the native language would again turn out to be a version of ours. Moreover, without a translation of '$*$', how do we know that we have identified P and Q? If P is 'this box is my soul', what makes that a correct translation? Why not 'this box is my spiritual identity card'? I contend that, without a translation of '*', the only answers are those mentioned at the beginning of this paper, and I would hope that the argument has by now advanced beyond them.

It may be as well to disentangle the *a priori* and empirical elements here. It is an empirical matter what ritual beliefs the natives hold, what sentences they express them in and how they express the connection between them. It is *a priori*, however, that any ritual beliefs which we can identify form a related set whose members supply reasons for each other. This is *a priori* in the sense that it is an assumption which determines the translation of native sentences and so cannot be shown to be false. It is not optional, in the sense that, if we try to make any other assumption, we cannot identify any native ritual beliefs at all.

Anthropologists are thus obliged, I suggest, to remove obvious incoherences, if they are to give their readers better reason to accept their account than to reject it. It may be of interest to note how Evans-Pritchard does so in his *Witchcraft, Oracles and Magic among the Azande*. He writes:

Azande see as well as we that the failure of their oracle to prophesy truly calls for explanation, but so entangled are they in mystical notions that they must make use of them to account for the failure. The contradiction between experience and one mystical notion is explained by reference to other mystical notions.[11]

Thus, for instance, an oracle can be bewitched and so its failure will reinforce beliefs about witchcraft. The connectedness of Zande thought is crucial to Evans-Pritchard's account. He finds that:

Witchcraft, oracles and magic form an intellectually coherent system. Each explains and proves the others. Death is a proof of witchcraft. It is avenged by magic. The achievement of vengeance-magic is proved by the poison-oracle. The accuracy of the poison-oracle is determined by the king's oracle, which is above suspicion.[12]

Elsewhere in the book he says:

[11] Evans-Pritchard, *Witchcraft*, Part 3, chapter IV, section viii, p. 338.
[12] *Ibid.*, p. 476. This is one of twenty-two reasons cited to account for the failure of the Azande to perceive the futility of their magic.

In this web of belief every strand depends on every other strand and a Zande cannot get out of its meshes because it is the only world he knows. The web is not an external structure in which he is enclosed. It is the texture of his thought and he cannot think that his thought is wrong.[13]

Although Evans-Pritchard may have changed his philosophical ground in later works, here he takes the line that Zande beliefs are empirically false but rational both for them and for us. If my argument is sound, this approach is the only one which allows the identification of ritual beliefs. Recently a belief in 'interpretative charity' has found widespread favour.[14] If interpretative charity means merely making the native society as rational as possible, I am all for it. But if it means making the notions of reality and rationality relative to the native conceptual scheme, in the belief that we should not claim the monopoly of these notions, then I maintain that anthropology is in consequence impossible. Without assumptions about reality and rationality we cannot translate anything and no translation could show the assumptions to be wrong.

In agreeing with Langer that ritual beliefs are to be identified by treating ritual utterances as acts of expressive, rather than presentational, symbolism, I am taking rationality for this realm as a relation between beliefs. A ritual belief P is rational if and only if there is a belief Q such that Q supplies a reason for holding P, and P does not entail the falsity of Q. This, I hope will 'extend the concept of rationality without breaking faith with logic in the strict sense'. In other words, outside the realm where one can plausibly argue that the correspondence theory of truth is presupposed in establishing the bridgehead, we must fall back on the coherence theory. To explore the point, I shall next draw an analogy between an anthropologist and an unbelieving theologian.

Most theologians are believers and hold their own religions to

---

[13] *Ibid.*, p. 195.

[14] Peter Winch's article, 'Understanding a Primitive Society', *American Philosophical Quarterly*, 1964, pp. 307–24, has been especially influential, although its relativistic implications have been restrained by Donald Davidson's treatment of the theme, particularly his essay 'The Very Idea of a Conceptual Scheme', in *Inquiries into Truth and Interpretation*, Oxford: Oxford University Press, 1984, which takes the line propounded here.

be internally rational. They may take religion to begin with faith and end with mystery but they also hold that every belief which can be made explicit either makes rational another belief or is made rational by another belief or both. An unbelieving theologian can take the same line. He can certainly judge that the system is in sum irrational but he may – and, I contend, must – hold that most individual beliefs are connected rationally. In short, he may disagree totally with a believing theologian, but he must also agree with him in most particulars. Otherwise the believer will be entitled to claim that the unbeliever does not understand what he is disagreeing with. Mystery is divine truth to the believer and human nonsense to the unbeliever. But both can agree where it sets in. A mysterious belief is presumably one for which some other (non-mysterious) beliefs supply reasons but which does not in turn supply reasons for other beliefs. This is, at least, as far into the unknown as I can stretch the notion of identifying a ritual belief. Here, however, both theology and my analogy stop: a complete mystery is unintelligible to all.

The analogy between anthropologist and unbelieving theologian may be missed, because it is easy simply to credit the theologian with an understanding of the language of the faithful. The theologian, in other words, is his own bilingual. If so, the price of drawing the analogy seems to be the collapse of my thesis, since, as remarked at the beginning, an articulate and intelligent bilingual can apparently make the anthropologist a gift of all the natives' ritual beliefs. But this presupposes that the bilingual has already identified the ritual beliefs and can present them in English sentences intelligible to the anthropologist. The conceptual problem remains the same, however, whether it is stated for two persons and two languages or for one person and one language. It is that of putting ritual beliefs into a form in which they can be classed as rational without ceasing to be the beliefs in question. This is one task of theology.

As proof of the pudding, let me offer as a model piece of anthropology a quotation from the Greek Cardinal Bessarion:

In the sacrament of the Eucharist there is one thing which is merely a sign, namely, the visible species of bread and wine; and another thing which is the reality signified, namely, the true body and blood of Our Lord, which he took from the pure flesh of the Blessed Virgin. But the body and blood of Christ, while it is a reality pointed to by the sign of the bread and wine, as we shall shortly show, nevertheless is, itself the sign of another reality, since it points to the Mystical Body of Christ, and the Unity of the Church in the Holy Ghost. This Mystical Body, however, and this Unity do not point beyond themselves to any other reality, but are only themselves pointed to.[15]

Bessarion is a believing theologian. How is the unbeliever to understand his account, without becoming a convert? He should, I submit, take it literally and test it for rationality, in order to understand it, and then deny that it corresponds to anything, in order to disagree with it. For, if it is taken as simply metaphorical or false or without truth value or irrational, then it is unintelligible, and, if it is taken not to make any empirical claims about a supersensible reality, then there is nothing to disagree with.

Unless we take the expression of some ritual beliefs literally, we shall again make anthropology impossible. I said earlier that a ritual belief P could be identified only if it was rational, and that it was rational if and only if there was a belief Q which supplied a reason for holding it. If Q is itself a ritual belief then we need a further belief R which supplies a reason for holding Q. In other words, if ritual beliefs form an autonomous system, we cannot understand one without understanding many or many without understanding one. We need, then, a belief Z which is expressed in practical, and not in expressive, symbolism and which supplies a reason for holding some ritual beliefs. Moreover Z must itself be identified and so must either be true or be traceable in the same way, to some further empirical belief which is true.[16] For, as has been argued all along, understanding is possible only if it advances from a bridgehead of true and rational empirical statements. Literal sense is as important to the temple as it is to the market place.

---

[15] *De Sacramento Eucharistiae*, P. G. 161, 496. The passage is quoted and discussed by Fr. Bernard Leeming, SJ., in his *Principles of Sacramental Theology*, London: Longmans Green and Co., 1956, p. 256.

[16] Peter Hacker has pointed out that the argument, if sound, should also hold against intuitionist theories of ethics.

But, it will be objected, people speak in metaphors, especially in ritual. The objects used in sacraments may be everyday things, like bread, blood and water, but they are used symbolically. If the upshot of this paper is that metaphor is impossible or unintelligible, so much the worse for the paper. My answer is that some metaphors are unintelligible, in the way that some mysteries are.

> Life like a dome of many-coloured glass
> Stains the white radiance of eternity.

This is what Carnap would call a Metaphysical Proposition and only a rash interpreter would claim to know what it means.[17] At any rate, since the claim is undemonstrable, we are free to reject it. Here, I think, we can at last settle for Langer's analogy between ritual and music. Shelley's metaphors cannot be rendered discursive.

Not all metaphors are so resistant. Some can be cashed (only indirectly, perhaps) in terms which can be understood literally. Thus the metaphor in 'It makes my blood boil', like the symbolism in the Statue of Liberty, is easily dissected. Metaphor, while it is still alive and not dead, is a new and self-conscious way of conceptualising experience and, although not purely descriptive, can be traced to descriptive statements. But this makes it a civilised phenomenon; a primitive who says 'It makes my blood boil', is likely to mean exactly what he says.[18] I am not pretending that there is no difficulty about metaphor. Indeed, I

---

[17] Lorna Sage tells me that any competent interpreter would spot the familiar Platonist image involved. She is clearly right; but, although somewhat chastened, I have left the sentence standing, as I am not convinced that this is enough to render Shelley discursive. If it is, there are more resistant examples.

[18] It is important also that a similar 'civilised' distinction between instrumental and symbolic behaviour does not always hold in primitive thought. Thus Evans-Pritchard remarks of the Azande:

> When a man chooses a suitable tree and fells it and hollows its wood into a gong his actions are empirical, but when he abstains from sexual intercourse during his labour we speak of his abstinence as ritual, since it has no objective relation to the making of gongs and since it involves ideas of taboo. We thus classify Zande behaviour into empirical and ritual, and Zande notions into common sense and mystical, according to our knowledge of natural processes and not according to theirs. For we raise quite a different question when we ask whether the Zande himself distinguishes between those techniques we call empirical and those techniques we call magical.

Witchcraft, p. 492. Taken in context, the passage does not imply the relativism which it may seem.

would agree that many metaphors have to be construed by analogy with music, and this requires a sense of 'understanding' which I do not grasp. I am saying only that claims to have identified the metaphorical uses of words and gestures must be rationally justified. This involves cashing the metaphors and therefore the notion of metaphorical use never has any independent leverage.

This chapter stands or falls with the claim that a theorist of social anthropology must budget for *a priori* elements which are not optional. It may be as well to finish by rehearsing the claim. The *a priori* elements are those notions which the natives must be assumed to have, if any identification of their ritual beliefs is to be known to be correct. To get at ritual beliefs, the anthropologist works from an understanding of the native language in everyday contexts. To establish a bridgehead – a set of utterances definitive of the standard meanings of words – he has to assume at least that he and the natives share the same perceptions and make the same empirical judgements in simple situations. This involves assumptions about empirical truth and reference, which in turn involve crediting the natives with his own skeletal notion of logical reasoning. To identify their ritual beliefs, he has to assume that they share his concept of 'being a reason for'. There will be better reason to accept his account than to reject it, only if he makes most native beliefs coherent and rational and most empirical beliefs in addition true. These notions are *a priori* in the sense that they belong to his tools and not to his discoveries, providing the yardsticks by which he accepts or rejects possible interpretations. They are not optional, in that they are the only conditions upon which his account will be even intelligible. In short, although it is an empirical fact that the natives hold any beliefs and have any language at all, and although it is a matter of hard work and huge expertise to discover what forms they take, anthropologists need conceptual tools before they can even begin. When packing their tool boxes they are philosophers.

Evans-Pritchard ends his book on Nuer religion with these words:

Though prayer and sacrifice are exterior actions, Nuer religion is ultimately an interior state. This state is externalised in rites which we can observe, but their meaning depends finally on an awareness of God and that men are dependent on him and must be resigned to his will. At this point the theologian takes over from the anthropologist.[19]

The theologian seems already to have taken over from the anthropologist. But why not? Sacred anthropology is sceptical theology.

[19] E. Evans-Pritchard, *Nuer Religion*, Oxford: Oxford University Press, 1956, chapter XII, p. 322.

CHAPTER 14

The social destruction of reality

It is evident that all the sciences have a relation, greater or less, to human nature; and that, however wide any of them may seem to run from it, they still return back by one passage or another. Even Mathematics, Natural Philosophy and Natural Religion are in some measure dependent on the science of MAN; *since they lie hid under the cognisance of men and are judged by their powers and faculties.*

David Hume, Introduction to *A Treatise of Human Nature*

That the formal determinants of belief are human, yet not intellectual, is an idea as old as scepticism. But it need not be a sceptical idea. Hume, for instance, saw in it the grounding of a new science, which would explain the human understanding as the work of custom and imagination. He was sceptical about Reason, but confident about science; and the tracing of our beliefs to custom and imagination was to be a scientific project. Philosophers have not, on the whole, taken kindly to his proposal, except recently in the philosophy of natural science, but sociologists of knowledge have carried it a great way. Of late a 'Strong Programme' has crystallised, intended to deprive Reason of all its traditional autonomy and to place the study of the social world on a thoroughly scientific footing. I find this a most instructive exercise, less for its results – witness my title – than for what it reveals about the understanding of beliefs. It forces friend and foe alike to think hard about the social world, the mental life of social actors and the very idea of a social science.

This essay first appeared in M. Hollis and S. Lukes, eds., *Rationality and Relativism*, Oxford: Blackwell, 1982, pp. 67–86. The present version is shorter but no less indebted to Steven Lukes for helpful criticisms and many discussions. I would also like to thank Richard Bernstein for perceptive comments and David Bloor for responses, which, although unpersuaded, I respect and appreciate.

221

Traditionally 'knowledge' has been regarded as belief which has passed an objective test and is held because it has passed the test. 'Reason' is the portmanteau name for the rules of proof, which aid the mind in securing *a priori* knowledge, and for the canons of empirical evidence, used in judging the truth of beliefs against the facts of an independent world, both for Mathematics and for Natural Philosophy. (It has also included whatever intuition is deemed needful to ground the first inferences.) Hence we have knowledge, only if we follow Reason; custom and imagination are never enough. So, traditionally, there is a basic asymmetry about the explanation of belief: someone who knows believes because the belief is true and justifiable; the explanation of beliefs which stem from custom or imagination is of a different sort. The Strong Programme rejects this distinction root and branch.

It is commonly a four-point programme:

1 *Causality.* The programme seeks the causal conditions which bring about beliefs (or knowledge), treating beliefs as effects, after the manner of any object of scientific study.
2 *Impartiality.* It is impartial between true and false beliefs (as between rational and irrational, or any other epistemic classification). All beliefs are equally grist to the explanatory mill.
3 *Symmetry.* Explanation, since it does not vary with the epistemic status of the belief explained, can be dubbed symmetrical.
4 *Reflexivity.* The programme makes no exception in its own case. It applies reflexively to itself; and the beliefs held by sociologists of knowledge are, in turn, objects for scientific study.

The four points are non-committal between imagination and custom (psychology and sociology), although a sociologist of knowledge of course opts for custom. But they are committed squarely to the side of science against the autonomy of Reason. There is nothing special about the beliefs which constitute knowledge. 'Knowledge for the sociologist is whatever men take to be knowledge. It consists of those beliefs which men confidently hold to and live by.'[1]

In what follows I shall take the four points in turn, raising queries and suggesting revisions. The programme is meant to rot away the props of a familiar notion of objectivity, and I shall resist by defending Reason. My aim is constructive. It is to clear the way for a sociology of knowledge helpful to an actionist theory of the social world as human handiwork. So I distinguish two kinds of rot spread by the programme. One is, so to speak, wet rot – a determinist picture of the shaping of beliefs by social conditions, which denies the scope of thought and action in weaving the social fabric. Here the blame will fall on the Causality clause, partly for making causation one-way and more for separating the intellectual from the social. The other is a lethal dry rot – a relativism implied in the other clauses, laudably meant to make us see the social world from within but resulting, I allege, in the social destruction of reality. By way of cure, I shall argue for an asymmetry in the explanation of beliefs, with those true and rationally held treated differently from those false and irrationally held and with mixed explanations for the mixed cases. Reason will thus advise a blend of charity and judgement in the understanding of social life and hence a damp-proof course for the sociology of knowledge too.

CAUSALITY AND BELIEF

The programme looks tempting in at least some areas of thought. Natural Religion, for example, has lost the place which Hume gave it in the citadel of the sciences and has long seemed a suitable candidate. This is not to say that a Strong Programme seeks to convict religious believers of some kind of global error by showing the ground of belief in God to be not God but society. The programme is not committed to any such functionalist innuendo. The idea is to tackle religious beliefs, like all others, without prejudice to their truth. The most ardent believer can agree that religion takes different forms in different social

---

¹ David Bloor, *Knowledge and Social Imagery*, London: Routledge & Kegan Paul, 1976, p. 2. See also the summary of the programme on p. 45 of Barry Barnes and David Bloor, 'Relativism, Rationalism and the Sociology of Knowledge', in Hollis and Lukes, *Rationality and Relativism*.

conditions and can profit from sociological help in applying the parable of the sower. The Causality clause is to be read not as asserting a brute social determinism but as seeking necessary and sufficient causal conditions.

There is no good reason, however, to insist that causation is all one-way. Beliefs helped to shape the Church, whose power extended to the social conditions which in turn helped to shape it and its beliefs. More generally, a Strong Programme is entitled to whatever a theory of ideology has to offer; and there ideas are commonly given work to do, for instance in masking and so perpetuating social forms. Perhaps the explanations of the last resort must be held to lie in social (or economic) facts, but meanwhile there can be interplay. Indeed the four points of the programme, taken together, demand it. For, we shall find, the attack on the autonomy of Reason is not meant to abolish all considerations of rationality. How the actors conceive their world is still important for understanding that world, even if their conceptions are rational by varying criteria, which finally have social determinants. Presumably then, the Causality clause permits causation both ways.

This amendment does more to strengthen the programme than to subvert it, provided that beliefs are never the explanations of the last resort. Deeper questions arise, however, when we reflect on the presumption that social and intellectual systems can be separated and then related as cause and effect. This seems to me a dangerous piece of rot. Ideas cannot, I submit, be described in isolation from the social world, which they let actors describe to themselves; nor can the social world be furnished without the aid of the actors' ideas. There is fusion in the identities of the actors, who can be treated neither, in idealist mood, as ambulating beliefs, nor, in materialist vein, as historically located bipeds whose beliefs are secondary. Consider, for instance, Catholicism, both as an intellectual system of doctrines, interpretations and precepts, and as a system of social positions within the Church affecting the everyday lives of Catholics. The distinction is real enough but it is got by abstracting in two different ways from the same charivari. No doubt the beliefs and the social life of priests (and of the faithful) vary systematically between New York, Dublin and Warsaw. Yet a priest is not essentially the occupant of a social position who just happens to hold Catholic beliefs. Nor is he a universal believer who just happens to live somewhere. His flock have social relations with their father confessor and his spiritual journey takes him through the streets and offices of a social world.

Each abstraction can itself be made in different ways. Sometimes it is useful to abstract a unitary Catholic view on say, contraception, sometimes it is more useful to emphasise the discord. Whichever is done, the beliefs are those of social actors; and the corresponding points can be made about abstracting to the political influence of the Church. Hence the units, which a Strong Programme connects, are each doubly abstracted from what the actors themselves usually manage to live as a single life. To treat beliefs as units, or even as properties of actors, is no doubt a proper and useful device. But it is a device; and nothing follows about the substantive reality of intellectual systems as entities. Conversely, social relations are partly ideal, in that norms and rules are real only given actors who regard (at least some of) them as real. They are external to each actor but only because they are recognised. They genuinely enable and constrain in the familiar way; but only because enough actors rely on them to enable and constrain. Although norms have material conditions and consequences, nothing follows about the reality of social systems for purposes of causal explanation. Social systems are detected by a double abstraction and to treat them as objects with causal powers is also a device.

I shall not defend here this view of social life as the life of actors with two aspects, each identified with the aid of elements from the other. Even undefended, it serves to put the Causality clause in question. What does the clause envisage as the basic causal relation? Presumably the explanation of beliefs needs something subtler than social mechanics, psychic forces or statistical correlations. At any rate, it should be possible to admit the interpenetration of ideas and things in the furnishing of the social world without abandoning the programme. In that case, however, we are owed more on the nature of causality than I find to hand. Equally, the programme would presumably rather retain a notion of agency than lose the actors in the interplay of the intellectual and the social. But there too an account of agency is owing. So I end this brief section with a query over the Causality clause. Read simple-mindedly, it seems to me to fall at once, partly because there has to be causation both ways and, at a deeper level, because the relation of intellectual and social cannot be that of distinct kinds of being related on the model of physical effect to physical cause. How then should the clause be read? With this question in mind for later, I turn to Impartiality.

IMPARTIALITY AND IDENTIFICATION

The second point of the programme is Impartiality, the refusal to confine itself to false beliefs or to irrational beliefs or to any other epistemic category. In so far as it differs from Symmetry, it has to do with what essential distinctions should be drawn among beliefs to be studied and I shall link it with the matter of how we are to identify the beliefs which people hold. Symmetry concerns the explanation of why they hold them. Under both headings I shall ask what kinds of judgement an enquirer must make, in order to understand a system of beliefs. I take there to be understanding, when one knows what one's subjects believe (identification) and why they believe it (explanation). But let no one forget that the two go together, lest we propose a canon for explaining beliefs, which would make it impossible to have identified them.

To clear the ground, some simplifying assumptions are needed. I assume that a society, culture or group holds a belief, if enough of its members do. (Thus I shall ignore questions of numbers, authority and the gap between publicly asserted and privately held belief.) I assume that beliefs can be ascribed to persons, as predicates to subjects, without first discussing intentionality, opacity and other issues in philosophical logic. I assume that a system of beliefs differs from a list in as much as there are connections in the minds of the holders, these connections taking the form of beliefs about beliefs, which mark out some as the reasons for holding others. Thus I assume that intellectual systems are internally rational for the most part, in a sense which even the strongest programme can accept. That should give just enough common ground to get argument going.

A belief can be warrantably ascribed to someone, I argued in the two previous essays, only as an element of a system, some of whose members are held because they are true, some because there is good reason for holding them and none without some reason. Here the notion of a reason is used objectively. In the previous paragraph I assumed that beliefs are rational from the actors' point of view, since they can always cite some other belief or an alleged fact, which, by some rule of justification, seems to them to warrant any belief. The thesis is that there are tests for whether a belief is objectively rational and that subjectively rational beliefs need not pass them; that there is a minimum score which all beliefs must attain and a maximum score which some must; and that 'good reason' is an objective term, to be applied with increasing warrant as the maximum is approached.

Yet much of what is believed is surely false or suspect. Mankind could hardly survive without beliefs which are incoherent, unlikely, disconnected or daft. Life is too short for constant Cartesian monitoring, even supposing that to be possible in principle. Social life often runs better on some false, or at least unquestioned, beliefs. Language cannot be understood solely as if all utterances were assertions or all assertions sincere. Nonetheless, the identification of beliefs requires a 'bridgehead' of true and rational beliefs. Before the theme is taken further, here is a brief reminder of the nub of it.

The evidence on which an enquirer ascribes a belief to an actor is got by interpreting what the actor and others say and do. Their sayings and doings must have been rightly understood. Hence, apparently, every interpretation requires a previous one. So how is identification possible? A tempting reply is that the air of paradox is spurious: each interpretation is provisional and subject to confirmation; a later interpretation can overturn an earlier one; so the need for a previous interpretation is genuine but harmless. Yet there are two reasons why there has to be more to it than the pragmatic assembling of a jigsaw. One is that even this pragmatic work presupposes internal relations among the beliefs – if you like, the existence of both a picture on the face of the jigsaw and a geometry to the shapes of the pieces which are not discovered by the confirming process. The other is that, in addition to internal relations, there must be an external determinant which is also presupposed and not discovered. This is not simply 'the world' – that begs too many questions – but an *a priori* guarantee of overlap between the perceptual judgements of the enquirer and of the informants. Putting internal and external constraints together, the enquirer must presuppose shared percepts, judgements, concepts and rules of judgement in the making of empirical discoveries about beliefs. So, although some individual interpretations are adjustable later, adjustment cannot be so thorough as to overthrow the bridgehead of interpretations it relies on.

Formally speaking, to know on evidence e that S believes p involves knowing that, on evidence e, it is more likely that S believes p than that S believes anything inconsistent with p, and that e can be relied on. This requires fixed rules for judging between rival interpretations and, if e depends in turn on e^*, requires that e^* (or whatever e^* depends on) be secure too. In upshot there has to be some set of interpretations whose correctness is more likely than that of any later interpretation which conflicts with it. The set consists of what a rational person cannot fail to believe in simple perceptual situations, organised by rules of coherent judgement, which a rational person cannot fail to subscribe to. All interpretation thus rests on rationality assumptions, which must succeed at the bridgehead and which can be modified at later stages only by interpretations which do not sabotage the bridgehead.

Where two languages are involved, the line is that translation presupposes some facts of the world described in both. Again, it does not assert flatly that there is a single, objective and neutral world but that translation needs to presuppose one. Whether or not the world is a fact, it is an indispensable presupposition. If expressions from two languages are to be rightly equated, any conditions for one meaning what it does in its language are conditions for the other in its language. Conditions for meaning should not, in general, be confused with conditions for reference; but, in the special case of defining without interdefining, understanding relies on a species of naming.

That the case is both special and crucial can be seen by asking how the enquirer can ascribe false and irrational beliefs to *S*. No doubt there are other options to try first – that *S* is lying, for example, or has unobvious but good reasons for the belief – but sometimes there is nothing else for it. Now the enquirer must decide whether it is likelier that *S* holds a deficient belief or that the translation is deficient. We cannot uphold the translation, unless sure of other translations, embodying identifications of other beliefs. It is crucial, then, that meanings can sometimes be established by ascribing true and rational beliefs. Such 'bridge-head' cases are special however, since otherwise false and irrational beliefs could not be ascribed at all. Falsity and irrationality need to be *prima facie* but not conclusive evidence against a translation.

The conclusion which I seek to draw is that some beliefs are universal. There are, because there have to be, percepts and concepts shared by all who can understand each other, together with judgements which all would make and rules of judgement which all subscribe to. If understanding is to be possible, there must be, in Strawson's phrase, 'a massive central core of human thinking which has no history'.[2] But the conclusion will come better after the next two sections, and it is enough for the moment that good sense is prior to bad. If Impartiality is a refusal to distinguish good sense from bad, it leaves us without reason for preferring one translation to other. In ascribing beliefs, we must be able to start by discerning the true and rational and to end with the false and irrational.

SYMMETRY AND EXPLANATION

The Strong Programme seems to me wholly wrong about symmetry and I shall contend that true and rational beliefs need one sort of explanation, false and irrational beliefs another. The intermediate cases – false and rational, true and irrational – will

---

[2] P.F. Strawson, *Individuals*, London: Methuen, 1959, p. 10.

be taken up at the end, with non-rational beliefs ruled out altogether.

That there is some asymmetry seems patent, offhand. In one of James Thurber's *Fables for Our Time* a man finds a unicorn browsing among the tulips in his garden.[3] He informs his wife, who, remarking with scorn that the unicorn is a mythical beast, summons the police and a psychiatrist, to have him certified. She tells them what he said and they ask him to confirm it. 'Of course not,' he replies, 'the unicorn is a mythical beast.' So they shut her up in an institution and the man lives happily ever after. It seems patent that the truth of the various beliefs makes all the difference. If there actually was a unicorn in the garden, his belief is not certifiable. If he actually said that there was, her belief that he did needs no psychiatrist to explain it. The psychiatrist intervenes only where beliefs are false or irrational. A Strong Programme which contests this patent asymmetry can surely be convicted of rot?

When we try to generalise the story, however, we find little to embarrass the Strong Programme. No doubt there are obvious facts of experience whose denial is a sign of mental disorder. But it is not true in general that beliefs about reality refer to the obvious contents of an independent realm. So, if we built on an apparent asymmetry for obvious common sense, we would pay for it when we came to beliefs whose objects were not obvious or of some other character. What of the beliefs of those engaged in Mathematics, Natural Philosophy and Natural Religion? I think it is important to treat these engagements as continuous with everyday life and not as radically peculiar in the ontological status of their objects of reference. Otherwise a bridgehead in common sense will be no basis for advance. It would be an exaggeration to say that all beliefs express the holders' understanding of reality. But those which do are the enquirer's road into unknown territory.

It might seem that my line relies on there being facts of the world independent of all theory. If so, a proof of the theory-dependence of facts might count in favour of the Strong

---

[3] 'The Unicorn in the Garden', also reprinted in *The Thurber Carnival*, London: Hamish Hamilton, 1945 and Harmondsworth: Penguin Books, 1975.

Programme and against making appeal to objective judgements. (It might also, incidentally, subvert the kind of objective causality which the Causality clause asserts.) But, to my mind, nothing said about a bridgehead forces a decision about theory-dependence; and it does not spoil Thurber's story, if unicorns and tulips are theory-dependent. The world, I said carefully, is an overlap rather than a fact. Presumably a Strong Programme is not intended to make it a matter of indifference whether to send for a psychiatrist or a zoo-keeper. So there is a distinction between reality and illusion, which the programme needs as much as anyone. When I argue later that the programme ends with the social destruction of reality, it will not be because it insists on the theory-dependence of facts. I see no threat, therefore, from treating common-sense beliefs as easy cases for whatever method is appropriate in general, rather than as a theory-free starting point.

The asymmetry in explanation, which I claim to detect, stems from elsewhere. It arises because beliefs are woven into a system by actors' beliefs about their beliefs. These are the actors' own reasons for belief and so their own explanations of why they believe what they do. Schematically, people who cite p as their reason for believing q, believe not only p and q but also that p is good enough reason to believe q. One of the enquirer's tasks is to discover these connections, not merely because the list of actors' beliefs will be incomplete without them, but also because the list must add up to a system. But he must also produce his own explanation of why the actors believe what they believe. In doing so, he cannot fail to endorse or reject the actors' own reasons or, where the actors are not of one mind, to side with some against others.

In the next essay, 'Hook, Line and Sinker', I shall offer a general case for holding that endorsing and rejecting are not symmetrical. For the moment, notice that a Strong Programme proposes a contentious theory of the relation between context and belief. The theory purports to explain belief (and utterance) and is thus committed to a contentious view of human identity and agency. Imprecise though it may be, it is certainly not shared by all actors. Indeed it is not fully shared by any, except for those who happen to subscribe fully to the programme. So (almost) every actor would reject some beliefs held by an enquirer who accepts a Strong Programme. The enquirer cannot fail to reject some beliefs of any actor who rejects some beliefs of the enquirer. Nor can the enquirer pretend not to judge, out of respect for the actor. The only way for the enquirer to respect actors' beliefs which imply that the enquirer is wrong is to treat those beliefs as false (or else to abandon the programme). Thus, in so far as reference to social context yields an explanation of the actors' system, the enquirer is judging some of the subjects' beliefs to be false.

Granted that an upholder of a Strong Programme disagrees with anyone who does not subscribe to it, why exactly might this obvious point imply an asymmetry in explanation? That will be plainer if we first consider two (tempting but incompatible) notions of rationality in belief, which might suit a Strong Programme. One is that rationality is a purely formal property, solely to do with the relation between premises and conclusions. If so, the enquirer can apparently trace the web of the subjects' beliefs without passing judgement. There is nothing odd about actors and enquirer each holding coherent beliefs which could not be combined into a single coherent set; and, since no one holds beliefs solely because they are coherent, the rationality of beliefs in this internal sense need not affect their explanation.

But, I reply, the enquirer is also interested in intellectual disagreements among actors. Such disputes are rarely battles in formal logic. They concern the content of the belief-system and what, in context, it is rational to accept. Coherence comes into them but so also do other tests of sound judgement. Unlike party-political manifestos, which suppress internal debate for the sake of an united front, belief-systems are fluid. For instance, as John Dunn has kindly pointed out to me, a historian of science needs to distinguish not only between the rival belief-systems of Copernicans and Ptolemeans but also between leaders, hacks and heretics within each evolving camp. The reasons earlier requiring more than tests of coherence in order to establish a bridgehead apply also to establishing the contents of any belief-system. The actors' own notion of rationality in belief involves more than coherence and that fact alone should suffice to establish that judgement cannot be confined merely to the actor's passage from premises to conclusion.

These considerations may tempt us to adopt a second notion of rationality, a contextual one. There seems plainly to be a relativity about what counts as a good reason for belief among different groups. If so, the enquirer may be excused judgement, because not required to judge on these differing rules of the game. Since to deem a reason for belief good in its context is not to endorse it, the enquirer can arrive at a system of beliefs (rather than a mere list) without taking an external standpoint.

But, I reply, one must still decide what is *explanandum* and what is *explanans*. Consider, for example, what account to give of Hobbes's thesis in *Leviathan* that civil society depends on the existence of an absolute sovereign with the power to keep all in awe. In explaining why Hobbes believed this, what significance attaches to his own supporting argument, to the fierce dissent of his contemporary critics, to the insecurity of the civil war period and to the underlying changes in the structure of English society? It seems to me crucial to decide whether *Leviathan* is well argued. If it is, then that is why Hobbes believed its message, even if the historical context can still help explain why he thought of it or why he presented it as he did. If it is ill argued, then his failure to realise this calls for an explanation, into which context can enter directly. Either way, the responses of his critics are to be given the opposite treatment. Even if rationality is somehow relative to context, we still have to decide which of conflicting beliefs are rational in their context, thus endorsing or rejecting the actors' own claims to hold rational beliefs and act rationally upon them.

Weber's recipe for the writing of history bids us ask what it would have been rational for an actor to do and then, when needed, to explain why he did not do it.[4] Where the actor did the rational thing because it was the rational thing, that ends that particular question. The recipe works equally well for a contextual notion of rationality, provided that there are limits to what is

[4] See, for instance, Max Weber, *Economy and Society* (1922), Berkeley: University of California Press, 1978, chapter 1.

contextualised. Thus, legal systems differ in what they regard as relevant to proving a case, for example whether particular theologians can be cited as authorities in a witchcraft trial, and the historian needs to identify such local rules of the game. But intersubjective standpoints are not to be confused with subjective ones, which might seem to guarantee vacuously that individuals always act rationally, once their subjective beliefs and preferences are taken into account. Nor can local rules be wholly local, as argued earlier. Limits need to be so set that, when actors in the same context are at loggerheads, their dispute can be described objectively and umpired. The historian needs scope for comparing the merits of the cases put in a witchcraft trial, taking local beliefs and rules into account but without allowing that there is nothing more universal to be said about their rationality.

Admittedly historians will not always know what would have been rational, neither absolutely nor even in context. But they must still lay their bets. They do so by issuing probable explanations, subject to revision. In issuing an explanation, they are forming their own reckoning of what would have been rational and applying it to judge the actors' reckonings and to judge between them. In revising an explanation, they are redistributing marks either between the historian and the actors or among the actors. They need not claim to be omniscient, but they cannot avoid laying bets; and this need stands, whether the notion of rationality involved is absolute or contextual. In sum, a Strong Programme is forced into judging between itself and the actors. The scope of an enquirer's explanations, when they conflict with an actor's own, either is or is not limited by how rationally the actors hold their beliefs. If it is, then the actors' own explanation stands, when it passes a test of rational criticism and falls when it does not; and there is asymmetry. If it is not, then the actors' own explanation stands when, for good reason or bad, it coincides with the enquirer's and falls when it does not; and there is again asymmetry. Asymmetry results not from imposing an absolute notion of rationality but from the fact that the actors justify their own beliefs to themselves in ways which often conflict with the metaphysics of a Strong Programme.

None of this puts the sociology of knowledge out of business.

Where beliefs are not rationally held, there is scope for the usual structural accounts. More to the point, even where beliefs are rational, there are further questions to ask about social conditions. Why, for instance, were Babylonians such conspicuous mathematicians in the ancient world or Holland a centre of scientific advance in the seventeenth century? There are social conditions favourable to the spread of knowledge and it is a valuable task to unearth them. I insist only that they differ relevantly from conditions which favour the spread of ignorance. There is not just one study, the spread of belief, treated as if it were like the spread of anthrax; and the enquirer must not only see the actors' world from within but also judge it. There can be a sociology of knowledge as well as a sociology of ignorance. But, while the social conditions of intellectual failure explain the failure, those of intellectual success do not explain why beliefs are held.

REFLEXIVITY AND RELATIVISM

I come, finally, to the promised fiasco, the social destruction of reality. There is an old paradox about a Strong Programme. If there is to be the same impartial and symmetrical style of explanation for all beliefs, it should, presumably, apply to the beliefs of those who advocate a Strong Programme. Yet these beliefs lay claim to a scientific status, which the programme dare not forfeit and dare not assert, since both would subvert the programme. The paradox, I hasten to add, has never stopped the sociology of knowledge in its tracks. Just as Hume saw nothing self-referentially absurd in the scientific reduction of science to custom and imagination, so too the traditional discipline has refused to blush for its canons of objectivity. But, equally, the traditional discipline has not included Reflexivity.

The reason, no doubt, is that older approaches relied on a stout distinction between relationalism and relativism. Relationalism merely introduces a notion akin to perspective. Just as the perceptual character of an object can be said to depend on perspective without impugning the objectivity of the relations involved, so too the sociologist was credited with a bird's-eye view of beliefs, social facts and the causal relations between them. Admittedly critics were not slow to complain that a bird's-eye view is strictly for the birds, since there is nowhere for a free-floating intelligence to perch in discerning these objective relations. But sociologists of knowledge were unselfconscious about making a perch for Reason, so that first-order accounts would not self-destruct at the second-order. In any event, this attitude illustrates the previous section. The beliefs of the sociologist were exempt from the general search for social causes of belief, because they were warranted by Reason. That is a nice example of asymmetry.

The recent addition of Reflexivity, however, is not prompted just by honesty. Older approaches have been strongly determin-istic. Even if the social world is identified from within the actors' consciousness, it has been explained from without and the actors have been left no initiative. The Durkheimian version is not materialist; yet there the important fact about norms is less that they are internal to all actors collectively than that they are external to each. That evocative phrase 'the social construction of reality' refers to a deterministic process whereby things collectively defined as real are real in their consequences. Self-reference is an embarrassment, not a selling-point. Recently, however, the sociology of knowledge has been harnessed to a search for an action sociology. Here 'the social construction of reality' refers to human handiwork. The actors create social facts, or even, in sweeping versions, all facts. The social world is both seen from within and explained from within. When a Strong Programme is harnessed to this sort of view of social life, it cannot avoid reflexivity and relativism, even if it wished.

Nor does it wish. The upshot of Impartiality and Symmetry is to insist that the actors' beliefs are always rational, when properly understood. This is guaranteed partly by making the criteria for rational belief relative to the conceptual scheme and social context in which they occur, and partly by taking reality to be whatever a social group who share a conceptual scheme take to be real. Belief is rational, if it is a legitimate interpretation of experience and legitimacy is a matter of coherence and consensus. The same applies to scientific beliefs, which can be studied in the sociology of science. So science, including sociology, is taken off the gold standard of truth and treated as a floating currency – or, rather, truth drops out and is replaced with a guaranteed rationality. The treatment meted out to Natural Religion earlier is extended to Mathematics and Natural Philosophy.

Old and new approaches coexist and the four-point Strong Programme does not discriminate between them. The difference lies in whether social constructions determine individual consciousness, with the actors' search for rational order a matter of their adjusting their beliefs to what they are expected to believe, or, conversely, whether norms and collective representations are the outcome of negotiations among rational actors. Either way, there will need to be more said about the meaning and implications of the Causality clause; but I shall here confine myself to Reflexivity, in the context of an actionist sociology of knowledge. Here Reason is dethroned but not abandoned. The idea is to treat rationality as variable and to make it an axiom of method that the social world is always rational from within. The sociology of knowledge becomes the study of internally rational social transactions. It is in many ways a liberating development, but I fear that it spreads a dry rot too vicious for anyone's comfort.

The snag is that there are now too many ways of making the actors' world rational from within. It is not as if the ascription of belief and desire were at least constrained by given criteria of rationality. For the dethroning of Reason must make it a contingent matter what criteria are in use among what groups of actors. Nor is it still as if there were objective furniture of the social (or even of the natural?) world. Now the furniture is accessible only through the actors' beliefs and can therefore be constituted in whatever way helps the final account hang together. Both ontology and epistemology are relative to shared belief and, in principle, variable without constraint, beyond that of overall coherence. Since the criteria of coherence are themselves included in epistemology, it ought to follow that there are no constraints at all. Indeed it does follow, I maintain, and only failure of nerve stops anyone who has gone this far drawing the conclusion. Moreover, since other cultures are, epistemologically, merely a case of Other Minds, there will no longer be any constraint on any interpretation of one person's beliefs and desires by another. What set off as an insight into the construction of social objects ends as the sceptical destruction of reality.

I can myself see only two ways of stopping the rot. One is to retrieve the given, to restore the independence of facts, to let there be at least an independent and objective natural world. With the present state of upheaval in the philosophy of natural science, this is easier said than done; but the reasons for wanting to attempt it are patent. Even if it can be done for the natural world, however, there is still a generic difficulty for the interpretation of belief. Behaviourism aside, there is no easy way round the 'double hermeneutic', which arises when the objects of study are themselves interpretations. Whether or not there is a veil of perception, there is assuredly a veil of thought. So I myself accept the reasons for refusing a social ontology independent of human beliefs and favour some thesis about the construction of *social* reality. But the 'bridgehead' argument still stands and the need for it arose because not enough was given in perception to set standards of judgement for choosing between rival under-standings of systems of belief. Empiricism cannot now be smuggled back in.

The other way, then, is to place an *a priori* constraint on what rational people can believe about their world. On transcendentalist grounds there has to be that 'massive central core of human thinking which has no history' and it has to be one which embodies the only kind of rational thinking there can be. The 'massive central core' cannot be an empirical hypothesis, liable in principle to be falsified in the variety of human cultures but luckily in fact upheld. Otherwise, as Sextus Empiricus remarked in ancient praise of scepticism, 'In order to decide the dispute which has arisen about the criterion, we must first possess an accepted criterion by which we shall be able to judge the dispute; and in order to possess an accepted criterion, the dispute about the criterion must first be decided.'[5] To escape Sextus, the existence of a core must be taken as a precondition of

---

[5] *Outlines of Pyrrhonism*, II.e.xx (Loeb edition).

the possibility of understanding beliefs. There has to be an epistemological unity of mankind.

The plain snag here is that such reflections yield at most an existence proof. What has to be in the core? Notoriously not everything which Kant said about the categories of human thought has remained intact. Not only does the core not include all categorial thinking (since, indisputably, cultures do vary in their ways of categorising experience) but there is also a distinction between what must be universal and what merely is universal (in the sense that, although it is not found only in some cultures, it might be). It is tempting to respond by making the core all form and no content, by assigning to it only the formal properties of coherent belief, and leaving all particular beliefs about what there is to empirical enquiry. But this line of division between the necessary and the contingent does not give enough to stop the rot. The enquirer needs a guarantee in advance that the actors' world makes basic sense to both enquirer and actors. The guarantee is expressed in the proposition that the actors are rational. It has to go beyond the assertion that the rational actor makes rational inferences from the unvarnished news supplied by the senses. For, even if there is such news, it brings with it neither categories nor principles of categorial organisation. Hence the plain snag remains. Without specifying the core, I cannot make this paper cogent. But neither can I make it short. So I simply enter a plea for metaphysics.

Meanwhile there are still the false-but-rational and the true-but-irrational. I have argued that the sociology of knowledge must distinguish the true-and-rational from the false-and-irrational. Without the former there is no entry into a system of beliefs and the actors' world cannot be seen from within. Without the latter, there is no accounting for intellectual change. The sociology of knowledge which I advocate starts with beliefs which are held for the good reason that they are true and advances by identifying beliefs which are held for the fairly good reason that others are true. It is then ready to deal with beliefs held for the indifferent reason that others are held. Thence it enters the realm of beliefs held when there was better reason not to hold them; and a fresh form of explanation is needed. With false beliefs irrationally held, the divorce between identification and explanation is complete: they are identified on the pretence that they are true and rational and explained in the recognition that they are neither. The two missing classes thus require a mixed explanation, from within to the degree to which they resemble one ideal type and from without for the rest.

If there are to be two forms of explanation for beliefs, what is the scope of each? Explanation from within is complete where the actors believe because they know. Explanation from without is residual. The size of the residue varies from case to case, with the restriction that the explanation must not overturn the identification of the belief explained. Mixed cases are those where the actors have incomplete reasons, and so the two forms of explanation coexist. Epistemologically, this makes correct explanation a function of the enquirer's omniscient judgement and I again wish to forestall the obvious objection that enquirers are human. Methodologically, we, as enquirers, are trying to strike a balance of probability between rival interpretations. Since we are fallible, we can only give our best reasons for the balance and must be ready to revise it in the face of better reasons. But we have to stake our judgement and, epistemologically, this requires a reference to objective truth. Without one, there is no balance to strike.

By way of summary, I revert to the four points of the original Strong Programme.

The Causality clause must be amended to allow causation both ways but its troubles go deeper. It relies on a distinction between social and intellectual which I cannot endorse and is fatally silent about the nature of social agency. All might be well in the end on a determinist reading of the social construction of reality. But the livelier enterprise of shaping the sociology of knowledge in the service of displaying the social world as a human construction depends on making actors for the most part rational. This sets a larger question mark over Causality than I have had space for.

The Impartiality clause makes the identification of beliefs impossible and I suggest that the sociology of knowledge needs to pass epistemic judgements, although it is indeed true that all beliefs are grist to its mill.

The Symmetry clause yields to a wholly crucial asymmetry, with one kind of explanation for the true-and-rational, another for the false-and-irrational, and mixed explanation for the mixed cases.

With Reason restored, the Reflexivity clause is no longer an embarrassment and the social destruction of reality is off the agenda. In all, I urge an account of social knowledge and social action which pivots on the concept of rationality and takes the side of judgement against that of charity.

This is an old but, I hope, durable line and the nub of it was well put by Vico two centuries ago:

There must in the nature of human institutions be a mental language common to all nations, which uniformly grasps the substance of things feasible in human social life and expresses it with as many diverse modifications as these same things may have diverse aspects.[6]

There must indeed!

[6] Giambattista Vico, *New Science*, section II ('On Elements'), paragraph 161.

CHAPTER 15

Hook, Line and Sinker

There is an old suspicion that the sociology of knowledge is caught in a paradox of self-reference. It might be dubbed the paradox of the free-floating intelligence. For example, the Strong Programme discussed in the last essay sets out to relate people's beliefs to their social context, with an apparent suggestion that beliefs are always finally determined by the social conditions in which they occur. How then, we ask, do advocates of the Strong Programme know that this is so? The reply, it seems, must be either that they have a perch, explicitly denied to the rest of us, from which to discern the truth of the matter, or that they do not. If there is such a perch, they refute themselves and, if not, we need not accept their claims. The version discussed in the previous essay faced the dilemma squarely, rejecting the first horn in favour of the second. In the name of 'Reflexivity', it insisted that there can be no exceptions: like all other beliefs, the beliefs held by sociologists of knowledge are objects of scientific study. Yet, since we may still doubt whether the second horn is more comfortable than the first, I shall now pursue the point from a fresh angle.

Traditionally the sociology of knowledge has weighed in on the 'structure' side of the recurrent dispute between those who maintain that social action is the product of social structure and those who take the opposite view. Indeed, the 'Causality' clause in its original version offered to treat belief-systems as the effects of social systems, thus apparently endorsing the traditional line.

The idea for this essay can be found embedded in chapter 7 of my book *Models of Man*, Cambridge: Cambridge University Press, 1977.

But that need not be so. Sociologists who regard social action as primary, or at least independent, can presumably subscribe to a sociology of knowledge which does not treat beliefs solely as effects. At any rate, let us suppose so, and then suppose, for the sake of argument, that sociologists of knowledge can be divided into two groups accordingly. Let the litmus test be whether social structures, including social norms and institutions, generate social actions and beliefs, or whether it is the other way about. Suppose that all sociologists subscribe uncompromisingly to one position or the other. I ask everyone to enter into the spirit of the game.

Now imagine three sociologists, Hook, Line and Sinker. Hook is researching into the beliefs of sociologists; Line believes structures to be the work of social actors; Sinker believes that structures explain action and belief. *Ex hypothesei* Hook agrees with one or other of them and the essay will have four phases. Firstly Hook, agreeing with Sinker, investigates Line. Secondly, still agreeing with Sinker, he investigates Sinker. Thirdly, switching to Line's point of view, he investigates Sinker again. Fourthly, still siding with Line, he again investigates Line. I shall assume throughout that the opening step for each phase is to identify the relevant beliefs from within, thus obeying what is sometimes called the hermeneutic imperative, this being without prejudice to whether they are finally to be explained in structural terms or understood in ways which give hermeneutics the last word.

In the first phase, Hook sets about Line, on the assumption that Line's beliefs have structural determinants. He opens by describing the social world, which he and Line share, from Line's point of view, including Line's own beliefs about how it works, with interpretive charity ensuring an account which makes sense to Line. Then he describes this same world again in structuralist terms, including the scheme of social positions in which he and Line are located, no doubt making special mention of departments of sociology and of universities as social institutions. Finally, treating the-world-according-to-Line as a belief-system and the-world-according-to-Hook as a correct representation, he explains Line's beliefs. For instance, he shows why it is functional for the higher education system to have some sociologists who think as Line does. If this then yields successful predictions about the prevalence of such beliefs wherever they suit the distribution of power, he cites this as evidence that social systems determine belief-systems.

The strategy involves judging the truth and rationality of at least some of Line's beliefs. In particular Line's beliefs about the direction of explanation and the nature of social action contradict Hook's. Were Line right, Hook's research would rest on so large an error that all its explanatory findings would be wrong. So here is one set of beliefs which Hook must judge and reject. He cannot maintain blandly that their truth is irrelevant to their explanation. Nor can he cover himself by saying that, although their rationality may matter, their truth does not. For, if Line has objectively good reasons for believing that explanation runs the other way, then Hook should accept them too; and, as argued in the preceding essays, subjective rationality is to be taken as derivative from objective. Nor can Hook suspend judgement on the pragmatic ground that his own approach is fertile rather than well evidenced. For, in so far as he is using it at all, he is to that extent betting against Line's beliefs. There is no impartial position.

Once impartiality is breached, the pace quickens. It is not only Line's explicit beliefs about sociological method which conflict with Hook's. Any belief will do, provided that it implies that Hook's explanation of why it is held is wrong. If Line were a Freudian, an existentialist or, indeed, anything but Hook's brand of structuralist, Hook would have to pass judgement. Nor need the conflicting opinions be academic. Were Line a disciple of Samuel Smiles or a capitalist with a Protestant ethic, who believed that he had taken to commerce on divine advice, he would hold beliefs whose truth would entail the falsity of Hook's explanation. Actors in every age and culture explain their beliefs to themselves; and Hook recognised this when he started by describing Line's world from within. Whenever the truth of Hook's explanation implies the falsity of the beliefs it explains, Hook cannot avoid passing judgement on those beliefs.

Hook is deep in ontology. To propose a method of explanation is to claim that the world works accordingly. If structuralism is true, then God does not prompt Calvinists to industrial enterprise through the small voice of conscience. A method for detecting causal laws commits the user to a world which contains them. If Hook chooses his methods pragmatically or relies on several, then he either asserts that there are in reality several sorts of connection or, as a merely tentative ontologist, must settle for equally tentative explanations. In general, the investigator, like the Other Mind investigated, tries to make the world intelligible to himself. In the act of explaining, he is asserting a metaphysic. Call it 'M', including:

M_1: methodological propositions about the criteria of explanation
M_2: theoretical propositions about the sort of sociological explanations which satisfy M_1
M_3: ontological propositions implied or presupposed by M_2
M_4: epistemological propositions justifying M_1
M_5: ontological propositions implied or presupposed by M_4.

He is committed to rejecting any of the Other Mind's beliefs which conflict with any implication of M. In other words, he tackles his subject armed with a method of enquiry, a set of sociological concepts, a model of humanity and of society, a theory of knowledge and a cosmology. His every explanation is therefore a judgement on the subject's own view of the world.

Secondly Hook, still believing that structure explains belief, investigates Sinker, who takes the same view. For the previous reasons, Hook must judge Sinker's beliefs, this time pronouncing them true and rational. But now there is a delicious snag. Why does Sinker believe that structure explains belief? The Sinkers of my acquaintance all give intellectual, epistemically charged reasons. So did Hook a moment ago, when we had him cite his findings as empirical evidence for the worth of his approach. But these are examples of the sort of beliefs which Hook is committed to rejecting. He need not reject them out of hand, as mere rationalisations or epiphenomena, since he can point to their role in the intellectual system to which he and Sinker subscribe.

Viewed internally to the system, the holding of one belief can be the cause or effect of the holding of others. Viewed externally, moreover, intellectual systems can have social effects, for example, to cite the Marxist theory of ideology, in masking, legitimating and perpetuating social systems. But he cannot stop there. It is not in his book to grant that any belief is held or any action done solely or finally because there is good reason for it. Social structure is the final explanation of belief. So Sinker's good reasons must finally be Sinker's 'good' reasons, reasons which satisfy criteria whose authority is finally the mere stamp of some socially significant body. By all means let Hook and Sinker explain why they believe that structure explains belief by appealing at first to the rules of the Logicians' Union and the Sociologists' Guild. But let them not forget to add a causal explanation of the power of these bodies and of why they endorse those particular rules. Even if reasons are causes, they also have causes. Otherwise, with structures no longer trumps, Hook cannot take all the tricks.

Hook is now in an impossible position. If he follows this advice, he destroys his earlier explanation of Line's beliefs. He earlier judged Line's beliefs false and Line's reasons for holding them bad reasons. He was not trying to convict Line of heresy by the prevailing norms of the Logicians' Union and Sociologists' Guild. Nor would he have succeeded, since the Union is neutral between consistent sociological theories and the Guild divided. What he believed, and needed to assert, was that Line was in error. Structuralism, he insists, has reason on its side or, in so far as reason is certified by some body, the body has good reason for its certificates. But there can be no final good reason for his holding the belief that every belief has a structural explanation, unless this crucial belief is itself false. He cannot afford to try for all the tricks.

When are structural explanations of belief not trumps? The exception just made soon proliferates, since it can only be a general one for any free-floating intelligence to justify the holding of a belief by showing it true and rational. In other words, an intelligence is *freischwebend* whenever it holds true beliefs for good reasons. Picture a stockbroker, who carries an umbrella because he knows that rain is likely and because he knows that an umbrella is the best way to keep dry and because he knows that it is against his interests to get wet. Where or in so far as these conditions do not hold, there is scope for causal explanation by reference to the institutional or ritual significance of the umbrella. In so far as the conditions hold, however, there is no more to be said. One can still raise further questions – why he owned an umbrella or why it had a gold handle – but they would be premised on recognising that he had solved the problem set by the weather. Similarly, historians can ask why Babylonian mathematics were ahead of Etruscan at the same date and show how the Babylonian social system helped what the Etruscan hindered; but, as any history of mathematics makes amply clear, they cannot set about accounting for the difference, without recognising explicitly that the Babylonians knew more about mathematics than the Etruscans. Hook's exception in his own case reinforces what was said before. To make the exception is to recognise an ideal type of self-sufficient explanation.

The moral is now wider. Hook must judge the believer's reasons for every belief and action to be explained. There is no structural explanation for what is its own explanation. I do not mean that there is a sociology only of ignorance, since it remains worth finding out what social conditions further the spread of knowledge. Also we often cannot judge where reason lies, and must bet that the believer does not know either. But we cannot avoid laying our bets, since the type and mixture of explanations depends on them. Hence there is a moral too for the study of ideologies, which can now be assigned to a superstructure and explained as products of a socio-economic base, only in so far as they are false. True consciousness is its own explanation.

For the third and fourth phases, Hook undergoes conversion to the rival camp and starts again. He still treats social and intellectual systems as distinct, but now reverses the direction of explanation. Like Line, he now believes that we construct the social world in our capacity as intelligent social actors. Sinker, meanwhile, still believes that social systems are always external, constraining and the source of explanations of the last resort.

Sinker presents a different target this time. Why does he hold these *mistaken* beliefs about the relation of intellectual and social systems? Hook's answer starts by giving Sinker credit for a reasoned position. Otherwise, in the spirit of the 'bridgehead' argument, it would be likelier that Hook had misidentified the beliefs than that Sinker actually held the beliefs being ascribed to him; and there is scope for dispute about how many of Sinker's beliefs are held because they are reasonably held. But, at some stage, Hook will follow Weber in insisting that an objectively irrational belief needs a different sort of explanation. There are many possibilities, for instance institutional pressure on Sinker to subscribe to a prevailing paradigm, with further social determinants, or a plunge into the subconscious demands of Sinker's personality. The field is open; but, whatever the type of cause sought, the crux is that such causes would not be called for at all, if the belief in question were held for good reason.

Hence Hook's new approach, unlike his old, is prescriptive. To trace the causes of Sinker's entrapment in a scheme of bad reasons is to show how the spell could be broken. Whereas the causes of beliefs held for bad reasons are external and constraining, beliefs held for good reasons are liberating. An actionist regards the external social constraints as, ultimately, a human construct; what humans can make, humans can change; what a single agent cannot accomplish alone, collective action often can.

This prescriptive aspect obtrudes further when, lastly, Hook renews his investigation of Line. Whereas Sinker's basic assumptions were now to be challenged, Line already accepts rational belief and action as their own explanation. Yet, although he and Hook are both trying to extend the scope of intelligent action, they need not be in total accord. Within the actionist camp there are disputes about the relation between rational action and, for instance, true interests or real wants or moral concerns, especially when it comes to questions of relating the good of each person to the public good. Hook is claiming to be able to stand clear of institutional context in mounting his enquiry; but he is not omniscient. He is a party to his own investigation and may find Line's beliefs more rational than his own. With all branches of social science and ethics at stake, each claim to identify a departure from the ideally rational will be contentious. Nonetheless he is committed to trying. If the type of explanation depends on the rationality of what is to be explained, every belief and every action has to be judged.

Now let us drop the coarse pretence that every sociologist is a Line or a Sinker. The real elements of the exercise were only the conflicting systems of belief. What spins beliefs into a system is the presence of beliefs about beliefs. The web includes purported explanations of its own elements. The point of the exercise has been to show that there are no impartial stances in the sociology of knowledge. Each stance commits one to judging the explanations proffered by those whose beliefs are being investigated. Investigators are committed, in particular, to rejecting rival metaphysical accounts to theirs. Thus an enquiry premised on the truth of social determinism in explaining beliefs must explain how actors of contrary persuasion have been led into error. Conversely, an enquiry premised on the autonomy of beliefs held for good reason must account for the prevalence of social determinists. Yet there is an asymmetry here. When these rival metaphysics are applied reflexively, both offer an intellectual case for accepting their approach. That sets no problem for the actionist view; but there is an old paradox about claiming ultimate truth for the view that belief-systems have no possible ultimate truth; and Sinker seems to me to illustrate it nicely.

If that is fair comment, then we can again draw the hermeneutic conclusion offered in the previous essays: understanding starts with true beliefs rationally held, continues with rational but false beliefs and switches to the passive mode only with the irrational. Then there may be a further conclusion. The final alternative to holding that social systems cause belief-systems need not be that the latter cause the former. A more fertile conclusion, I suspect, is that we are not dealing with distinct objects, causally related, at all. But, since I have not argued this case here, the thesis about understanding will suffice for the moment.

CHAPTER 16

Say it with flowers

Historians have only the husks of action, the traces of what once were episodes played out between past and future. To recover these passing moments they rely on texts of all sorts, on utterances in ink and stone, metal and paint, which once had meaning for living actors. Even written, reflective texts are not as if the tape-recorded voices of authors prevented by death from addressing us in person, since they were meant for other audiences, couched in local idioms and fired by unfamiliar concerns. Historians must read in before they can read out and there is a plain danger of their finding what they put there themselves. Even written texts are not just strings of propositions. In uttering them, their authors were acting and interacting, and the historian must interpret the actions as well as the words. Here lie circles of the most daunting kind but Quentin Skinner has braved them before and I seize the chance to dissect them with him. It goes without saying that what so visibly troubles him in the dark of the archives also afflicts anyone trying to understand the social meaning of action.

To broach a huge topic, I shall assume that historical actors have at least some autonomy within a context which both enables and constrains them, that their actions are their solutions to problems set by circumstance and by other actors,

A longer version of this essay, with more said especially about group action, formed part of a symposium with Quentin Skinner under the general title 'Action and Context' in *The Proceedings of the Aristotelian Society*, Supplementary Volume 52, 1978, pp. 44–56, reprinted in part here by courtesy of the Editor. Both versions owe an immense debt to his many articles on aspects of historical interpretation and the understanding of action, and to many fruitful conversations with him. My dispute with him about the relevance of motives signals no general rejection of his approach.

and that their particular skill at solving problems is crucial in interpreting their actions. This picture needs a general defence, but, since Skinner shares it, I shall concentrate on the specific objection that the attempt to construe historical action as manoeuvre within a context is caught in a vicious hermeneutic circle. The question will be whether a notion of rationality affords an escape.

'Say It With Flowers', the florists urge. Very well, let us do so in a story intended to sketch Skinner's approach to historical interpretation, to exhibit the circles which threaten it and then to usher in the one disagreement between us. Suppose that, soon after the balcony scene of some real-life Romeo and Juliet, Romeo sends Juliet a bunch of red orchids with a card inscribed, 'A beauteous flower for when next we meet'. This episode is the text and I shall be using 'text' to refer not just to speech but to any act whose author intends others to understand something by it. What is its interpretation? The question is ambiguous between meaning and explanation and I propose splitting it into four.

> First, there is the *overt meaning* - in the case of speech 'What did he succeed in saying?'
> Secondly, there is the *covert meaning* - 'What did he intend to say and intend in saying it?'
> Thirdly, there is the *overt explanation* - 'Why was the utterance apt?'
> Fourthly, there is the *covert explanation* - 'What was his motive in uttering the text?'

The historian's primary task, according to Skinner, is to answer the first three parts of the question but not the fourth. Having extolled the subtlety of this approach, I shall nevertheless insist that the question of motive be answered too.

The division into overt and covert has to do with the importance of context. It is not as if the sending of the flowers means just whatever Romeo means by it. 'In "action" is included all human behaviour', says Weber in chapter 1 of *Economy and Society*, 'in so far as the acting individual attaches subjective meaning to it.' The dictum is not to be read as saying that subjective meaning is all. Romeo cannot succeed in meaning what he pleases by the flowers. The gesture is taken from stock, its meaning restricted to a conventional list. It may be a mark of love, respect, gratitude or sympathy, perhaps, but not of hate, scorn or support for the Verona football team. (I ignore hidden codes or conventions, like irony, which exploit conventions.) This is just as well, since utterances constituted wholly by subjective meanings would be quite beyond the historian's reach. So let us suppose the episode to be one in a courtship, expressing something conventionally said by lovers. What exactly is said is then determined by the message on the florist's little white card, provided that it is within the list of proper meanings. (If the card reads 'The cat sat on the mat', Romeo succeeds in meaning nothing by the flowers.) A sort of social grammar is at work.

Here, then, is one notion of context, where the actors engage from socially recognised positions, attended with normative expectations. We may call it the normative context, the set of rules governing what a person must do, may do and shall not do in each social capacity. The rules both constitute and regulate. Romeo is not Juliet's lover at all, unless he stays within the rules of courtship; he is a sorry lover, unless he courts her with grace, unselfishness and fervour. Admittedly, the notion of a norm is an elusive one, witness my swift transition from 'position' to 'capacity', and requires nuance, for instance to allow for differences between what is publicly prescribed and what is tacitly permitted. But the idea that social action is constituted and regulated by legitimating rules is clear enough to accept.

It has been held that the normative context exhausts the meaning of action, at least for purposes of historical explanation: although Romeo has more than one option as a lover, he also has other social positions or capacities, which together determine a uniquely legitimate course of action. This approach, which could be dubbed 'normative structuralism', depends on seeing norms as the social category of the last resort and on absorbing the actor into them. If we refuse the first move, on the ground that norms have further social determinants, we need a wider notion of structural context. If we refuse the second, on the ground that actors also express inner states in a way which may be rule-governed but is not role-determined, we need a notion of what we might call expressive context.

In speaking of a wider structural context, I have Marx's distinction of structure and superstructure in mind, although not excluding other ways of distinguishing between the normative and non-normative for the purpose. But I shall not pursue this topic, since, even if there is an ultimate wider structure, the normative context is intermediately important enough to keep us busy. In the same cavalier way, I shall ignore other external factors of, for instance, geography, biology and even technology, presuming them to enter the interpretation of social action through the normative context and the actors' consciousness. These are pieces of ontological impudence which lack of space demands.

The expressive context, however, is as crucial as the normative. Romeo's flowers are not just a lover's insignia, like the wig on a judge. They are red for passion, expressing fire within. This is a symbol, not a natural sign, and belongs to a language of the heart. Romeo's gesture in its normative context is that of a suitor; in its expressive context it is that of a man in love. The expression of feeling is governed by rules too and, in doing what is normatively proper, Romeo also conveys a claim to inner sentiment. That the claim can be false shows that there is an external and enabling context for it. By citing the normative and expressive contexts, the historian gives the overt meaning of the text. But, if that is what the flowers mean, it does not exhaust what Romeo means by the flowers. Or so it will seem to anyone who denies that actors are mere vehicles of norms and sentiments. Romeo also intends his gesture to be read in particular ways and intends to achieve something by it. In part, no doubt, he means what the flowers mean, uttering their overt message with the intention that others recognise this intention. But, anticipating Henry James, he can be addressing several messages to several audiences with the one text. Conscious perhaps of Lady Capulet's intercepting eye, he intends the formality and the plush orchids to bespeak an admirer of solid substance but slight acquaintance

– an intention likelier to succeed, if it goes unnoticed. At the same time he intends Juliet to catch the echo of her own words on the balcony:

> This bud of love by summer's ripening breath
> May prove a beauteous flower when next we meet.

He intends her to relish the incongruity of these intentions. He means, in a common sense of that nimble term, whatever he intends insiders to understand. That is the covert meaning of the text.

The overt explanation is got by parading the overtly legitimate elements of the covert meaning and showing why the actor was justified in context in acting as he did. Much is forgiven a man in love and much can therefore be achieved by laying successful claim to the title. Exactly what needs doing to regain the sense of an action in the eyes of contemporaries for the benefit of posterity will depend on the particular case. In Skinner's hands the idea that texts are to be interpreted by recovering the context, the actors' intentions and their legitimating reasons becomes a sharp tool, as cogently witnessed by his books and articles. What does not depend on particular cases, however, is his contention that the historian need not and should not tackle, still less prejudge, questions of motive. Hence the overt explanation stops with what is legitimate. We are not to infer that it tells us what the actor was really moved by: the principles and sentiments which someone professes in action are the key to explaining his actions in context, *whether or not he expresses them sincerely*. The crux is that actors cannot succeed without legitimating their actions in the eyes of others.

So when, fourthly, we ask whether Romeo's intentions were honourable, Skinner's answer is that we neither know nor need to know. Romeo is sighing like a furnace, his orchids are aflame, he is every inch a man on fire; yet it may all be sound and fury, signifying nothing. Actors are neither mere creatures of norms nor mere vehicles of sentiments. They stand back not only from what their actions mean but also from what they mean their actions to mean. Once the historian has found them sufficient reason to have acted as they did, he can penetrate no further but

	OVERT	COVERT
WHAT?	Rules	Intentions
WHY?	Reasons	Motives

Figure 1

he has done enough. To sum up schematically, Romeo illustrates Figure 1.

The four boxes correspond to the opening four questions and, in strong, ingenious support of Collingwood's dictum that all history is the history of ideas, Skinner offers to do history with the first three only.

We are now ready for the circles which beset any hermeneutic account of historical understanding. They arise because rules, reasons, intentions and, indeed, motives are interrelated both ontologically and epistemologically. Ontologically, the rules of courtship are those binding lovers in the expression of love; lovers are persons subject to the rules because they are in love; love is the sentiment expressed by observing the rules of courtship. Are these relations constitutive? The case for saying so is that love is surely not a universal condition which people catch like colds in all climes and contexts and then express in what happens to be the local idiom; that, even if courtship rules from many cultures are all so classified because they govern expression of the same sentiments, the sentiments are the same because their expression is governed by courtship rules; that in general the covert is a discrimination within the overt, no less than the overt is an expression of the covert.

Epistemologically, to be warranted in ascribing an intention to express love, the historian must know that the relevant rules are those of courtship and that the actors are as lovers; and hence must already be warranted in ascribing the intention. The overt is to be understood as the context of the covert, and the covert as what the actors means by the overt. Nor is the problem an empirical one, to be overcome by tacking back and forth from overt to covert in advancing zig-zags, since apparent success will not guard historians against a charge of imputing what they purport to discover. The problem is a theoretical one of conceiving the relation between rules, actors and intentions in such a way that the merit of rival interpretations can be judged. Even if we know it to be soluble, on the general ground that actors do succeed in interacting with one other, the exact solution makes a difference and we await one.

The way in, Skinner and I agree, is to make the actors as rational as possible. But we are not fully in agreement. In his version to deem Romeo rational is to say that he knows how to legitimate and so achieve his intentions. The idea is to treat meaningful action as a text which, construed with an apparatus of locutions, illocutions and perlocutions and on the assumption that it was rationally uttered, is its own explanation. The attraction is that the historian can spin a yarn, knit the actor a cap, and, if a critic doubts whether the actor was actually wearing the cap, retort that we need not ask. A rational actor, in recognising good reasons for acting, makes those reasons his own. Motives are not needed, because the actor in that context would have acted in the same way from more than one motive. For instance Romeo would have sent the flowers, whether he was sincerely in love or merely bent on an alliance with the house of Capulet; so we want a form of explanation which leaves the matter of motive open.

This attractive line seems to me, nevertheless, to involve two *non-sequiturs* and a lacuna. First, if the actor emerges with more than one possible motive, it does not follow that the matter of motive is left open. If Romeo is rational, then motives which would have led him to act differently are thereby ruled out and so the matter of motive is only partly open. Secondly, just because two possible motives would yield the same action in the context, it does not follow that explanation can proceed without deciding between them. To know why Romeo acted as he did involves knowing how he would have acted in other conditions, for instance those where the two motives would move him along differing paths. It also involves knowing when he wanted but failed to achieve, as opposed to when he seemed to want but covertly was not really trying. So it looks as if motive does matter – a suspicion confirmed by noticing that Romeo has as yet no reason for action at all. He has legitimating, overt reasons but his being rational depends on his having a covert reason for taking advantage of them. His intention cannot be this reason, nor can his expressions of principle and sentiment, while all are being conceived as tactical devices. There is thus a lacuna when we ask why he wants what he is overtly pursuing; and it must be filled, if his tactics are to be interpreted as those of a rational man.

Motives do matter then; but, in the face of the hermeneutic circles, they must be the sort of item which can move a rational actor. The heart has its reasons; yet not such as reason knows nothing of. Mere wants will not do. Someone may complain that whether there is a reason for Romeo to send flowers is one thing and whether Romeo himself has a reason another, the difference depending on whether he has a motivating desire. I reply that having a desire to do something does not in itself make it rational to do it, even when no other stronger desire would thereby be frustrated. The rational actor not only has good reasons for his actions, given his desires and projects, but also has good reasons for his desires and projects. What makes the difference between there being good reason for him to act and his having good reason to act is his recognising the good reason, which he thereby makes his own.

The point needs proper argument; but it is enough for the moment that a circle turns vicious without it. If we are to discover Romeo's motive by asking what desires he must have had for his action to be identifiable as rational, we cannot then hold that whether his action was rational depends on the desires he happened to have. An action which is the incompetent effecting of one want is wrongly interpreted as the competent effecting of another. Hence we can find the rational actor's motive only on the assumption that it is a rational one.

There is now no case for assuming that all action is always equally rational. Indeed there never was in the eyes of anyone who finds subjective logic-of-the-situation explanations vacuous. But the rationality postulate still stands, now revealed as an ideal-type assumption and a yardstick for assessing what needs to be explained. Fully and objectively rational action is explained by showing how it matches the ideal case; imperfectly rational

	OVERT	COVERT
WHAT?	Action's meaning	Actor's meaning
WHY?	Legitimating reasons	Actor's good reasons

Figure 2

action needs a further account of why it fell short. Either way, the historian starts by trying an intellectual interpretation and, even where only partial explanation results, will have determined what is missing. This is what is involved in making the actors out as rational as possible.

As soon as we insist on rational desire for rational actions, we embark on a theory of real interests, *eudaemonia* or some such unnerving concept. But there is no turning back and, if Skinner jibs at the notorious problems thus set, I can reply that, in truth, he relies on one himself. My admiration for his writings is due, *inter alia*, to my belief that he writes as a rational actor who rationally desires to find the truth. Would he wish to deny it?

In this spirit, Figure 2 is offered as a slightly revised scheme for interpreting individual action. The emended version retains the idea that legitimating reasons are crucial, whatever the actor's true motive, and still tries to elicit what is covert by treating the actor as objectively rational. It differs only by insisting on motive after all, but in the face of the hermeneutic circles, recasts motives as reasons, in so far as the actor has good reasons for his desires.

The proviso leaves a large issue unresolved, however, as becomes clear when we turn to groups of actors. Any success with Romeo can be generalised to small groups confronted with a given context and either wholly of one mind or wholly under the command of one member. But these are tight conditions, not applying to less united groups or to those with a collective power to shape the normative context. Indeed they do not apply to an individual actor who has this sort of scope for manoeuvre. Since the power exists not only for wielders of law or force but wherever norms are fluid or ambiguous, and since historians are crucially interested in groups, movements and classes in transition and imperfect unity, Romeo cannot be pressed straight into further service.

There is a fundamental difference between individuals and groups. While Romeo and Juliet act singly, the likely response of each is a strategic factor in the planning of the other. When they join forces, they acquire a joint power to decide what both will do. Since what was external to each becomes internal to both collectively but not to either, the power of joint decision is an emergent property. Since it can include deciding the rules of their relationship, context is no longer the external, fixed frame which it has been hitherto. With larger groups in permanent and more embracing alliance, there starts to be a control not only over relations within the group but also over some of the previously external norms which enabled and constrained its growth. Rational manipulation of context emerges as a possibility, and much of what was *explicans* becomes *explicandum*.

If we want to take the idea of emergence seriously, while retaining the scheme of meanings and reasons, we might try regarding the group as if it were a single actor. In a traditional Marxist analysis, for instance, classes are single actors, whose overt motivations belong to ideology and covert ones to class interests. But, for this and other examples, the analogy between a single actor and a unitary group breaks down when we consider the process of deliberation and decision. Whereas the actor's real reasons are presumably those he would give to himself correctly and in secret, the group's are not those it would agree on in private session. The private session, although similarly closed to outsiders and although determining the public stance of the members, remains an internally public session of individual members. Debate about what the group should do reflects not only uncertainty about strategy and tactics but also manoeuvre within an alliance of actors with conflicting covert motives. So the puzzle of recovering Romeo's reasons is translated not into that of laying one's hands on the private-circulation-only minutes of the meeting but into that of recovering the various covert real reasons of the several members present.

The impasse stands. To interpret the overt utterances and actions of a group, we need access to real reasons. If the real reasons are those of individual actors and if we conceive the actors as closed individuals, real reasons are irrecoverable. If the real reasons are those of the emergent group and if we conceive the actors as deriving their human identity from membership of groups, we lose the thematic analogy between individuals and groups. So we still need a way to conceive actors so that, provided they are rational, we can warrantably read off the good reasons they act from. And we still need to show how groups of actors can be judged rational or irrational in their manipulation of context.

Someone may protest that there is an impasse only because I have insisted that rational action has objectively good reasons; whereas perceived reasons will surely suffice. But, however great the difficulties, I remain unrepentant. How actors perceive their situation is presumably meant to be a variable whose value is to be settled empirically. To settle the value we must know how rational the actors are. If we shrug this off by holding that everyone always does what seems a good idea at the time, there is no limit to possible interpretations. So we must make it matter how accurately they perceive their situation. A circle threatens: to know how accurate their perceptions are, we must know how rational they are and vice versa. To cut into this circle, we must treat rationality as a skill in judgement which can be ascribed *a priori* in some measure to anyone capable of communicating with others. Unless the actors are basically rational, we cannot know how accurate or inaccurate their perceptions are. This is, once again, the nub of the 'bridgehead' argument, whose detail is presented in 'Reason and ritual' above.

How then are the actors to be conceived? If their identity is not to be derived from that of constitutive groups, we must still try to show how what is collectively rational is so because it is rational for those taking part. Granted the puzzles arising when the actors are conceived as egoists, this means refusing once again to make instrumental rationality primary. The question is then squarely what it is about human beings (or some at least) which makes it rational for them to act uninstrumentally.

The objection to assuming egoism is not that it involves predicating the wrong basic motivation of the right sort of subject but that it mistakenly abstracts from human actors to timeless, universal monads. So a corrective tempting to historians is to give human nature more substance by having it vary with place and time. If different cultures are peopled by different sorts of men and women, historians must be able to identify what sorts they are dealing with. The point of assuming rationality is then to let them discover by asking what kind of actor would have found it rational to act as the ones in question did. This again threatens to be circular, however, if the apparent relativism implies that actors are the creatures of their culture, who accept the ends and means prescribed by their cultural context. We would need to understand the norms in order to make sense of the actions and vice versa, and, incidentally, then be left foxed to account for cultural change. In other words, we would once more be confined to actors' meanings, actions' meanings and legitimating reasons, with the circularity complained of earlier. Rescue again depends on an objective notion of rationality and an appeal to the actors' good reasons for what they did.

It seems to me, then, that actors must indeed be conceived in a timeless, universal way, so that historical explanation is given enough *a priori* to avoid the circles. The mistake was not abstraction itself but the form which it took. Human beings are not monads but persons who create their human identity by using social capacities in social relations. They succeed not by achieving any old equipoise between desires and norms but by creating a rational identity, one which expresses what it is rational to value. The key lies in a connection between rationality and autonomy, coupled with a thesis about the social character of autonomy.

This is to claim that there is what might be termed 'an epistemological unity of mankind' and to do so in a way which crosses the border into ethics. That is beyond my present scope. So, having flaunted my colours, I shall end more soberly with some summary remarks.

Skinner's explanatory method works admirably in general with Romeo and other single actors, and I find especially fertile his advice that written historical texts should always be seen as episodes of strategic action in a context. I object solely that the historian also needs to identify the actors' motives or, rather, since what is needed must be recoverable, their real reasons. But the method seems at first no help in interpreting combined action. This cannot be because group action has a logic independent of what is rational for the members individually. So presumably the problem is set by the frequent discrepancy between the interests of each and the interests of all, typified by the free-rider problem.[1] That calls for a logic able to tell us when and why it is rational for individuals to pool their divergent interests. When and why is it rational for groups to try to reshape the norms internal and external to them? These are the ontological questions, the former being acute for anyone who still wishes to be silent about motive, and the latter acute in so far as the identification of social meaning and explanation of group action always presuppose a definite social context.

Epistemologically, the daunting circles can be broken only by assuming that actors are rational enough for even their irrational acts to be intelligible. But it needs to be more than a platitude that the social world makes sense when interpreted, and the assumption must have an edge. The edge comes from an objective, not a subjective, notion of rationality, which involves the historian in judging how well the actors did. Rational action is a skill. At what? Is it just the effective translation of consistent preferences into the most promising course of action? I have claimed that the rationality of motives is needed in judging that the actors' real reasons were good reasons. A fresh way of conceiving the actors is required. Since a vicious relativism results if human nature is made to vary empirically with historical context, I hold out for something universal. 'Wherefore art thou Romeo?', Juliet asked. The question invites a blend of metaphysics and ethics, too heady, I fear, for sober historians. Yet, if rational action is its own explanation, every historical explanation judges and partly endorses a claim to rationality. How exactly do such endorsements stop short of moral approval? This daunting question is the subject of the next essay.

---

[1] cf. the discussion in 'Reasons of honour' below, and 'Penny-Pinching and Backward Induction', *The Journal of Philosophy*, 88, 9, 1991.

CHAPTER 17

Reasons of honour

Marcus Atilius Regulus commanded the Roman Army in the First Punic War, until captured by the Carthaginians in 255 BC. After a time in captivity he was despatched to Rome to try to arrange the return of some high-ranking prisoners. To kindle his ardour, the Carthaginians extracted an oath that, if he failed, he would return to Carthage to be put to death by torture. On reaching Rome, however, he urged the Senate to refuse, since the prisoners were worth more to Carthage than he was to Rome. His advice carried the day. Then, unmoved by the pleas of friends and peers, he insisted on keeping his oath and sailed back to Carthage. There he was returned to prison and kept awake until he collapsed and died.

This is a famous story and one easy to remember. It came readily to mind when I was casting around for a way of setting a puzzle about the understanding of action, although I had last heard it in the schoolroom over quarter of a century ago. To make sure, however, I checked with Cicero and have just given the version set down in *De Officiis* (Book iii, chapter 26) where it is introduced into a discussion of duties as 'a real event in our history'. There is a twist to it, as will be revealed, but, meanwhile, it will do nicely as a starting point. The tale is not only easy to remember but also, it seems, easy to understand. Regulus embodies the heroic virtues of the Roman Republic and those virtues still have resonance even in our own unheroic

This essay began as the 1986 Presidential Address to the Aristotelian Society, and is reprinted, with revisions, by courtesy of the Editor, from *The Proceedings of the Aristotelian Society*, 1987. I am grateful to Richard Gordon for his classical scholarship and to Timothy O'Hagan for his comments on an earlier draft.

times. No doubt few of us would be inclined to do the same or even to expect it of others. Would an American general, captured by the Vietcong and sent to Washington on the same terms, have been likely to keep his oath and return after sabotaging his mission? Do we believe that he should? The answer is presumably no; and, to that extent, had an American general behaved like Regulus, we would be a little puzzled. Perhaps we would echo Maréchal Bosquet's comment on the Charge of the Light Brigade: *c'est magnifique mais ce n'est pas la guerre*. That wry comment would show, however, that we had at least understood the action, even if we found it more gallant than rational.

Even that slight puzzlement seems to disappear with Regulus. The moral framework of the Roman Republic was a robust and encompassing one, Cicero assures us, and governed the giving of oaths to legitimate enemies. The gesture was not only *magnifique* but also very much *la guerre*. So does that make everything clear? On reflection, no, it does not. It might do so, if traditional frameworks, especially codes of honour, truly bound and dictated in ways which our looser modern moralities do not. Thus Cicero suggests that Regulus' heroic virtue lay not in returning to Carthage, since no true Roman could have done otherwise after taking an oath, but in urging the Senate to reject his mission. That was a virtuous choice beyond the call of duty, whereas returning was not a choice at all. Yet Cicero cannot mean quite what he seems to say, since he also cites cases of men similarly placed who broke their word. Admittedly he presents such base fellows as weak or selfish, but, even if they were, that still shows obedience to the code not automatic. Nor is it plain that Regulus' duty lay all on the side of returning to Carthage. He could legitimately have wondered whether the interests of Rome would have been better served by his soldiering on or whether his duty to his family should tip the scales. Meanwhile Cicero himself makes it a matter of choice for Regulus whether to speak against his mission, thus implying (rightly, I think) that even the sternest code leaves discretion both in interpreting it and in deciding whether to conform.

In that case we do not yet understand the story. Why, then,

did Regulus do what the old *mores* help, but only help, to explain? That is really two questions: why they were reasons for him and why they were his own reasons. Provisionally, they were reasons for him because he was so placed that they applied to him. Provisionally, they were his reasons because he wanted to do what was required or virtuous. These answers, let me stress, are only provisional and I mean to show that they will not do. But they serve to cue in our common assumption that action is to be explained by reference to the agent's beliefs and desires in his particular situation.

Before taking the cue, let us see what is at stake. Anyone tempted by the hermeneutic tradition, as I am, needs to play up the distinction between *verstehen* and *erklären*. The goal is a definite, usable and justified way of explaining action. It will not be achieved, if *verstehen* is simply a heuristic device for hitting on promising interpretations, which stand or fall by their adequacy at a causal level defined in terms of causal laws or mechanisms. Nor is it enough, in my view, to make *verstehen* crucial for identifying what actors are doing, if nothing follows for how those actions are to be explained. Understanding involves both identifying and accounting for; and both, if the hermeneutic tradition is worth its salt, in the same mode. The mode cannot merely be insight or empathy (*direktes Verstehen*), since, even allowing the claims of insight to identify, it offers no obvious way of accounting, still less of justifying an account.

The concept which springs to mind for the mode is Rationality. To grasp why an action was rational is not only an aid to being sure what the actor has done but also at least a large step towards knowing why. This much is familiar, especially when glossed with the help of the standard model of rational choice, as for instance in the theory of economic behaviour. The gloss is admitted not to work quite convincingly for cases like Regulus and there is dispute about why. I shall contend that it fails with Regulus finally because it makes a subtler nonsense even of the 'economic' cases which it is supposed to manage best. For purposes of both diagnosis and cure, I shall advocate another criterion for judging an action irrational.

Very broadly, the standard model has it that Regulus acted

irrationally, if, placed as he believed himself to be, he did not do what he thought likeliest to satisfy his current desires. Or, if that is too subjective a version, then he acted irrationally if, placed as he was, he failed to do what truly was likeliest to satisfy his current desires. Either way, the crux is in the interplay of situation, calculation and desire. To make it precise let us invoke a Parsonian 'unit act'.

The 'unit act' specifies an actor, an end, a current situation with given conditions (or parameters) and with a choice of means, and a 'mode of orientation' with at least one standard of value. Thus we have Regulus in his time and place with more than one way of transforming his situation into one outranked by no other. This is not exhaustively precise and, in one way at least, is usefully vague. It says not a word about 'self-interest' and that will save us from carelessly building selfishness into the model and then having to remove it later, so as to construe 'self-interest' as broadly as possible. No advance restrictions are to be placed on what a rational agent may value. In another way the 'unit act' is instructively precise. It involves an instrumental, means-ends notion of rationality, which excludes sloppy talk of expressively rational acts. Instead it offers a device for treating expressive acts as instrumental, since they are means to an end to which the actor is oriented; and this, we shall find, is not the same thing.

By this account, Regulus can have acted irrationally, if he has misread the situation, misconstrued his options, miscalculated likely consequences or misapplied the standard of value. He cannot be at fault, however, for accepting the parameters or the standard of value. That seems to yield a neat distinction between pilot error on the one hand and instrument failure, defective instructions and natural hazard on the other. But this is too quick, as emerges if we fill in the 'unit act' by reference to microeconomic theory. Group the end, mode of orientation and standard of value together as 'preferences' and call the alternative means (his feasible actions with their consequences) 'the domain of his preferences'. In the ideal-type case the agent has complete and consistent preferences and is fully informed also about their domain. But, since life is uncertain and agents finite, and so as to be able to apply the model without making all actual agents irrational, let us settle for preferences which are complete and consistent over the relevant range, and information which is perfect for the (subjective) probability of the various consequences and their associated costs. Pilot error now becomes a miscalculation of net expected utility and occurs, formally speaking, if and only if the agent does *a*, when there was a *b* with greater net expected utility.

The telegraphic nature of the last paragraph should not be allowed to mask the power of the approach. By construing rational action as the maximising of expected utility within parameters, we can harness the technicalities of decision theory and the theory of games to the persuasive general thought that rational action results from consistent preferences plus rational belief. It offers a way of turning *verstehen* into a precision tool for economics in the first instance and then for whatever areas of social life can be analysed *in more economico*. I want to capture and retain the power of the approach. But, I shall contend, in offering an account of Regulus which makes him rational, so to speak, on the cheap, it is deeply at fault in ways which also apply even to the more obviously marketeering behaviour which it seems to analyse so well.

An agent acts irrationally, if and only if he does *a*, when there is a *b* with greater net expected utility. Regulus, the Samurai, the US President in election year and the shoppers in Piggly Wiggly supermarkets are grist to the same mill. That is an interesting prospect but it depends on treating desires (or preferences) in a way which proves less and less satisfactory. A common complaint about rational-actor models in that they are specific to market exchanges and extend at best only to rational-legal social systems with individualistic norms. The apparent retort is that rationality is an instrumental notion with a timeless and universal structure, which can be applied anywhere just by filling in the local parameters. Let us see.

The model contains both a deliberative and a motivational component. The deliberative one is straightforward. It is an algorithm for maximising the value of the expected utility variable, commonly drawn from Bayesian decision theory. Does the algorithm in fact correspond to the actual process of deliberation which real people go through in flesh and blood? Allegedly, it does not matter, provided that it is *as if* they did. That leaves an obvious question about the truth conditions for this 'as if' but I shall put it in the margin. Meanwhile there is the motivational component. As noted, it would be a mistake to suppose that the model ascribes a self-seeking egoism to every human being. The actual component is far blander. It merely relates action to preferences by stipulating that what moves an agent is the state of his preference schedule, after discounting for likelihoods, costs and other constraints on what he would otherwise have preferred. In philosophical terms it is merely a Humean assumption that action is the product of desire plus belief, with desire supplying the motor. This is so bland that it can seem wholly non-committal. Indeed, if mere logic connects preferring *a* to *b* with choosing *a*, when *a* and *b* are suitably in competition, as in revealed preference theory, there seems hardly to be a motivational component at all.

In truth, however, there is one and it does a great deal of work. It does it by specifying both a locus and a direction of preference. Here lies the difference between self-interest and selfishness. Edgeworth's oft-cited remark from his *Mathematical Psychics*, 'the first principle of economics is that every agent is actuated only by self-interest', still catches the guiding spirit. But two senses of the principle need separating. One is that people are moved solely by personal gain, and Edgeworth himself, although thinking it a useful rule of thumb for analysing some kinds of commerce, did not suppose it true of people at large. The other is that people are moved to seek the satisfaction of their own desires. This remains primary and specifies that every agent is moved by his own preferences ('locus'), which are ordered by how well they serve his own interests ('direction'). Neither clause is non-committal.

An ordering or direction is needed because preferences can be very various and the 'complete and consistent' clause requires them to form a single rank. The obvious point is that not all Regulus' preferences are self-regarding. Some are other-regarding and some are not easily cast as related to desires at all. For instance the claims of duty are often presented as independent of what the agent wants for himself or for anyone else. The ordering must homogenise self-regarding, other-regarding and what we may call 'principled' desires. Less obviously, each category has to reckon with time. Suppose that Regulus will wish that he had not chosen to return to Carthage and knows now that he will wish it. How, if at all, can this future desire influence his choice? The force of saying that desire plus belief produce action, with desire as the motor, is to insist that only present desires can move an agent. So his future desires enter the reckoning only in so far as he has a present desire to satisfy them. The same is true of the past desire, which moved him to make a promise with the intention of keeping it. That too can move him now only if he has a present desire to satisfy his past desire. Similarly, if he is moved by the desires of others, he can admit those desires only by ranking them so as to be clear which matter most – what his wife wanted, wants and will want may be distinct – and by finding a suitable desire in himself to satisfy them. Principles too can enter in only by the gate of his present desires.

At this point let us declare a silly answer, to be avoided on pain of destroying the model. The silly answer is that a rational agent follows his most urgent present desire. This would make a rational man of a shipwrecked sailor, who slakes his urgent thirst with sea-water, knowing that he will go mad and die. When told to wait for the rain which will fall at dusk, he replies, 'But I do not now want water in a few hours; or not nearly as much as I want water now. I shall regret it; but that will be urgent only later.' If the model makes it rational to be governed by the pleasure principle in complete defiance of the reality principle, it is a worthless account of rationality.

The silly result is meant to be blocked in two ways. One is by insisting that to choose is to choose the likely consequences. So the sailor must rank as inseparable package of sea-water and madness. The other is to regard future desires as present desires discounted only for uncertainty. Otherwise investment of time or resources becomes irrational. In themselves, however, both moves leave it rational for someone strongly enough gripped by the pleasure principle to act on the pleasure principle. Whether madness later is an acceptable price for water now depends so far solely on how strong the desire is for sea water now against rain-water later. This is curious but not surprising, seeing that rationality is so far an internal relation between what are, in effect, tastes and the likely consequences of gratifying them – *De gustibus non est disputandum*. The stronger the taste, the higher the price it is rational to pay, even after consideration of consequences. Equally, whether it is rational to repay a debt is bound to depend at least partly on how much I now want to repay it, since only present desire can move me. So Regulus must weigh his present desire to satisfy the earlier desire, which prompted his oath, against his present desire to avoid a future desire not to have done so. He is irrational, if he then acts contrary to the heavier pan of the scales.

This yields a very queer account of principled choice. It does so, however, because it also yields a very queer account of prudence. It is plain that Regulus will need to be moved in part by the fact that he is the very same person who made the oath; otherwise he can brush the past aside by refusing to accept that an oath's having been made by someone last month is of any concern to him. Similarly prudence will be no guide, unless the person to be tortured will be him. At the very least, a notion of personal identity over time is called for, otherwise there will be nothing to anchor the reflective consistency which a preference schedule is supposed to display. Yet the model provides only a notion of personality, in the sense of an organised bundle of preferences, and treats the agent over time as a series of bundles linked by overlapping similarities. Since the utility of any choice varies at different points in the series, and indeed at different points in a contemplated possible series, we need a locus for rational decision. 'Now' will not serve as one.

The point obtrudes further, if Regulus is offered a marked change of personality. Suppose that he has the option of exile in Babylon, where, he knows, he will come to scorn his old Roman life and values. That would present him with a choice of the currency in which utilities are to be measured. At Roman prices, exile is a craven option and scores below martyrdom; at

Babylonian prices it will come to have scored above. The model as yet provides no way of judging the value of a currency. This is a serious lack, granted that everyone, in growing up and passing through the stages of life, experiences changes of currency. The old pay for the sins of their youth with rheumatics which did not worry them, when young, even in prospect. 'Tastes' change over a lifetime and hence, since we are dealing so far only with matters of degree, they can change a little even over five minutes. Once again we need a better standpoint than Now.

The plot thickens if Regulus gallantly tries to do what best satisfies the desires of others. Is he to respect the past, the present or the future desires of his fellows? Of which of his fellows? family? friends? Romans? human beings at large? The obvious retort is that these are questions of morality and not of rationality. But, even allowing the distinction, the retort will not suffice. Rational action is the efficient choice of means to ends. It depends, in the model, on a complete and consistent ordering of possible outcomes. So he cannot act, unless he can order his other-regarding desires; and he cannot do that without knowing which utilities at which stages of whose life to respect. Here too he needs a notion of unitary persons. Once again the maxim 'act according to the present strength of thy present desires' is hopelessly indeterminate.

If the model is really so hopeless, how do economists and many others get on so happily with it? The answer, I submit, is that they add assumptions about the locus and direction of preferences. The usual one for direction is self-interest; and the locus needs to be an enduring self, whose real interests are served by rational action. So even an instrumental theory of rationality is committed to some notion of real interests and of persons as more than bundles. The tricky question is how specific this notion must be. On the one hand it must be specific enough to gauge utilities by. For instance it is specific enough (for many purposes) to assume that producers seek to maximise their own profits and consumers their own consumer surplus. But, on the other hand, it must not be too specific, if the model is to be exported to other realms of life and to other cultures. To see that profit-maximising is a too local a motive, we need only recall the

Victorian 'pawn-broking hymn' which has lately disappeared shame-facedly from the hymn books. The key verse went thus:

> Lord, whate'er I lend to Thee
> Repaid a thousandfold will be
> So gladly will I lend to Thee.

We cannot decide whether Regulus acted rationally by judging whether he had hit on the best investment in his own future hereafter.

Can we not? At first sight it is a straightforward matter of fact how widely the profit motive operates and, offhand, many societies have managed without it. On second thoughts, however, profit is only one instance of the variable x, whose value any rational agent maximises. If, say, social approval, status and power are others, then it becomes unclear what the scope of the model is. By the same token it is also unclear whether its scope is an empirical question. At any rate, the model is not straightfor-wardly refutable. Its account of rational agents as utility-maximisers operates in a buffer zone between the all-but-*a-priori* claims of a general view of human nature and the all-but-empirical hypotheses about the actual currencies of human value. The maximisation thesis regulates what descriptions of human actions are allowable. Whether we can succeed in construing Regulus as a rational economic man depends, partly at least, on how stubbornly we insist on doing so.

Hume once remarked rashly:

It is universally acknowledged that there is a great uniformity among the actions of men, in all nations and ages, and that human nature remains still the same, in its principles and operations. The same motives produce the same actions: the same events follow from the same causes. Ambition, avarice, self-love, vanity, friendship, generosity, public spirit: these passions, mixed in various degrees, and distributed through society, have been, from the beginning of the world, and still are, the source of all actions and enterprises, which have ever been observed among mankind. Would you know the sentiments, inclinations and course of life of the Greeks and Romans? Study well the temper and actions of the French and English: You cannot be much mistaken in transferring to the former most of the observations which you have made with regard to the latter. Mankind are so much the same, in all times and places, that history informs us of nothing new or strange in this particular. (*Enquiries*, VIII.I.65)

The real Humean reason that history has no news for us is not, I think, that mankind happen to be the same in all times and places but that Hume's analysis of action as the work of desire-plus-belief holds timelessly, if it holds at all. Ancient Romans, medieval merchants, Victorian labourers and American Senators are equally grist to its analytical mill. Specific motives, like avarice and public spirit, on the other hand, ought to be news, since it could be false that they turn up everywhere. Indeed, I venture to bet, it is false. If so, there is something missing in the middle distance between a background of the analytically timeless and a foreground of the historically specific. The middle distance should contain a way of fleshing out variable x in a way which is both historically interesting and analytically guaranteed. At this point the stock model of instrumentally rational action is exhausted.

In summary so far, there are three possible answers to the question whether Regulus acted rationally. We might deem him rational, because, with due allowance for time and context, we find that he maximised his net expected utility. We might deem him irrational because he missed a line of conduct with higher expected utility or, more cryptically, better attuned to his real interests. We might deem him non-rational, because the Roman Republic is beyond the scope of the model. It seems to me somewhat arbitrary so far which answer we give; and I confess to not liking any of them. That is because they all construe social relationships as exercises in the satisfaction of desire. Since I think this mistaken even in the best case of a shopper distributing a household budget among the goods in a supermarket, I shall next suggest another angle of vision.

It is time for the promised twist to the tale of Regulus, which Cicero recounts so graphically. The twist is that this 'real event in our history' seems to have been pure fancy. At any rate modern authorities do not believe a word of it. Mommsen, for instance, describes the episode and its details as 'incongruous embellishments, contrasting ill with sober and serious history.'[1] Scullard declares that Regulus died in captivity in Carthage, without ever returning to Rome. The yarn about the barbarity of the Carthaginians, he says, was a cover-up for the barbarity of Regulus' wife, who, on hearing of his death, had some Carthaginian prisoners of war killed by torture.[2] Although one should not take it as self-evident that the moderns have it over the ancients, let us assume for the sake of argument that the 'real event in our history' never happened and see what that does to the discussion.

Focus now shifts from the First Punic War to the Rome of Cicero's time. By then Regulus was plainly a well-established epitome of the Republican virtues[3] and that is why Cicero cited him. *De Officiis* is a thesis about duty and virtue, aimed at contemporaries who maintained that moral rectitude conflicts with expediency. Cicero argues that it was expedient for Regulus to return to Carthage, since it is always truly expedient to do what is right.

When he came to Rome, he could not fail to see the specious appearance of expediency, but he decided that it was unreal, as the outcome proves. His apparent interest was to remain in his own country, to stay at home with his wife and children, and to retain his rank and dignity as an ex-consul, regarding the defeat which he had suffered as a misfortune that might come to anyone in the game of war. Who says this was not expedient? Who, think you? Greatness of soul and courage say that it was not. (*De Officiis* III, xxvi, Loeb translation)

Plainly Cicero is having to use his heaviest guns to make his case, against what was therefore serious contemporary opposition. The question about whether Regulus acted rationally becomes one about the concept of rationality prevailing in the decline of the Republic.

In shifting the focus, we have passed judgement on Cicero's grasp of his own history. How do modern historians manage to know better than an ancient Roman? I do not doubt their

---

[1] T. Mommsen, *The History of Rome*, vol. II, p. 184 n., London, 1894.
[2] H. H. Scullard, *A History of the Roman World 733–146 B.C.*, London: Methuen, 1935, p. 152.
[3] Witness also Horace *Odes* iii, 5 and Livy's summary of the (missing) Book XVIII of his *Histories (periochae XVIII)*.

scholarship, which I am anyway quite incompetent to review, but I do want to point out that a test of plausibility is being applied. Scullard, for instance, is willing to reconstruct the battle which Regulus lost and hence willing to rely on later sources sometimes. But he cannot swallow the legend. He does have some earlier sources, I grant, where the legend is conspicuously absent, when it surely should have been present (Valerius Maximus, for example). Even there, however, he is judging it unlikely that there would have been such an omission; and, in general, he reckons much of the later Romans' own history of early Rome implausible in itself and all too convenient for their ideological purposes. In brief he is judging what it is rational, on the one hand, for actors of Regulus' vintage to have done, and, on the other, for later Roman historians to believe to have happened. If he is right, then it is rational for us to believe that it was rational for ancient historians to believe that Regulus had rationally chosen to do what, even allowing for our own distance from 250 BC, we find unlikely.

How does the rational-actor model bear on this tangle? It seems at first to simplify it. It separates rational belief from rational action, so that it is one question what the norms of Roman life were at the time of the First Punic War, another question what Cicero might rationally believe them to have been and yet another question how we shall rationally decide the first two questions. But that is, alas, too simple. Underlying all three questions is a thesis about the relation of norms to action. It surfaces most obviously in the general view that the history of early Rome as seen from the first century BC is both implausible on the one hand and ideologically too convenient on the other. This general view integrates the notions of rational belief and rational action after all. It does so in a way which Cicero might well protest at. Cicero was looking back to an age when men acted from honour not because they reckoned it a paying proposition but because they were men of honour; and that is how a truly rational man acts. That would at once remove the basic implausibility of the Regulus story, although one might, of course, still doubt the sketchy evidence.

Cicero, however, is arguing a case in ethics, and by his time the conceptual connections were plainly disputed. We see him trying to head off opponents, who drew the modern distinction between what is expedient and what is right. So he cannot fairly present his own interpretation of 'a real event in our history' as independent evidence that the event was really as he describes it. Furthermore, by his own admission, there were other real events of early Roman history where the old Roman actors notably failed to do the honourable thing and were thus quite capable of separating expediency from right. Even Cicero thus found dishonourable conduct intelligible enough and hence, it seems, is using 'rational' strictly as an ethical term, as opposed to a synonym for 'intelligible'. To put it in modern words, even he concedes that an actor may act rationally on a false belief about what is expedient. In general, therefore, the stock theory of rational choice seems correct in separating means from ends and can always be applied, whatever ends people may happen to have.

In shifting the focus, we have transferred the model from social action to Other Minds. That is a move from analysing rational choice to reconstructing the motives of rational actors. If the model were right about choice, it should be possible to identify and explain the actions of Other Minds by finding the mixture of desire and belief which produced them. In other words, given the formula $(D + B \rightarrow A)$ and given A, we could find the values of the variables D and B, such that A solves the actor's maximising problem. So far, however, we have too many unknowns. Even A is not exactly given, since it is at least plausible to hold that the character of an action depends on the agent's own description of it or on the social rules which it instances. For example, A would typically be 'the swearing of an oath' rather than 'a motion of the lips'. Oaths, it can be argued, need intention and convention in ways which behaviourism finds awkward. But that is too intricate a matter to press here. Let us focus on D and B.

At first sight D and B are in free variation, even granted that the actor is sane. ('Sane' means that he is at least trying to maximise his expected utility as defined by his preference schedule.) For, given D and A, we can still credit him with almost any set of (false) beliefs, provided only that someone who holds those beliefs would find it rational to do A. Equally, given B and A, we can credit him with whatever desire could produce A as a maximising move. But initially, we have neither D nor B. So we seem to have an almost free hand in cooking up a set of desires and beliefs, provided only that they would yield A. If that were truly so, the writing of history would be almost arbitrary.

In fact historians, anthropologists and all who try to find the mind's construction in the face cut down their options by strengthening their assumptions. They do it in part by assuming that actors are objectively – and not merely subjectively – instrumentally rational, at least on the whole. If only true, or at least rationally held, beliefs connect D to A, then B is much easier to specify exactly. But that will suffice, only if the relevant beliefs have to do solely with likely consequences and ordered preferences, as in the case of instrumentally rational shoppers in supermarkets; and, if my earlier arguments are allowed, it will not do even there. Meanwhile it begs the question of whether men of honour are instrumentally rational.

That is still an ambiguous question. Certainly the beliefs behind principled action are not solely about consequences and preferences. Or, rather, they concern consequences as judged by principle and preferences ordered by principle. That granted, there is no harm in calling principled action 'instrumentally rational' but to do so is not yet to put it within the scope of the economic model, for reasons given earlier. In other words, historians do indeed solve the Other Minds problem by treating principled action as tactical choice. But they do not necessarily do it by treating principles as givens, which constrain the tactics of historical actors. Sometimes they do it by explaining the actors' choice as an affirmation of what one might term their identities.

That both readings are intelligible, at least on the surface, is shown by Cicero's text. He holds that people always do what they think expedient; but he identifies two ways of judging expediency. The heroes of the golden age equated what was expedient with what was right, whereas base or foolish persons in all ages contrast expediency with right. The difference thus lies in the judgements which actors make; and the way to render action intelligible is to look for those judgements. The moral which I draw from the story of Regulus is thus neither that there was a golden age nor that there was not. It is that, unless we make both possible, Cicero cannot be translated into English. To manage it, we too must tie rationality to the judging of what is truly expedient, so that we can speak in the same breath both of men of honour and of men of markets.

Even this modest moral helps to remove some puzzles. What is right about applying the stock economic model to primitive or traditional societies is that they too contain rational and irrational actors. So the initial thought, that the first step to explaining action is to show why the actor might have deemed it rational, is upheld. What is wrong, however, is the stock equation of expediency with market ideas of expected utility. That is itself a substantive proposition in ethics and, I believe, a mistaken one. But, once it is seen as just one way of filling in the wider formula that rational action is expedient action, we can understand what is done in its name. This is not particularly a point about the difference between traditional and modern societies. Witness Cicero, both ways of filling in the formula can often be found together. Action on principle remains common enough, I am happy to say.

A second puzzle concerns the notion of contextual rationality. It is tempting to make what is rational relative to social context. For instance, given the supposed norms of the golden age, it becomes rational for Regulus to keep his word, but, given the norms of our age, an American general who returned to Vietnam would be off his head. The merit in this thought is that what it is rational to do depends both on what it is rational to believe at a particular stage of human knowledge and on the demands of a particular social and moral framework. What is wrong about it, however, is more serious. I leave aside the general question of the sense in which rationality in science may be relative to context, since the Ancients could distinguish as clearly as we between not sailing straight out to sea because the gods have forbidden it and not doing so because one might fall off the edge of the earth. The context relevant to Regulus is the social and moral one. It should not be thought of solely as imposing demands, which are automatically obeyed. Such a context is the actors' world and it enables as much as it constrains. If there was a golden age, then it defined their problems and their resources for dealing with them, just as their typical solutions defined the age. This puzzling two-way traffic need not be thought of as mechanical. The agents acted rationally in context, in the sense that they did their intelligent best. The context is their collective self-portrait and, until they reject it, rationality is a matter of applying the paint expediently in a good cause.

Cicero writes:

of all that is thus praiseworthy in the conduct of Regulus, this one feature above all others calls for our admiration: it was he who offered the motion that the prisoners of war be retained. For the fact of his returning may seem admirable to us nowadays, but in those times he could not have done otherwise. That merit, therefore, belongs to the age, not to the man. (*De Officiis* III, xxxi)

I pointed out earlier that 'could not have done otherwise' is not to be construed strictly. But it does hold the key to the job done by context in explaining action. There has to be somewhere for a rational-actor explanation to stop. Cicero marks it for the old Republic Roman by saying in effect that it is the breaking and not the keeping of oaths which needs explaining, since no ancient Roman needed a further reason to keep his oath. By the first century, when he was writing, however, he feared that priorities were fast reversing. The keeping of oaths was becoming strange and the breaking of them natural. We need not unravel his discussion of ethics to see what this implies for the problem of Other Minds.

Actors' expediencies, then, are governed by what sort of actors they are. That is the point about the locus and direction of preferences again. The question is still what is involved in being a 'sort' of actor and it still needs an answer which balances the timeless against the historical. Historically different types of action can be picked out for different societies as an explanatory grid. I have nothing interesting to say on this score, as the importance of social position, religion, gender, race and so forth seems to me to vary and I have no firm set of categories to recommend. Broadly, however, to propose a type of action is to answer a question in advance. For instance, it is not surprising if typical business people maximise profit and only surprising if they do not. Timelessly, however, mankind still has to be so much the same in certain ways that history can inform us of nothing new or strange in this particular. Otherwise cross-cultural comparisons will be impossible.

The self-portrait which all people have always painted is one of themselves as intelligent judges of how to achieve what they value. 'Intelligent' does not mean 'super-intelligent'. So brilliant solutions to the problems of choice facing an actor may be as much in need of explanation as incompetent ones. 'Intelligent' implies only that human judgement is usually goodish and, where it is, explains action. Meanwhile the emphasis is on 'judgement'. In the stock account of rationality the actor is a clockwork toy whose output is some direct function of desire plus belief, with desire supplying the motor. I want to distance human beings from their desires and beliefs, making them judges of what they do desire and should desire, do believe and should believe. On this showing, they are not the prisoners of their own inputs, neither social nor psychic, and no social science should proceed as if they were.

The force of calling such a metaphysic 'timeless' is to deny the discontinuities between traditional and modern, primitive and developed, prescientific and scientific. Instead we find everyone trying to understand the world and to act for the best as they see it. Equally there will be continuity between the theoretical and the practical, and between the rational and the moral. Different activities, like different cultures, make different sense from within their context, but not radically different sense. This sounds like mere optimism, no doubt, and far beyond what I have given argument for. However, I am not stating it as a metaphysical truth (although I take it for one) but as a precondition of understanding others. In this sense, there has to be an epistemological unity of mankind.

So did Regulus act rationally? That question has by now become several.

Firstly, does Cicero tell an intelligible tale, one which makes the taking of an oath both a good reason for Regulus' conduct and Regulus' own reason too? That is a hard question because the early history of Rome is so misty; but the story does, I suppose, pass the tests of internal coherence which we place on narrative fiction and is thereby intelligible.

Secondly, and more interestingly, does Cicero make a rational first century Roman of Regulus? Yes, he does convince us, I think, that even in the late Republic the keeping of an oath could be judged expedient and that a Roman might rationally act on this moral judgement by going to his death.

Thirdly, would a modern Regulus still act rationally, for example by returning to Vietnam? It is tempting to reply that the historical displacement is too great for an answer. But that ignores the epistemological unity of mankind, which involves recognising that the actor's moral identity is at stake in every action. We might still wish to repeat '*c'est magnifique mais ce n'est pas la guerre*'; but, in pointing out that this was no way to win a war, we do not thereby imply that, for a rational soldier, war is solely about winning. We mean only that action on principle is not made rational by displaying the simple-minded consistency of a rhinoceros.

What set off as a question about the rationality of action has ended as one about the interpretation of texts. The link is our need to identify the principles which guide action and to identify what actors take themselves to be doing. These identifications have to pass a test of reasonableness and so, therefore, do the actors as we present them. The hard-nosed version of the economic model failed to supply this test and the underlying softer version from Humean psychology did no better. The moral, I suggest, is that to be truly instrumentally rational (or 'useful'), an action must serve an expressively rational end. In identifying the ends we determine which choices of means shall be puzzling and which self-explanatory. Cicero refused to be puzzled by actors who chose what it was expedient to do by deciding what was morally right. He has my support.

Index